The
Alzheimer's
ADVISOR

The
Alzheimer's
ADVISOR

A Caregiver's Guide to Dealing
with the Tough Legal and Practical Issues

Vaughn E. James

⁴AMACOM

American Management Association

New York • Atlanta • Brussels • Buenos Aires • Chicago • London • Mexico City
San Francisco • Shanghai • Tokyo • Toronto • Washington, D.C.

Special discounts on bulk quantities of AMACOM books are available to corporations, professional associations, and other organizations. For details, contact Special Sales Department, AMACOM, a division of American Management Association, 1601 Broadway, New York, NY 10019. Tel: 212–903–8316. Fax: 212–903–8083.
E-mail: specialsls@amanet.org
Website: www.amacombooks.org/go/specialsales
To view all AMACOM titles go to: www.amacombooks.org

This publication is designed to provide accurate and authoritative information in regard to the subject matter covered. It is sold with the understanding that the publisher is not engaged in rendering legal, accounting, or other professional service. If legal advice or other expert assistance is required, the services of a competent professional person should be sought.

Library of Congress Cataloging-in-Publication Data

James, Vaughn E.
    The Alzheimer's advisor: a caregiver's guide to dealing with the tough legal and practical issues / Vaughn E. James.—1st
        p.   cm.
    Includes bibliographical references and index.
    ISBN-13: 978-0-8144-0924-4
    ISBN-10: 0-8144-0924-5
    1. Alzheimer's disease—Patients—Legal status, laws, etc.—United States—Popular works.   2. Caregivers—United States—Handbooks, manuals, etc.   I. Title.

    KF3803.A56J36   2009
    344.7304′36831—dc22

                                                                              2008020258

Printing number

10   9   8   7   6   5   4   3   2   1

To
Marva, Vijhay, Etienne, and Maelys
Thanks for the love and support . . .

and to the memory of
Franco, Ol' Oak, Co'n Rosie, and Ma Di
Gone but not forgotten . . .

and to

Debbie
Que sera, sera . . .

CONTENTS

FOREWORD

The current and projected statistics regarding the incidence and prevalence of Alzheimer's disease (AD) and related dementias are staggering, as we increasingly become victims of our own wonderful success in employing advances in medical science to keep more people alive longer. However, raw statistics alone fail to convey the real impact and meaning of AD. Each "case" of the scourge represents an individual human story about a particular human being's life. In this book, attorney, law professor, and author Vaughn James beautifully illustrates for the reader—through the rich and revealing narratives about his family and himself, as well as various hypothetical examples interspersed throughout the text—the adage generally attributed to pioneer health services researcher Ruth Roemer, "Statistics are people with the tears removed."

AD is a multifaceted phenomenon. Each situation involves a somewhat unique trajectory, but the affected person's decline is ultimately inevitable and the final result the same. Adapting to this human tragedy is a life-changing process not only for the affected individual but for family, friends, and the larger society. The challenges that emerge present physical, mental, emotional, financial, ethical, and (the primary focus of this book) legal ramifications for all of the involved parties. *The Alzheimer's Advisor* is not a self-help book for confronting these challenges with dignity and grace as much as a guide for getting help from the cadre of trained and compassionate professionals who have dedicated themselves to improving quality of life for people with AD and those who care for and about them.

Both victims and caregivers (professional and informal) need to maintain a combination of reality, reason, and hope. They need to be both strong and feeling. There is no magic formula for achieving the ideal mix, but this book should inspire readers to try to eliminate some of the uncertainty that is an inescapable part of AD by acting (not just contemplating) proactively and in a timely manner, especially concerning legal affairs. In the absence of purposeful planning assisted by competent multi-professional expertise and experience, important decisions get made through default mechanisms that may produce results inconsistent with the values and preferences of affected persons and their loved ones.

It is my fervent hope that one day in the not too distant future literature on this subject will become irrelevant to everyone except historians. As this book describes, significant ongoing scientific research is aimed at producing medical interventions to effectively treat and eventually prevent AD. The glimmers of success already apparent from these efforts will someday soon blossom into the creation of products that convert this biological abnormality with enormously adverse human consequences into a readily manageable inconvenience, if not a total relic of the past. Until that awaited day, though, we are fortunate to have this book and its wisdom.

Marshall B. Kapp, J.D., M.P.H.
Garwin Distinguished Professor of Law and Medicine
Southern Illinois University Schools of Law and Medicine

PREFACE

Late in 2003, I met Glen Provost, then Vice President for Health Policy and Public Affairs and a faculty member at the Texas Tech University Health Sciences Center in Lubbock, Texas. Glen invited me to join him in writing a book on the legal aspects of Alzheimer's disease. The book would focus on Texas law and would be a handbook for medical and legal practitioners, in particular, law and medical school students. I liked the idea. By the time I went to teach summer school at the University of Tennessee College of Law in 2004, I had produced an outline for the last ten chapters of the book. Glen was to work on the first two chapters.

Alas, a few months later, Glen announced that he would be retiring from his position at Texas Tech and that he would not be able to be my coauthor. I turned to Marshall Kapp, a member of the faculty at Southern Illinois University School of Law and School of Medicine, and asked him to join me. Marshall had a counter-suggestion: I would write the book and he would serve as my personal editor and a member of my support team. I agreed.

Shortly thereafter, I came across Stan Wakefield, now of Amacom Books. Stan liked the idea for the book and guided me as I put a book proposal together. Here is the finished product: *The Alzheimer's Advisor: A Caregiver's Guide to Dealing with the Tough Legal and Practical Issues.*

When I began the research for this book early in 2004, it was an academic exercise for me. I had known only one person who, in my opinion then, had exhibited Alzheimer's-like symptoms: my great-uncle who had died of pneumonia in December 2002 after exhibiting Alzheimer's-like symptoms for three to four years. The family is still not sure whether he really had Alzheimer's (no doctor ever made the diagnosis, and there was no postmortem autopsy of his brain).

Researching and writing the book has made me more aware of the symptoms of Alzheimer's disease. Since I left Tennessee in August 2004, I have seen one good old friend (I use "old" in both senses of the word—our friendship went back many years, to 1975, and she was elderly when she died in January 2006) exhibit symptoms of the disease and eventually die of pneumonia. I have also watched as four members of my family began exhibiting symptoms of the disease. One of them died recently— yes, of pneumonia. (As stated later in the book, most Alzheimer's patients die of pneumonia or asphyxiation.) Years before his death, his doctors confirmed—with 95 percent certainty—that he was indeed suffering from Alzheimer's disease.

The most recent diagnosis for a family member came four months before I completed the manuscript for this book. The doctor who made the diagnosis—and who spoke to me about his findings and conclusions because he had heard I was writing this book—believes the condition could be either Alzheimer's disease or a related condition, vascular dementia.

Surrounded as I am by Alzheimer's disease and other forms

of dementia, this book is no longer an academic exercise for me. Over the past several months, I have spent much time preparing many of the legal documents the book discusses and dealing with many of the issues contained herein. Moreover—and I am thankful to Stan Wakefield and Marshall Kapp for this—my attitude toward whom the book is for has changed. This is not a book only for medical school and law school students. It is a book for members of the public, for anyone who wants to prepare for the future just in case he or she or a relative ever develops Alzheimer's disease or any other form of dementia.

The truth is, we have no way of knowing if Alzheimer's disease will strike. As I said in a lecture to the Midland Estate and Business Council in Midland, Texas, in November 2007, given my family history, I would not be surprised if I developed Alzheimer's disease; I am therefore preparing for that eventuality. However, there are people with no family history of Alzheimer's who develop the disease. They, too, should prepare for the eventuality, if for no other reason than by the year 2050, 50 percent of all people over age 85 will be suffering from Alzheimer's disease.

I hope this book will help each of you in making preparations just in case Alzheimer's comes by some day. I also hope the book will help those who are already into the first stage of the disease. Finally, I hope the book will be of help to the caregivers of Alzheimer's patients, both those who are caregivers now and those who will have caregiving responsibilities thrust upon them some day.

As you read this book, I urge you to digest what you read slowly and seriously. The stories contained in the book are sometimes funny. For the most part, they are true. To protect the identity of the patients and their family members, I have changed their names, changed the names of the towns where they live, and made some minor changes to the facts.

Each story introduces a legal issue. Sometimes, I have had the actors and speakers ask me questions, to which I have responded with information in the chapter. I confess that sometimes I created the questions (that is, the speakers did not ask them in the way I presented them). Still, as you read, understand that the people in the stories are real human beings suffering from a real disease or, in some cases, real human beings trying to cope with the ravages of the disease in their loved ones.

ACKNOWLEDGMENTS

So many people played a part in getting this book to press. I'll try here to acknowledge and thank them all, hoping that I do not inadvertently leave someone out. If I do, please forgive me.

First, I give thanks to Almighty God, my Creator and Sustainer, who gave me the strength to write this book and helped me through some difficult times during the researching and writing period. But if not for You, oh Lord, I would not have completed this work.

Next, my family—Marva, Vijhay, Etienne, and Maelys—who endured my roaming the house at night and my ceaseless travels as I researched and wrote the book.

I dare not forget my wonderful colleagues at Texas Tech University School of Law who have been so supportive throughout this process, and my equally wonderful and supportive colleagues at the University of Tennessee College of Law.

And, of course, the wonderful staff at the Texas Tech University School of Law library, especially Sharon Blackburn and Judy Ford. You are the best.

The idea and the inspiration for this book came from Glen Provost, formerly of Texas Tech University Health Sciences Center. Thanks, Glen.

Professor Marshall Kapp of Southern Illinois University School of Law and School of Medicine, my personal editor, has been a source of constant and strong support. In addition, his writings helped me through some difficult times.

I had four wonderful research assistants: Tanya Johnson, Ariya McGrew, and Shirlyn Solas-Edwards of Texas Tech University School of Law, and Leigh Rhodes of the University of Tennessee College of Law. Without their help, I would have been lost.

As I turned out the drafts, I had to rely on my readers to catch the typos and legalese. For an excellent job in helping me keep this book simple and readable, I thank Ricky Sabar-Neelley and Dail Moise.

I was also blessed with the assistance of three very capable people who helped me perform difficult tasks like making copies, using a hole puncher, keeping files in order, and formatting files. For this, I am truly grateful to three of the world's best secretaries: Melinda Moore and Pamela Best of Texas Tech University, and Tammy Neff of the University of Tennessee College of Law.

Stan Wakefield of Amacom Books—you know what you've done. I am so thankful for the day our paths crossed. May these paths keep crossing.

Ellen Coleman, Mike Sivilli, Jacqueline Laks Gorman, and the others at Amacom Books have been a pleasure to work with. Let's do it again some time.

Dr. Claudine Smith has been more than gracious with her advice and guidance. I am grateful.

I am also grateful to the writers and publishers who have allowed me to use their copyrighted material: the Alzheimer's Association, the Family Caregiver Alliance, the National Association of Elder Law Attorneys, the Associated Press, Fair Winds Press, Lexis-Nexis, Thompson/West, Todd E. Feinberg, M.D. and Winnie Yu, and Professor Marshall Kapp.

Last, but by no means least, I am eternally grateful to the people who allowed me to drag them—kicking and screaming, sometimes—into the story: Andy, Arlette, Christie, Dail, Grandpa, Jasma, Kaisha, Sheila, Viktor, and Vilna. Of course, there are the wonderful people—who will remain nameless—of Monmouth County, New Jersey, and Amarillo, Texas, who helped this story take shape. For my part, I appreciate the opportunity to tell the story.

NOTE TO THE READER

Although this is not a work of fiction, the real names of the persons portrayed in the stories at the start of each chapter and in the hypothetical cases presented throughout the book have been changed to protect their privacy. Any similarity in name between a named character and anyone living or dead is purely coincidental and was not thus intended by the author.

CHAPTER 1

THOSE MEMORY LAPSES!

GRANDPA'S STORY

*G*randpa has been acting strangely of late. Last Monday, I told him I was heading to the movies. When I got back home, he asked, "So, how is Aunty Sheila?"

"Aunty Sheila?" I asked, startled. Aunty Sheila, Grandpa's sister, had been dead for some five months.

"Yes," Grandpa replied. "Didn't you tell me you were going to see her?"

"No, Grandpa. Aunty Sheila died in January. I went to the movies."

"Aunty Sheila is dead?" Grandpa asked, surprised. "What happened to her?"

"Grandpa, she died of pneumonia. Have you forgotten?"

"Pneumonia? I never knew that."

How could Grandpa, one of Aunty Sheila's pallbearers, have forgotten that his beloved sister had died? I put the episode down to hearing problems (Grandpa must have heard me say

*"Aunty Sheila" when I had said "the movies") and a tempo-
rary memory lapse (these lapses happen to us all, right?).*

*On Tuesday morning, I gave Grandpa a $100 bill to pass
on to Granny. He placed the bill on the coffee table. I left the
house and headed to the library. I had forgotten to take one of
the books I had to return to the library, so I turned around and
headed back home. Granny met me at the door. "You forgot to
leave the money," she said.*

"No," I replied, "I gave it to Grandpa."

*When we asked Grandpa about the money, he denied that
I had ever given him any. Yet there on the coffee table sat the
$100 bill. When we asked Grandpa how the money got there,
he simply replied, "I have no idea."*

*On Wednesday, all hell broke loose. Grandpa woke up early
and announced that he had to do some work in the yard. He
said that he "was tired" of seeing the yard open to stray dogs
and cats, so he wanted to spend the day building a 4-foot-high
concrete fence around the perimeter of the property. I agreed to
stay home to help him. We worked through the morning, and
by the time we were finished, we had built a 4-foot-high concrete wall around the perimeter of our property, with an 8-foot-
wide space for the cars to drive into and out of the property.*

*About an hour after we were finished, Grandpa took a
shower, got dressed, and announced that he was heading to the
supermarket. He took his keys, got into his car and—yes, you
guessed it—instead of heading through the 8-foot-wide opening, backed straight into the wall we had just built! Maybe, I
thought, Grandpa is losing his eyesight. Imagine my surprise
when Grandpa got out of the car and began asking who had*

built the wall and who could be so dumb as to put a wall around the perimeter of the property, followed by saying that whoever had done this "stupid thing" should pay to fix his car.

By Wednesday night, I was beginning to believe that Grandpa was experiencing more than hearing loss, poor eyesight, and temporary memory lapses. I had heard the words "dementia," "senile dementia," and "Alzheimer's disease" before, but I knew nothing about them. In fact, I wasn't sure whether the three terms referred to the same condition, if one was just a type of the other, or whether someone could suffer from all three conditions simultaneously. Still, I did begin to wonder from which, if any, Grandpa was suffering. I set myself to doing the research.

Some of you may recall moments when you apparently forgot to do or say something or when some event or person "slipped your mind." Some of these lapses are minor, like searching for your glasses while they are perched on your nose; searching for the car keys, only to discover they have been in one of your pockets all along; trying to remember the words of a hymn you sang so well at church two weeks ago; or trying to remember the name of the actor or actress in a favorite movie. We typically dismiss such instances as part of the aging process. Even young people sometimes joke with each other about "old age creeping in" or "Alzheimer's taking its toll."

Yet sometimes these memory lapses are no laughing matter. Indeed, especially in the elderly, they could be—and often are—the result of some form of dementia.

WHAT IS DEMENTIA?

Dementia is not itself a disease but is the name given to a group of symptoms including memory loss, reduced ability to reason, impaired judgment, and progressive loss of ability to understand either spoken or written language. Put in simple terms, dementia is somewhat like a fever. A fever is not a disease; it is merely a symptom of some disease. This, though, is where the similarities end.

A person suffering from dementia generally behaves in ways that others find irrational. He or she usually suffers from severe mood or personality changes, is physically aggressive, becomes easily agitated, and experiences altered perceptions such as hallucinations (accepting mental phenomena as being real), misperceptions (the inability to organize perceptual information), and delusions (holding on to unfounded, unrealistic beliefs without supporting evidence). In the later stages of the condition, the patient may become disoriented in time (i.e., not knowing the day of the week, the date of the month, or the month), place (not knowing where he or she is), and person (not knowing who he or she is—or who anybody else is, for that matter). The mere nature of these symptoms reveal why they are termed "dementia." After all, the term *dementia* comes from a Latin word that means "apart or away from the mind," or in common parlance, "irrational."

To define a medical condition as dementia, medical professionals generally look for the presence of at least two types of impairment: (1) significant memory problems, and (2) impairment of at least one other cognitive function, such as speech, the ability to think abstractly and exercise judgment, and the ability to articulate or manage previously learned information. As you can imagine, a dementia diagnosis can have serious implications for the patient, family members, and other caregivers, if any. After all, the condition results in a restriction in the patient's daily activities and, in most cases, leads to the long-term need for care.

While relatively young people (i.e., those between forty and fifty years of age) are sometimes afflicted with dementia, the incidence and prevalence of the disease are age-related. According to Professor Marshall Kapp of Southern Illinois University, almost 5 percent of persons age 65 and older are severely demented, with another 10 percent of that group in the moderate dementia category. Among persons age 85 and older, Professor Kapp states, more than 15 percent are severely demented.[1]

While people often speak of dementia as a single disease, in reality at least seventy-five distinct diseases belong to the "dementia group." Of these, Alzheimer's disease is the most prevalent, accounting for more than two-thirds of all dementia cases.[2] Other forms of dementia include senile dementia, vascular dementia, Pick's disease, and AIDS-induced dementia. Let's take a look at senile dementia and Alzheimer's disease in more detail.

SENILE DEMENTIA

As the name indicates, senile dementia is a type of dementia. It is caused by the degeneration of brain cells. Someone suffering from senile dementia experiences a gradual deterioration in brain function, resulting in the progressive loss of memory and mental abilities and noticeable personality changes.

Like its "parent," dementia, senile dementia encompasses several other forms of dementia. Foremost among these are Alzheimer's disease and Binswanger's disease. Senile dementia is the result of an underlying disease or condition that damages the patient's brain tissue and, as a result, causes brain function to diminish. While some forms of senile dementia, such as Alzheimer's disease, are irreversible, other forms—such as senile dementia caused by depression, poor nutrition, thyroid dysfunction, drug poisoning, and alcoholism, to name a few—can often be healed by treating the underlying problem.

ALZHEIMER'S DISEASE

As previously stated, Alzheimer's disease accounts for approximately two-thirds of dementia cases. Unlike some of the other forms of dementia, Alzheimer's disease is a brain disease that physically attacks the brain itself. Accordingly, the memory loss experienced by the Alzheimer's patient is merely a symptom or function of the brain disease, not the disease itself.

Because Alzheimer's physically attacks the brain, it is, in all senses of the word, irreversible. Over the course of its progression, it robs the patient of memory and cognitive skills and causes him or her to have severe changes in personality and behavior. While the disease itself does not cause death, it causes conditions (such as pneumonia, pressure ulcers, and the inability to swallow) that eventually lead to the patient's death. Although some people have lived up to twenty years with the disease, the average post-diagnosis life span for an Alzheimer's patient is eight to ten years.

The disease takes its name from a German physician, Dr. Alois Alzheimer. On November 26, 1901, Dr. Alzheimer began treating a 51-year-old woman who has become known as Auguste D. Auguste D. died on April 8, 1906, after having suffered for years from memory loss, progressive deterioration of her cognitive functions, and severe alterations in her personality. After Auguste D. died, Dr. Alzheimer performed an autopsy on her, including an autopsy of her brain. He noticed many unusual lesions and entanglements in her brain, which resembled those he had seen in older people who had been diagnosed with senile dementia. But Auguste D. was different. She had died at such a relatively young age that Dr. Alzheimer figured she was too young to have developed senile dementia. He therefore termed the condition pre-senile dementia. In the century since Dr. Alzheimer made his discovery, scientists have developed a much better understanding of the brain lesions and entanglements and their effects on the human brain. They have dubbed the condition caused by them "Alzheimer's disease."

WHAT WE KNOW AND DO NOT KNOW ABOUT ALZHEIMER'S DISEASE

Alzheimer's disease is a form of dementia. The disease, also known as Senile Dementia of the Alzheimer's Type (SDAT), is an irreversible disease that slowly erodes the brain. It robs the patient of memory and cognitive skills and causes changes in personality and behavior. The rate of progression of the disease is different for each person. Typically, if the disease develops rapidly, it continues to progress rapidly. On the other hand, if it progresses slowly to begin with, it will likely continue on a slow course.

In the century since Dr. Alzheimer first noticed the lesions and entanglements in Auguste D.'s brain, scientists have made giant strides in understanding the disease. They have, for example, developed an understanding of the lesions and entanglements noticed by Dr. Alzheimer and have given names to them: beta-amyloid plaques and neurofibrillary tangles. Scientists now acknowledge that the presence of these plaques and tangles in the brain is one of the classic signs of Alzheimer's disease. Indeed, they are what differentiate an Alzheimer's-stricken brain from a normal one.

Under normal circumstances, human beings undergo several changes as they age. For example, many parts of the human body change: bones become more brittle, vision diminishes, skin loses its elasticity and wrinkles easily, the brain shrinks, and nerve cells shrink. Unfortunately, nerve cells, unlike other cells in our bodies, have a limited capacity to regenerate; therefore, once they are gone—or shrink—no new nerve cells develop to replace them. As a result of these changes and other changes to the nervous system, as a person ages, short-term memory is less able to store information, which in turn inhibits a person's ability to learn new tasks. The person may have a harder time paying attention for any considerable length of time and may become less coordinated, less balanced, and more clumsy.

While these changes and their effects may scare the person experiencing them, they are not life-threatening. They are normal. They are part of the aging process. On the other hand, what occurs in Alzheimer's disease is not a normal part of the aging process, and in many ways, it *is* life-threatening.

WHAT YOU NEED TO KNOW ABOUT ALZHEIMER'S DISEASE

As of the middle of 2007, more than 26 million people worldwide had Alzheimer's disease; an Alzheimer's Association estimate forecasts that this number will quadruple by the year 2050.[3] This number is alarming. If it is correct, it would do well for today's generation to know more about the disease and its risk factors. After all, who knows who among us will develop the disease or which of our family members and loved ones will develop it?

CAUSES OF ALZHEIMER'S DISEASE

First, the bad news: No one knows exactly what causes Alzheimer's disease. Yet hypotheses abound. When I first heard of the disease several years ago, it was from a friend living in Columbus, Ohio, who advised me to throw away all my aluminum pots and pans and never use aluminum foil because, she said, aluminum deposits caused Alzheimer's disease. Another friend advised me to stop using my microwave oven because, she said, the radiation emanating from the machine caused Alzheimer's.

Scientists have disproved and discarded these theories as well as others involving lead, mercury, and other substances, but they haven't yet found a theory to replace them. What they can say is that genetics do play a role in the development of the disease. Indeed, 30 percent of all people with Alzheimer's disease have a family history of dementia. But that means that 70 percent of people with Alzheimer's have no family history of dementia! Some other factor or factors must be at work.

Unfortunately, no one knows just what these other factors are. Some scientists argue that the beta-amyloid plaques found in the brains of dead Alzheimer's patients are themselves the cause of the disease. Others contend that the neurofibrillary tangles are the culprits. Still others speculate that inflammation—

the immune system's normal response to injuries and foreign invaders such as cuts, viruses, and disease—may play a role in the development of Alzheimer's. Finally, others think it could be oxidative stress, which is a process triggered by inflammation and the brain's excess production of beta-amyloid.

All interesting theories, but they are only theories. Perhaps more disheartening, scientists cannot say for certain that a person has Alzheimer's disease because the only way to know for sure is by a microscopic examination of a sample of the person's brain, which can only occur *after* the person has died.

RISK FACTORS FOR ALZHEIMER'S DISEASE

Although the cause of Alzheimer's disease remains a mystery, scientists have been able to determine certain risk factors that may increase someone's chances of developing the disease. These risk factors include age, family history, a history of head trauma, the person's gender, cardiovascular disease, strokes, and poor education.

AGE

Advancing age is the number one risk factor for Alzheimer's disease. For every five-year age group of people over the age of 65, the percentage of people with Alzheimer's disease doubles. Hence, by age 85, an individual has a 50 percent chance of developing Alzheimer's. This is an unsettling phenomenon, because with the improvements in medical technology and the subsequent increase in life span that we are seeing today, more people are living to age 85 and beyond, and consequently, more and more people are being diagnosed with Alzheimer's disease. Yet Alzheimer's disease is not a normal part of aging. Age, then, is just one risk factor.

FAMILY HISTORY

We have already discussed the discovery that genetics plays a role in the development of Alzheimer's disease and the relationship between family history and the likelihood of someone developing the disease. However, the mere fact that a family member has the disease does not mean that any other family member will eventually develop it. All it means is that a person with a family history of Alzheimer's has a *greater chance* of developing the disease than someone who does not have that family history.

HISTORY OF HEAD TRAUMA

Although scientists have yet to discover how strong the link is, current research suggests that head injuries also increase a person's chances of developing Alzheimer's disease. A 2002 study by researchers at the University of Pennsylvania found that mild, repetitive head injuries accelerate the onset of Alzheimer's disease.[4]

GENDER

Women are more likely to develop Alzheimer's disease than men are. The reasons for this are unclear. However, it may well be because women generally outlive men. According to the Centers for Disease Control and Prevention, women in the United States have a life expectancy of 80.4 years, while men have a life expectancy of 75.2 years.[5] Since the risk of developing Alzheimer's disease increases with age, and since women live longer than men, it stands to reason that more women will develop the disease during their lifetimes.

CARDIOVASCULAR DISEASE

People with high blood cholesterol levels and high blood pressure are at risk for conditions like cardiovascular disease and diabetes. Recent research suggests that these same risk factors may also play a role in causing Alzheimer's disease.[6] Indeed, high blood pressure, diabetes, high blood cholesterol, and cardiovascular disease can damage blood vessels, affecting their ability to supply oxygen to the brain. This in turn disrupts the important neural circuits that humans use to perform cognitive functions. The result could well be Alzheimer's disease.

STROKES

A stroke occurs when the arteries carrying blood to the brain suffer a blockage or leakage, depriving the brain of the oxygen and glucose it needs to function properly. Moreover, when someone suffers a stroke, part of the person's brain literally dies, just as it does when the plaques and tangles that cause Alzheimer's disease form in the brain. Because of this death to part of the brain, people who have suffered a stroke are more likely than others to develop two types of dementia: vascular dementia and Alzheimer's disease.

POOR EDUCATION

Scientists believe a correlation exists between education—or the lack thereof—and the likelihood of developing Alzheimer's disease. An ongoing project known as the "Nun Study" appears to support this theory.[7] In this study, hundreds of nuns consented to be part of a research project. They also agreed that upon their deaths, they would donate their brains to the project's research.[8] On average, at the time they entered the convent, the nuns were twenty-two years old. When they joined the project, the nuns wrote autobiographical essays, which researchers measured for grammatical complexity and density of ideas (the number of ideas per ten words).

As the nuns aged, researchers tested them on such things as how many words they could remember minutes after reading them on flashcards, how many animals they could name in a minute, and whether they could count coins correctly. As the nuns died, the researchers studied their brains. They discovered that the nuns who in their twenties had written essays rich in ideas had fewer neurofibrillary tangles in their brains; those whose essays were not idea-rich tended to have these tangles.

This research suggests that low levels of education might be associated with Alzheimer's disease. Conversely, people who are better educated may well enjoy some protection from the disease. It may well be that the cognitive functioning required for intellectual pursuits fosters more neuronal connections, which may help keep the onset of Alzheimer's at bay.

Yet a high level of education does not necessarily protect a person from Alzheimer's disease. After all, both the Irish writer Iris Murdoch and former U.S. President Ronald Reagan—intelligent people by any standard—suffered from Alzheimer's.

WHAT THESE RISK FACTORS MEAN TO
YOU AND YOUR LOVED ONES

These are by no means the only risk factors associated with Alzheimer's disease, and the presence of one or more of them in no way indicates that you will eventually develop Alzheimer's. Instead, you should be aware that your chances of developing the disease are higher than those of a person without any of the risk factors, and it therefore would be prudent to start to prepare for the possibility.

THE STATISTICAL REALITY: WILL YOU OR
SOMEONE YOU KNOW DEVELOP
ALZHEIMER'S?

Alzheimer's disease is the most common form of dementia in people age 65 or older. Current estimates suggest that 4.5 million to 5 million people living in the United States have the disease. Approximately 3 percent of people between the ages of 65 and 74 have the disease; nearly half of all people over age 85 have it. Of those 85 and over, 15 percent are *severely* demented. Moreover, with the significant increases in life expectancy brought about through improvements in medical technology, better healthcare practices, and increases in better lifestyle awareness, Alzheimer's disease has become more prevalent. Looking into the future, as we continue to live longer, more of us will be diagnosed with the disease. If scientists are unable to develop preventive treatments and the population continues to age at its current rate, by 2050, 13.2 million Americans will have Alzheimer's. Worldwide, 106 million people will have the disease.[8]

Although Alzheimer's currently is and will remain to be more prevalent among the elderly, it sometimes affects people much younger. The disease occasionally emerges in adults in their forties and fifties. This sad fact provides sufficient reason for people of all ages to be aware of the disease, its effects, and the legal implications of an Alzheimer's diagnosis.

NOTES

1. Marshall Kapp, "Legal Standards for the Medical Diagnosis and Treatment of Dementia," *Journal of Legal Medicine*, Volume 23, September 2002.

2. National Institute on Aging, *Progress Report on Alzheimer's Disease*, NIH Pub. No. 00–4859, 2001.

3. Associated Press, "Alzheimer's Cases to Quadruple by 2050," June 11, 2007.

4. "Researchers Find Definitive Proof that Repetitive Head Injury Accelerates the Pace of Alzheimer's," *University of Pennsylvania Health System News*, January 15, 2002.

5. National Center for Health Statistics, *Deaths: Preliminary Data for 2004*, September 11, 2007.

6. "Cardiovascular Disease Leads to Higher Risk of Dementia," *Science Daily*, May 10, 2002.

7. The Nun Study is a longitudinal study of aging and Alzheimer's disease funded by the National Institute on Aging. Current participants are 678 American members of the School Sisters of Notre Dame religious congregation who are 75 to 106 years old.

8. Associated Press.

CHAPTER 2

IF IT *IS* ALZHEIMER'S: WHAT THE FUTURE HOLDS

AUNTY ARLETTE, AUNTY DAIL, AND UNCLE ANDY

*M*y research was proving interesting. I now knew more about dementia, senile dementia, and Alzheimer's disease than I'd known before. I decided it was time to do some research on real people. Two of my great-aunts, Aunty Arlette and Aunty Dail, were supposedly suffering from memory impairment, and my great-uncle, Uncle Andy, was beginning to exhibit some of the same symptoms as his two sisters—at least so the reports from other family members indicated.

Not knowing any better, the family members who had broken the news to me had simply said that Aunty Dail and Aunty Arlette were senile and that Uncle Andy was "somewhere between senility and plain old insanity." Of course, "senile" was the popular term for any form of memory impairment. I knew better; my research had already taught me that "senility" was actually a term that had fallen out of use and that the condition manifested by memory impairment was actually "dementia" in one of its many forms.

I figured I would pay my great-aunts and great-uncle a visit and simply observe their behavior. I was intrigued that these relatives were all Grandpa's siblings. Was this condition—whatever it was—hereditary?

I called my cousin Vilna (Aunty Arlette's daughter) to say that I'd be visiting the following week. She called me back an hour later to tell me that when she told Aunty Arlette of my pending visit, my aunt smiled and said, "Vaughn is coming to see me? That would be nice."

Encouraged, I made the six-hour drive to Aunty Arlette's home. Vilna greeted me at the door and, after the usual long hug and kisses on both cheeks, ushered me into the bedroom where Aunty Arlette was sitting up in bed staring blankly at Mother Angelica on EWTN (an elderly nun who appears on a religious cable station). "Mommy," Vilna announced, "Vaughn is here."

"Vaughn?" Aunty Arlette asked. "Who is Vaughn?"

"Mommy," Vilna replied, "remember, last week, I told you Vaughn was coming to visit you and you said, 'That would be nice'? Well, it's that same Vaughn, and he is here now." With that, Vilna left us alone.

Aunty Arlette shifted her blank stare from Mother Angelica to me. I saw a spark of recognition in her eyes. "Ah," she said, "why is Vilna trying to play tricks on me? Telling me some Vaughn came to see me! This is my own son, Edward! Ed, come kiss Mommy."

I decided to play along. I went and kissed her on both cheeks.

"So," Aunty Arlette stated matter-of-factly, "you came to see your little sister? She's been taking good care of me, you know. It's just that every now and then she goes away and some other lady comes in to care for me. That one is mean."

Alarmed, I asked, "Do you know the name of that mean woman?" "No, no," she replied, "she has never told me her name, but she is mean and vicious. Always giving me orders— eat this, eat that, go to sleep, wake up. Mean woman!" I made a mental note to talk to Vilna to see what could be done about this situation.

"So," I asked, "apart from that mean woman, is everything okay?"

"Almost," she replied. "But sometimes that picture of the Blessed Virgin on the wall talks to me. I don't understand what she is saying, but her chatter keeps me up at night. I guess she is scolding me for my sins, but I wish I could understand what she is saying."

After that revelation, Aunty Arlette and I had a fairly normal conversation. She told me tales of what life was like for her growing up back home in Dominica and related aspects of our family history, while I listened attentively and smiled or laughed. We never touched on current affairs, but that was fine with me: I loved delving into our family history and thoroughly enjoyed the afternoon. One thing, though, did puzzle me: I was Edward all afternoon. Eventually, I went to the guestroom where I would be spending the next two nights. I decided to hold off asking Vilna about the mean caregiver, hoping that I'd get to see her myself when she showed up the following morning.

The next morning, I woke up early, showered, got dressed, and went to Aunty Arlette's room. She was sitting in a chair close to her bed. She looked up as I came in. "Vaughn!" she exclaimed. "It is so good of you to come see me! When did you arrive? How are the wife and children? Oh Vaughn, it is so good to see you!"

That was good. I was "Vaughn" again. For the next two hours, Aunty Arlette and I had a very normal conversation—a far cry from the one about the Virgin Mary of the previous afternoon. This time we talked about the weather, politics, the CNN newscast of earlier that day, the day's edition of Good Morning America, and, of course, today's news from our homeland. Aunty Arlette was very coherent through it all. At around 11:30, she told me she was getting tired and needed to rest her eyes. I left her, went to the local library to read, and then visited some old friends who lived in town. I returned to the house shortly before five o'clock and, after the obligatory hug and kisses from Vilna, went to Aunty Arlette's room. "Hello," I said as I walked through the door.

Aunty Arlette looked away from the local news and said in a low, stern voice, "Edward, I am happy you stopped by. You really must talk to your little sister about what she made that man do to me today."

"What man? What happened?" I asked, again alarmed.

"That man, Dr. Osborne," Aunty Arlette explained. "He came to see me today. He touched me in places he had no right to. I am a respectable woman! No man—doctor or otherwise—should touch me in such places."

"I'll go talk to Vilna right now," I said.

"Good," Aunty Arlette replied. "Come tell me what happens after you spank her skinny backside."

I found Vilna in the living room catching up on the local

news. *"Vilna,"* I said, *"what happened when Dr. Osborne visited this afternoon?"*

"Who?"

"Dr. Osborne. Aunty Arlette says he examined her today."

"Oh dear," Vilna responded, *"Mommy has been saying this for the past four years, ever since Dr. Pascal gave her a thorough exam. It was around then that she began acting crazy."*

"So who is Dr. Osborne?" I asked.

"He was Mommy's doctor when she was a young woman. Last I heard he retired and moved to St. Thomas."

This seemed a good time to ask about Aunty Arlette's caregiver, whom I was beginning to suspect might not be real. *"Caregiver?"* Vilna replied. *"Vaughn, I haven't hired a caregiver. I do everything by myself, all alone. I quit my job to take care of Mommy. I am the only one here with her."*

Despite all this, I slept relatively well that night. The following morning, Aunty Arlette was as cheery as ever and very nice to both Vilna and me. After an enjoyable two hours with them, I got ready to leave for home. *"Vaughn,"* Aunty Arlette said, *"come see me again soon, you hear?"* I promised I would.

Four days later, I flew out of Lubbock Preston Smith International Airport to go visit Aunty Dail. I had telephoned her daughter, Christie, to say that I was coming for a visit. I pulled into the driveway shortly after one o'clock. Christie and her boyfriend were tending to the family's small grocery store located next to the house. Aunty Dail was sitting in a lawn chair on the front porch slowly eating her lunch. After the usual hug and kisses from Christie and firm handshake from her boyfriend, I went to see my aunt. *"Hello, Aunty Dail,"* I said, coming to stand behind her chair and hugging her around the shoulders, planting a kiss on each of her cheeks.

"Hee, hee, hee."

After a moment's pause, I said, "Aunty, I came over to see how you're doing. It is good to see you."

"Hee, hee, hee."

"Well, I hope you're enjoying your lunch."

"Hee, hee, hee."

Our initial conversation—if you could call it that—lasted for about ten minutes. No matter what I said, the only response I could elicit was "Hee, hee, hee." Later, she added a gesture. If a car passed by, she would point and say, "Hee, hee, hee." If a bird chirped, she would point at it and say, "Hee, hee, hee." As the afternoon wore on and the sun began to head toward the horizon, streaks of light showed up on the legs of my trousers. You guessed it: Aunty Dail pointed at those streaks and said, "Hee, hee, hee."

The next morning brought more of the same. From the moment we sat down to breakfast to the time I jumped into my rental car for the journey to the airport, the only words I heard Aunty Dail utter were "Hee, hee, hee," and the only "meaningful" activity she engaged in was pointing at various people and objects. Through it all, Christie just watched me and shrugged her shoulders. I drove to the airport filled with despair. I had visited two of my elderly relatives, and clearly, something was drastically wrong with both of them. Moreover, that "something wrong" seemed to be with the brain or the mind.

Two days later, I set out to visit Uncle Andy down in Dominica in the Caribbean. I got to his home late that night to find *that he was asleep. I went to bed and woke up the following morning delighted that I would be seeing my dear great-uncle again.*

I walked into the dining room to find Uncle Andy having breakfast. When he saw me, he was ecstatic. "Vaughn," he said rather loudly, "it is so good to see you. When did you arrive?"

"I came in last night, but you were asleep."

"Someone should have awakened me," Uncle Andy said. "I would have loved to have seen you last night."

"Yeah, right," his wife, Aunty June, responded. "Can anyone ever awaken you when you go to sleep?"

"Vaughn, my boy," Uncle Andy said, "I worked hard all my life. Right now, I am old and tired. I need rest. So, when I go to sleep, I sleep. Is anything wrong with that?"

Not wanting to get involved in a family squabble, I said, "Well, come on, let's eat." We ate heartily, enjoying a wonderful conversation on the differences between the 1960s and 1970s. I did notice, however, that Uncle Andy occasionally spilled some food on his shirt; however, he did not seem to notice what he had done. I wondered if he did that all the time.

After breakfast, Uncle Andy announced that he wanted to watch The Price Is Right. *He parked himself in front of the television set and was soon lost to the rest of us. I quietly left the room and headed to the beach. Upon my return to the house several hours later, Uncle Andy was sitting in the living room. He stared at me, but there was no sign of recognition in his eyes. After a minute, he said, "Gabriel, what on earth are you doing in my house? You rascal! After all you did to me, you have the nerve to show up at my house! If it wasn't for June, I'd kick your backside out!"*

I was taken aback. I was certainly not Gabriel (Aunty June's nephew), nor did I even look like him. I was at a loss for words. Aunty June saved the day by calling me into the kitchen and explaining that Uncle Andy behaved "strange" every afternoon.

Later, at dinner, Aunty June told Uncle Andy that I was Vaughn, not Gabriel. He appeared to accept that fact. However, he sat at the table staring at his food but not eating. I eventually asked him whether he was going to eat. "I already ate," he said.

"No," I told him. "You haven't eaten a thing."

"Oh, oh, I thought I had."

Uncle Andy then picked up some food with his fork, brought the fork up to his mouth, then put the fork right back down without eating any of the food. He did this a few times. Then I said, "Uncle, you still have not eaten any of the food."

"Oh, oh," he replied, "I thought I had."

I decided to help him complete his meal. I picked up the fork and fed him like a small child. He dutifully opened and closed his mouth as I requested while I fed him. All the while, my heart was breaking. My great-uncle, with whom I had shared many happy moments, was like a toddler, and I, who had depended on him for so many years, was now feeding him.

The job of feeding Uncle Andy his dinner became mine for the rest of the week I spent in Dominica. At the end of the week, as my plane took off for Texas, my heart was heavy. In the space of one month, I had visited three of my elderly relatives, three relatives who were very dear to me. It was obvious that they were all suffering from some mind-altering diseases, be they dementia, senile dementia, or Alzheimer's disease.

It is safe to say that almost everyone experiences bouts of forgetfulness. I confess that I have often been in the middle of a lecture and lost my train of thought. On many occasions, too, I temporarily forget the name of the actor who starred in both *The Quick and the Dead* and *Absolute Power*—especially when I recognize him in another movie, such as *Unforgiven* or *The Firm*—but just cannot remember his name (Gene Hackman). Often when I recount these episodes to family and friends, they have the same reaction: "Shakes, you're getting old!"

Well, it is true: As we age, our memories falter. Indeed, people as young as age 30 experience episodes of faltering memory. These episodes are not necessarily symptoms of Alzheimer's disease or any other form of dementia. However, if they develop into or are part of a more disturbing trend, they may well indicate that a person is developing Alzheimer's disease. When a person is in the early stages of Alzheimer's, the episodes of forgetfulness progress to the point where the person frequently has trouble remembering things that happened earlier in the day. Soon, the person begins to forget events that happened just a few days before. He or she also has great difficulty learning and recalling new information. If family members see someone who exhibits these characteristics, they should begin thinking about the possibility of Alzheimer's disease.

DIAGNOSING ALZHEIMER'S DISEASE

Because Alzheimer's disease resembles several other forms of dementia, no one, including a physician, knows for sure whether it is in fact Alzheimer's. To make the diagnosis, the doctor employs tools such as neurological exams, cognitive screening exams, blood tests, and brain scans. However, the doctor must also rely heavily on reports by the patient, family members, and close friends. In discussing Alzheimer's, it is important to remember that the development and progress of the disease vary from person to person. No two people have the same experiences, and no two people experience the same symptoms. Further, in some people the disease progresses rapidly; in others, it progresses slowly. In all patients, though, the disease progresses in stages.

Some scientists have broken down the progress of Alzheimer's disease into three broad stages: (1) mild, (2) moderate, and (3) severe. The Alzheimer's Association, on the other hand, divides the disease into seven stages: (1) no cognitive decline, (2) very mild decline, (3) mild decline, (4) moderate decline, (5) moderately severe decline, (6) severe decline, and (7) very severe decline. In this book, we follow the classifications of those scientists who say that Alzheimer's progresses through three stages. Regardless of the number of stages you adopt, you must keep in mind that these stages are mere guidelines and not strict definitions of what the patient will experience or loved ones will notice at each phase of the disease. It is quite possible—and it does happen—that some people display symptoms from a more advanced stage of the disease at what seems to be an earlier stage. Other patients may simultaneously display symptoms from more than one stage. For this reason, it is not always easy to determine the disease stage the patient is going through.

SYMPTOMS OF ALZHEIMER'S DISEASE

There are two types of Alzheimer's disease: early onset and late onset. Early onset Alzheimer's can run in families. In fact, scientists have identified three early onset genes.

In early onset Alzheimer's disease, symptoms first appear before age 60. Early onset is much less common than late onset, accounting for only 5 to 10 percent of Alzheimer's cases. However, when the disease strikes that early, it tends to progress rapidly. Late onset Alzheimer's develops in people age 60 and over. Although late onset Alzheimer's may run in families, the role of genes is less direct and definitive. The genes may not cause the disease but may simply increase the likelihood of formation of plaques and tangles or other Alzheimer's-related pathologies in the brain. Regardless of the type or the cause, the stages of progression and the symptoms are the same.

STAGE I: MILD ALZHEIMER'S DISEASE

Early in Stage I, as the nerve cells first begin to deteriorate, there may be no signs or symptoms of Alzheimer's disease. In fact, the person may not notice anything different. However, as the plaques and tangles build up in the brain and the destruction of the nerve cells worsens, noticeable changes in behavior occur. At this stage, the symptoms of the disease may include memory loss, difficulty reasoning, poor judgment, language difficulties, confusion about time and space, a decreasing ability to interpret sensory stimuli, an inability to concentrate, loss of initiative, extreme mood changes, and changes in personality. Let us examine these symptoms in some detail.

MEMORY LOSS

In Stage I Alzheimer's disease, the person experiences memory loss, especially of recent events. This happens because the disease first strikes in the part of the brain called the hippocampus, where short-term memories are stored and then converted into long-term memories. With the hippocampus under attack from plaques and tangles, short-term memories disappear completely.

As a result, the person begins to neglect appointments and to forget to complete important tasks like paying the bills. These lapses soon begin to interfere with daily functioning. Because of missed doctor's visits, the individual goes without adequate medical care. With the utility bills unpaid, the utility companies may disconnect their services, leaving the person without electricity or telephone service. In one recent case, an Alzheimer's patient—a medical doctor with more than enough money in her bank account to meet all her financial obligations—forgot to make the monthly mortgage payments on her house.

Interestingly, while the person is unable to recall recent events, he or she can still remember things that occurred a long time ago, such as during childhood or young adulthood. I met one Alzheimer's patient who, although unable to recall where her daughter now lived, could talk animatedly about the day her daughter was born and events that took place soon thereafter.

There is a medical explanation for this. Stage I Alzheimer's disease does not affect the temporal and parietal lobes of the brain, where long-term memories are stored. Hence, while short-term memory is erased, long-term memories are alive and well.

DIFFICULTY REASONING

Logical or "abstract" thinking is necessary for human beings to perform their daily tasks. Human beings engage in abstract thinking every day, almost without thinking much about it. We drive cars, balance checkbooks, prepare meals, and take showers. We know the steps involved in each of these activities and follow them to their logical conclusion.

For the person with Stage I Alzheimer's disease, however, such thinking is difficult, becoming increasingly harder with each passing day. Alas, without the ability to engage in abstract thinking, it is difficult for anyone to perform tasks that require sound reasoning and judgment, to determine what needs to be done with a series of numbers, or to comprehend information. Accordingly, the person in Stage I Alzheimer's finds it difficult—almost impossible—to perform tasks we take for granted, such as balancing a checkbook, following a recipe, preparing a meal, following directions to a friend's house, or completing a form.

POOR JUDGMENT

The difficulties the Alzheimer's patient faces because of memory loss and problems in reasoning combine to create a new problem: poor judgment. Put simply, judgment refers to a person's ability to act upon information he or she possesses. This information consists of both currently received information and information stored in the person's short-term and long-term memories. The person pieces the information together in a logical manner to make a decision or to arrive at some conclusion. To exercise good judgment, a person must have sound memory, the ability to think logically, and the ability to reason. However, we have already discovered that the person with Stage I Alzheimer's has difficulty reasoning and has no short-term memory. This person is not able to exercise good judgment. Rather, he or she is prone to make choices and decisions that are faulty or even dangerous. Indeed, people in Stage I Alzheimer's may purchase expensive objects they cannot afford; transfer their homes to others for far less than what they are worth (some end up homeless); guarantee loans for unscrupulous family members, neighbors, and friends; or dress in ways that are inappropriate. Some have basements, garages, or attics filled with tools and equipment they will never use; others write checks on long overdrawn or nonexistent accounts; and some dress in shorts on winter days and then wonder why they are cold.

LANGUAGE DIFFICULTIES

Occasionally, all of us struggle to find the right word to express a thought, whether in a casual conversation or in the middle of delivering a lecture. We eventually find the right word or a substitute and move on. However, the person with Stage I Alzheimer's finds it impossible to find the right word or phrase. As the disease progresses, the person's vocabulary and ability to say just what he or she means diminishes. In response, the person may (1) substitute similar-sounding words for the correct word although they have very different meanings, (2) talk less to avoid making embarrassing mistakes, and (3) repeatedly ask the same questions. The person may also cover up his or her language difficulties by smiling, nodding, and agreeing in order to make others believe he or she has understood and is expressing an opinion. This makes this symptom difficult to spot.

CONFUSION ABOUT TIME AND SPACE

A person in Stage I Alzheimer's disease may frequently become confused about what day it is and where he or she is. One New York woman drove to the mall and then forgot where she was, why she was there, and—most important—how to get back home. Another woman in Maine, left alone by a lake for a few minutes, did not then walk to the house where she had been living for years but to the location of the house in which she had grown up. She was totally exasperated that the ice cream shop that used to be on the street corner was no longer there.

Forgetting the day of the week, the month, or the year is common at this stage. A Stage 1 sufferer may get up and get dressed for church on a weekday or vice versa, get dressed for work on a weekend.

DIFFICULTIES ASSESSING SENSORY STIMULI

Very often, the first sense affected by Alzheimer's disease is sight. The person in Stage I Alzheimer's whose visual perception is distorted may lose depth perception, misjudge the appearance of objects, and become disoriented while driving. It is not unusual for people in Stage I Alzheimer's to drive the car into the back wall of the garage or to miss the driveway completely and drive into the fence.

INABILITY TO CONCENTRATE

People with Stage I Alzheimer's have great difficulty reading a passage and making sense of it. They find it hard to track conversations. Further, because the person loses the ability to remain focused, even doing familiar things may become difficult.

LOSS OF INITIATIVE

Most of us are energized by doing things we enjoy, whether it is writing short stories and poetry, singing, gardening, taking a walk, or just watching television. A person with Stage I Alzheimer's may lose his or her desire and energy to engage in these activities. Hence, the person may spend countless hours sitting in front of the television set (though not really *watching TV*), sleep more than usual (in fact, sleep quite a lot), and express a lack of interest in activities.

EXTREME MOOD CHANGES

Sudden and dramatic mood shifts for no apparent reason are common. Sufferers can be sweet and quiet one moment, then boisterous and rude the next.

CHANGES IN PERSONALITY

In Stage I Alzheimer's, the person's inhibitions give way to a loss of control. As a result, the person undergoes a dramatic personality shift: The extrovert becomes a recluse, the "lady" becomes outspoken and rude, the outgoing and friendly neighbor withdraws into himself and stops seeing friends, and the church-lady swears at any and everything. Indeed, some of these behaviors may be antisocial, offensive, and embarrassing. One woman whose father is going through Stage I Alzheimer's told me that her dad—formerly a quiet man who never swore—became so foul-mouthed that she no longer allows her children to visit him.

In some cases, the disease brings to the fore subtle personality characteristics the person previously was able to keep under control. For example, a suspicious person may become very paranoid, and a frugal person may become miserly.

OTHER SIGNS OF STAGE I ALZHEIMER'S

These are by no means the only symptoms of Stage I Alzheimer's. Following is a list of things you may notice being done by a person going through Stage I of the disease:

- Misplacing things and/or putting things in odd places. The person with Stage I Alzheimer's may put things in strange places, like a wallet in the freezer.

- Repeating the same phrase or story, completely unaware of the repetition.

- Resisting making even simple decisions.

- Taking longer to do routine chores and becoming upset if something unexpected occurs.

- Forgetting to eat, eating only one kind of food, or eating all the time.

- Neglecting hygiene and wearing the same clothes day after day, insisting they are clean.
- Becoming obsessive about checking, searching, or hoarding things of no value.

STAGE II: MODERATE ALZHEIMER'S DISEASE

In Stage II, the plaques and tangles affect more nerve cells and more parts of the brain. During this stage, the person with Alzheimer's develops new behaviors and exhibits more personality changes. The symptoms are now so glaring and the person's thinking so hazy and sound judgment so diminished that family members recognize that something more than simple aging is at work. Behaviors that manifest themselves during this stage of the disease include:

- Loss of interest in appearance, manners, and hygiene. The person may require help with basic hygiene such as toileting and dressing
- Difficulty sleeping or sleeping for extended periods
- Confusion or inability to identify familiar objects and people, for example, thinking the person's wife is his sister
- Increasingly poor judgment, which may pose safety risks, such as getting lost, accidental poisoning, and falling
- Difficulty organizing thoughts, making logical explanations, or planning
- Restless, repetitive movements or actions, including pacing, opening and closing doors, and telephoning
- Constant repetition of stories, favorite words, statements, or motions

- Inappropriate and unusual behavior, for example, accusing loved ones of illicit acts and making threats or cursing, even in public
- Inventing stories to fill gaps in memory
- Seeing, hearing, smelling, or tasting things that are not there
- Inappropriate sexual behavior, such as disrobing in public or masturbating in front of others

STAGE III: SEVERE ALZHEIMER'S DISEASE

By the time the disease progresses to Stage III, it has eroded the person's ability to think or reason. The person requires assistance for the most essential tasks of day-to-day living. His or her personality may be entirely changed. In some cases, the person may be bedridden. Because the sufferer's body is also considerably weakened, he or she is at risk for other illnesses. It is no wonder, then, that many Alzheimer's patients die, not from Alzheimer's disease itself, but from pneumonia. Common changes in the patient at this stage include:

- Complete memory loss: The person is no longer able to recognize him- or herself or close family members.
- Difficulty speaking: Speech becomes increasingly difficult, garbled, and slurred. Sometimes the person stops speaking altogether.
- Difficulty eating, including refusing to eat, choking when eating, or difficulty with or forgetting how to chew or swallow. Weight loss, malnourishment, and related conditions can result.

- Repetitive crying out, as well as constant patting or touching things, groaning, and grumbling for no apparent reason.

- Loss of control of bowel and bladder and frequent incontinence.

- Discomfort, sometimes extreme, when being transferred or touched.

- Difficulty or inability to walk or even stand unaided as a result of unsteadiness.

- Seizures and frequent infections.

- Excessive sleep.

- Inability to perform the activities of daily living, including personal care, using the toilet, bathing, dressing, eating, and getting around.

THE FIRST REACTION: DENIAL, DENIAL!

Because Alzheimer's is a disease that affects the mind, many people equate it with "madness" or "craziness." It is not uncommon for both patients and family members to react with denial when the disease first strikes. As the symptoms begin to manifest themselves, patients and family members—especially the family members—look around for any explanation except the most obvious: Alzheimer's disease.

Even after a doctor makes the diagnosis and the patient begins living with the knowledge that he or she has Alzheimer's, family members may still deny the reality and look to alternative causes for their loved one's forgetfulness, mood swings, excessive sleeping, and other symptoms. In one case I encountered while writing this book, family members clung to the belief that their Alzheimer's-stricken husband and father was losing his eyesight rather than his memory. In another instance, a husband, rather than acknowledging that his wife had Stage I Alzheimer's and needed care, opted to call her lazy because of her inability to continue working and her new "habit" of sleeping for long hours every afternoon. In a third case of early onset Alzheimer's, the patient looked healthy; if you had not known her prior to the onset of the disease, you would not know that she was an Alzheimer's patient. Perhaps for this reason, when the doctor made the diagnosis, one of her parents told me, "I just cannot accept it!"

These denials are somewhat understandable (remember, Alzheimer's and diseases of the brain and mind still carry stigmas in some people's minds). However, the denials are unhealthy for both the patient and family members, who may delay seeking adequate care and making necessary preparations for living with Alzheimer's. Rather than deny the new reality, the patient's family members should accept it and prepare the patient to live out the rest of his or her life in relative comfort, even as they prepare themselves to serve as caregivers and guardians of their loved one and to continue to meet the demands and needs of their own lives.

CHAPTER 3

OKAY, IT *IS* ALZHEIMER'S: THE LEGAL IMPLICATIONS

AUNTY ARLETTE BUYS A NEW CAR

I woke up to the incessant ringing of the telephone. Confused, I grabbed the phone and mumbled, "Hello."

The ringing continued. "Hello," I said, "hello!"

The ringing continued. Then I realized I was holding the alarm clock, not the phone! I picked up the phone—the real one, this time—and answered, "Hello?"

It was Vilna, a breathless, crying Vilna. "Vaughn," she said, "you have to help me. Yesterday morning, Mommy woke up saying she felt fine and that she wanted to go take a walk. She was gone for several hours, and when she came back, she was driving a new car. I asked her where she got it. She said she'd gone to the car dealership, and that the 'nice man' asked her some questions, asked to see her Social Security card, typed some things 'on something like a typewriter but with a TV

attached,' then let her have the car for $98 down and her prom-
ise to make monthly payments of 'just over $300' for the next
'few years.' I asked her just where she got the $98. She said she
wrote a check."

"Just a minute," I interrupted. "Does Aunty Arlette have a
checking account?"

"Yes," Vilna replied, "a convenience account that lets me
make transactions for her. It has been ages since she wrote a
check herself."

"And is there a balance in the account?"

"Yes, a few thousand dollars."

"Enough to pay over $300 for the next, say, five years?"

"Certainly not!" Vilna said. Then she continued: "I asked
her whether the 'nice man' realized she was sick. 'Sick?' she
asked. 'Who's sick? Me, I am as fit as a fiddle!' Vaughn, I am
worried that Mommy got involved in something that will come
back and bite me in the butt. Is there anything you can do?"

My mind began churning. How could we turn this around?
Did Aunty Arlette have the necessary mental capacity to enter
into a contract to purchase a car? Was she even legally compe-
tent? Was she even able to drive? And should she be driving, for
her own safety and that of others?

When family members begin to suspect that something is amiss
with their loved one's cognitive functioning—and that it might
be Alzheimer's—they begin to think of ways to cope. Typically,
they begin to think of physicians and other healthcare or health-
related professionals that they and the patient might consult,

such as psychologists, psychiatrists, neurologists, and the family doctor. They seldom think they need to see an attorney.

The reality is that many legal challenges lie ahead for the patient, family members, and even friends. Some of the issues, like the need for estate planning documents or advance directives (documents that relate someone's medical care and end-of-life wishes to doctors, medical personnel, and family members) are simple enough. Others are complex and have far-reaching consequences, like determining the patient's liability for his or her actions while under the influence of the disease.

The remaining chapters of this book focus on the legal aspects of Alzheimer's disease, from pre-diagnosis to end-of-life decisions. These chapters introduce terms and concepts you may never have contemplated before, but a firm understanding of them is necessary if you are to adequately care for a loved one stricken with the disease.

Consider this: I recently spoke with a woman who had been caring for her incapacitated sister for several years. I asked her whether she and her family had purchased a long-term care insurance policy for her sister. Not surprisingly, she had never heard of long-term care insurance. She said that she and her family had always assumed that somehow, one or more of them would always be around to care for their sibling. They had never considered the possibility that they could all predecease her. Not only did she and her family not know about long-term care insurance, but they had never considered obtaining powers of attorney (documents that enable others to act on behalf of someone who is unable to act for him- or herself) or advance directives while her sister still had the capacity to sign them.

My hope is that reading this book leads you to consider not only long-term care insurance but also many of the additional estate planning and other tools that you might need as you care for a family member succumbing to Alzheimer's. When you are dealing with family members who have Alzheimer's, legal assistance is needed sooner rather than later.

In understanding the need for legal assistance when Alzheimer's strikes a loved one, you need to understand two legal terms: *mental capacity* and *legal competency*. Because Alzheimer's attacks the brain, causing it to deteriorate, people suffering from the disease are unable to function like other members of society, even those with life-threatening diseases that do not affect the mind.

Most if not all Alzheimer's patients suffer from an impaired ability to make decisions. This impairment has serious consequences for the patient and his or her family members and caregivers. From a legal standpoint, family members and caregivers must be concerned with whether the patient possesses the mental capacity to engage in certain transactions or make certain decisions or has the legal competency to retain his or her autonomy.

MENTAL CAPACITY AND ALZHEIMER'S DISEASE

Mental capacity and legal competency, though related, are not synonymous. In fact, they are two distinct concepts. Mental capacity relates to someone's ability to perform a certain task. For example, a normal adult has a number of different capacities, including the capacity to:

- Enter into a contract.

- Prepare (or have prepared) and execute a last will and testament.

- Consent to medical treatment.

- Manage one's financial or personal affairs or appoint agents to make such management decisions on one's behalf.

Each of these capacities involves a distinct combination of functional abilities and skills, and accordingly, the mental capacity—or level of alertness or functional ability—for each one is different.

Although different jurisdictions in the United States set different standards for determining these requirements, all jurisdictions are interested in the same thing: Is the individual able to make the decision required for this particular task? Thus, legally speaking, capacity implies that there are varying levels of ability, depending on the level of the decision-making task.[1]

To guide you, we'll look at some generally accepted requirements for the various types of decisions that someone with Alzheimer's disease might be called upon to make.

THE CAPACITY TO MAKE A CONTRACT

Even a casual listener to the news must have heard horror stories about unscrupulous people taking advantage of people who have developed Alzheimer's disease. In the first half of 2007, ABC News broke the story of a real estate agent in New York who purchased a home from an Alzheimer's-stricken doctor for about one-quarter of its value. As this book went to press, the

Kings County District Attorney's office was investigating the transfer of the doctor's home to the real estate agent.

I recently spoke to a car dealer who told me of a young woman who took advantage of her Alzheimer's-stricken grandmother by getting her to cosign a car loan. When the dealer realized that the grandmother had Alzheimer's, he rescinded the contract and repossessed the car.

That doesn't compare to the news story presented in Figure 3-1.

These incidents raise some important questions. First, does someone suffering from Alzheimer's have the capacity to enter into a valid, legally binding contract, and second, how do we define the term "capacity to enter into a contract"?

For a contract to be valid, the people who enter into the contract (called "the parties") must be capable of doing so, which means they must possess both the legal capacity and the mental capacity to enter into the contract. If one of the parties entering into the contract lacks the requisite legal or mental capacity, the contract is invalid and not legally binding.

A person lacks the legal capacity to incur contractual duties—and thus enter into a valid, legally binding contract—if, at the time of signing the contract, he or she is:

1. Under guardianship
2. A minor
3. Mentally ill
4. Intoxicated

The courts have for years grappled with the definition of mental capacity as it relates to someone's ability to enter into a

Figure 3-1. **The story of a car dealer taking advantage of an Alzheimer's patient.**

Christy Karras, "Oregon Auto Dealer Agrees to Pay Fines in Alzheimer's Case," Associated Press, August 19, 2001.

Oregon Auto Dealer Agrees to Pay Fines in Alzheimer's Case

PORTLAND, Ore (AP)—The family of a man with Alzheimer's who was sold seven cars in one month said they would drop their lawsuit after the auto dealer agreed to pay $120,000 in fines and restitution.

In an agreement with the attorney general's office, Hillsboro Chrysler Jeep warehouse agreed to reverse the sales and pay $90,879 to James D. Rickards, 78, who bought the cars in February and March 2000.

The dealer also paid the Department of Justice $31,000, most of which will go into a consumer protection fund.

"Families dealing with aging parents have enough challenges without having unscrupulous sales people prey on their loved ones," Attorney General Hardy Myers said.

Rickards' family agreed to drop a lawsuit. Attorney John Shadden, who now handles Rickards' financial affairs, said he was satisfied with the deal.

The agreement stops short of saying the dealership violated the law.

Dealership manager Kevin Chimienti said his salespeople not only didn't break the law but also didn't know the victim had bought that many cars.

"We weren't aware we had sold him seven cars. He dealt with different people," Chimienti said.

Rickards, who has no driver's license, traded in two of his own vehicles and bought sports cars and sports utility vehicles totaling $244,708.

"This would be hard to explain even for a non-Alzheimer's customer," Myers' spokeswoman Jan Margosian said. "In every case, he paid more for the car than it was worth."

contract. One Illinois court has held that the ability to legally enter into a contract requires that a person entering into the contract possesses sufficient mental ability to appreciate the effect of what he or she is doing. Two other courts, one in Tennessee and the other in Minnesota, have held that contractual capacity requires that the contracting party understands in a reasonable manner the nature and consequences of his or her transactions.

These legal principles hold great significance for Alzheimer's patients. Based on our knowledge of the disease, it would seem no one would deny that an Alzheimer's patient most likely lacks the capacity to enter into a valid, legally binding contract. Indeed, courts have held that a contracting party suffering from a disability like Alzheimer's disease could not exchange promises that would give rise to an enforceable agreement, and such a contract is not only voidable but also void from the start.

Yet the nature of Alzheimer's disease is such that while the patient may lack mental capacity at one particular point in time, he or she may well possess the requisite capacity at some other point. For example, Alzheimer's patients suffer from a phenomenon called *sun downing*, meaning they experience increased confusion, agitation, and memory impairment toward the end of the day and are often at their best early in the day. During that early time, they may hold reasonably intelligent conversations, read and understand books or documents, or watch the news on television and, to some degree, understand its meaning. As the day progresses, however, the patients' memory and ability to perform tasks deteriorate, causing them to suffer increased confusion and agitation.

The legal ramifications of sun downing for Alzheimer's patients, their caregivers, and legal advisors are important. While it is true that a person who lacks the requisite mental capacity may not enter into a valid, legally binding contract, if a person possesses legal capacity *at the time* of entering into a contract, later incapacity generally does not invalidate the contract.

Thus, an Alzheimer's patient might be lucid enough to negotiate the terms of a contract early in the morning, but if that patient suffers from sun downing and becomes confused in the afternoon of the same day, he or she would lack the requisite mental capacity for executing the contract in the afternoon. This is why I am very wary about and avoid at all costs having Alzheimer's patients—even those in Stage I of the disease—execute contracts and other documents in the afternoon or evening.

The issue of the contractual capacity of the Alzheimer's patient also holds implications for the non-Alzheimer's party to the contract. The law holds that where a contract is entered into on fair terms and the other party is *unaware* of the patient's condition, the contract is not easily voidable. Rather, if the other party has performed in whole or in part or the circumstances have so changed that voiding the contract would be unfair to that person, a court would be authorized to grant relief as justice requires.

The key determination here is whether the healthy party was aware that the patient was suffering from Alzheimer's disease. Admittedly, it is difficult for someone to determine that another is stricken with Alzheimer's. It is difficult for a car dealer to determine whether the elderly man sitting across from her, who wants to purchase an expensive car and has the financial resources, is an Alzheimer's patient. Likewise, it is difficult for a banker to know whether the elderly woman sitting across from him, who is seeking a $15,000 loan for which she has adequate collateral and an enviable credit score, is an Alzheimer's patient. If the dealer sells the car or the banker makes the signature loan knowing of the patient's condition, the contract will be void and invalid. However, if the provider was unaware of the patient's condition and conducted the transaction in good faith, the Alzheimer's patient and his or her family would have to wait upon the court to grant some form of relief as justice requires.

TESTAMENTARY CAPACITY

Something strange happens when someone dies; not to the dead person (who is already dead), but to the relatives and friends who are left behind. Often, these survivors change: They become greedy and begin thinking of what they may inherit. Sometimes, while some members of the family are at the church, synagogue, mosque, temple, or funeral home for the memorial service, other family members are at the home of the deceased, removing items that now belong to the estate. On other occasions, even before the ailing person has died, family members begin squabbling about what they will inherit. This is no exaggeration of events that can occur. Consider this: The majority of court challenges to wills ("will contests") are initiated, not by strangers and creditors of the deceased but by the deceased's own family members who are disgruntled with what they received or failed to receive from the estate.

No will is valid if, at the time the individual executed (that is, signed) it, he or she lacked the requisite testamentary capacity. Simply put, to possess the requisite testamentary capacity, at the time a person signs a will, the person must:

1. Understand who his or her family members and friends are.
2. Know what assets he or she owns.
3. Know to whom he or she wants to pass these assets.
4. Know that he or she is making or signing a will and the implications of doing so.

This legal standard is very significant for the Alzheimer's patient. First, if the patient is at an advanced stage of the disease, there is no way that person possesses the necessary capacity to execute a will. After all, the patient does not possess any of the four abilities listed above. Therefore, if the patient has not executed a will before entering late Stage II or Stage III of the disease, he or she is most likely unable to execute one now and will die intestate (without a will, which means that the laws of the state where the patient lives dictate how the estate is distributed). This sometimes results in unloving, uncaring, and greedy relatives receiving the deceased's property, while the friends and others who cared for the patient and whom he or she regarded as "family" receive nothing.

It is, however, possible that a patient in Stage I or early Stage II of the disease, at some point, possesses the necessary mental capacity to prepare and execute a last will and testament. It is important, though, to ensure that *at the time the document is signed*, the person possesses the requisite testamentary capacity contained in the four requirements listed above. In addition, because of the sun-downing phenomenon, it is wise to have the patient execute the last will and testament in the morning, when he or she is not agitated and not suffering bouts of confusion and increased memory impairment.

Finally, it is very important that all of us prepare and sign wills either (1) while we are young and healthy, or (2) at the first sign of some form of memory impairment. The following story is cautionary:

Some time ago, a moderately wealthy elderly woman began exhibiting Alzhiemer's-like symptoms. Two close friends eventually took her to see a doctor who confirmed that the woman was indeed suffering from Alzheimer's disease. From then until the woman died, these two friends served as her unpaid caregivers. They prepared her meals and helped her eat, did her laundry, cleaned her house, drove her to and from doctor's visits, and generally did all they could to help her during her illness, which was still in a relatively early stage. Family members never visited her or did anything to help her. Grateful to her friends for all they were doing for her, the woman asked an attorney to draft her last will and testament. During a period of lucidity, she completed the will questionnaire detailing how she wanted her assets to be distributed after her death. She wanted to leave her estate to various charitable organizations and to the two friends who had been caring for her. She specifically wanted to leave nothing to her family members. The woman asked the attorney to draft the will and to return the following day with two witnesses so that she could execute it.

Unfortunately, the will was never executed. That night, the woman began having chills. The following morning, she was admitted to the hospital. She soon lost consciousness and died of pneumonia a week later. She died intestate. Pursuant to the state's intestacy statute, her relatives shared her estate. The charities and close friends listed as beneficiaries on the will questionnaire and on the unsigned, incomplete will received nothing. The attorney (now a law professor named Vaughn E. James) could do nothing to convince the probate court to transfer the deceased's property to the intended beneficiaries.

The moral of this story is clear: Whether you are healthy or in Stage I Alzheimer's disease, it is time to prepare and sign your last will and testament.

CAPACITY TO CONSENT TO MEDICAL TREATMENT

Impairment of a person's medical decision-making capacity is an inevitably frequent consequence of Alzheimer's disease. Medical decision-making capacity is the ability to give *informed consent* to how you are treated medically. This *doctrine of informed consent* requires that a person's consent to medical treatment must be informed, voluntary, and competent. Medical ethicists have determined that medical decision-making capacity consists of the following different consent abilities or standards:

1. *The capacity to make a treatment choice.* This focuses on the presence or absence of a decision and not on the quality of the decision.[2]

2. *The capacity to appreciate emotionally and cognitively the personal consequences of a treatment choice.* This emphasizes the patient's awareness of the consequences of a treatment decision and its emotional impact, rational requirements, and future consequences.[3]

3. *The capacity to reason about a treatment choice or make a treatment choice based on rational reasons.* This tests the patient's ability to use logical processes to compare the benefits and risks of various treatment options and weigh this information to reach a decision.[4]

4. *The capacity to make a treatment choice based on an understanding of the treatment situation and alternatives.* This re-

quires that the patient has memory for words, phrases, ideas, and sequences of information and understands the fundamental meaning of information he or she receives about his or her treatment.[5]

These standards represent different thresholds for evaluating a person's medical decision-making capacity. Each threshold requires that the patient be able to perform a different set of tasks. For example, the first standard—making a choice—merely requires that the patient be able to choose a course of treatment from among options the treating physician presents. The patient can decide whether to take one type of drug over another or whether to take no drugs at all. If he or she were able to do that, the patient would be deemed to have the requisite medical decision-making capacity. In contrast, the fourth standard requires that the patient engage in reasoning and thus be able to enunciate a rational reason for his or her chosen course of treatment.

Depending on the severity of the disease and how far it has progressed, people who have developed Alzheimer's may find it difficult to achieve even the first level of medical decision-making capacity. When that happens, third parties step in to make the decisions for them, often without the patient's consent and sometimes contrary to his or her previously expressed desires. This is avoidable if the Alzheimer's patient prepares advance directives (see Chapter 5) prior to losing medical decision-making capacity.

THE CAPACITY TO MANAGE FINANCIAL AND PERSONAL AFFAIRS OR TO APPOINT AGENTS

No law exists regarding the capacity necessary for someone to make financial or personal decisions or to appoint an agent to make them on his or her behalf. Indeed, the law assumes that competent adults may manage their financial affairs and personal lives in any way they choose so long as they act within the confines of the law. The only requirement is that they be competent to make such decisions.

That said, to the extent the financial management or personal decisions involve contract law, for the decisions to be valid, the individual would have to possess the requisite capacity for entering into a contract. The same capacity would be necessary for the person to appoint an agent to make these decisions on his or her behalf. In short, the individual would have to know and understand the act in which he or she is engaging and must have the desire to engage in the act or transaction. For example, if Albert wants to appoint Giftus his attorney-in-fact under a durable power of attorney, Albert would have to know and understand the nature and effect of a durable power of attorney and must have the desire to both execute the instrument and appoint Giftus as his attorney-in-fact or agent.

LEGAL COMPETENCY (OR THE LACK THEREOF) AND ITS CONSEQUENCES

A significant difference exists between someone's lack of mental capacity and his or her lack of legal competency. While an individual's lack of capacity to perform certain functions or to execute certain documents affects only the functions or documents for which he or she lacks capacity, a determination that the person lacks legal competency has far-reaching consequences because it means the person is unable to do anything that would have legal ramifications. It does not mean that the person is insane or lacks intelligence, but it does mean that the person, for one reason or another, is unable to make his or her own decisions—or at least those decisions that truly matter.

Only a court can determine, or adjudicate, whether an individual is legally incompetent. Once the court has made this determination, the adjudicated incompetent individual loses more rights than an accused felon whom everyone saw commit the crime. After all, while the hypothetical felon enjoys the presumption of innocence and the state has the heavy burden of proving his or her guilt beyond a reasonable doubt, an adjudicated incompetent has his or her rights virtually stripped away and is put under the care of a court-appointed guardian, who will then make every decision for that person. If the adjudicated incompetent individual wants to contest the appointment of the guardian, he or she has to retain the services of an attorney and submit to the adversarial process practiced in U.S. courts.

Even in the absence of a guardianship, the state can force certain decisions upon an incompetent. For example, if an individual is incompetent, the state may override his or her refusal of medical treatment. States have traditionally justified their actions in such cases by maintaining that the injury caused by denying the individual's autonomy is exceeded by the harm that would be caused by honoring his or her choices.

With Alzheimer's disease becoming more prevalent and society seeking ways to protect Alzheimer's patients from themselves, some commentators have suggested that the courts should impose restrictions upon them. Some of the suggested restrictions include:

- Curtailing driver's licenses and fining caregivers who permit patients to drive without a license

- Removing access to working firearms or other objects that could be used as weapons
- Requiring the installation of special controls in cooking and electrical appliances to control the risk of fire
- Permitting the police to take individuals into custody if they appear disoriented (for example, if they are wandering out of doors or in a public place such as a shopping mall)
- Involuntarily placing a person with Alzheimer's disease who is living alone in a long-term care facility
- Requiring persons with Alzheimer's disease to carry a special kind of identification card
- Creating a widely accessible database of Alzheimer's patients
- Requiring the use of some form of electronic monitoring technology (worn externally or implanted) that could track the whereabouts of people with Alzheimer's disease

While the last two recommendations in this list border on an invasion of privacy, the recommendations are actually quite sound and, in my opinion, should be implemented as far as possible. Not only would they protect Alzheimer's patients but they would also give peace of mind to the family and friends who love these patients and are caring for them. Even without the implementation of these recommendations, though, a determination that an Alzheimer's patient is incompetent has serious consequences for the patient, his or her family, and caregivers.

DETERMINING LEGAL COMPETENCY

No universal method exists for determining legal competency. In the final analysis, the decision is left to the judge who hears the matter. Horror stories abound of harried judges who, in the space of five minutes, determine that an individual is legally incompetent and sentence that person to life with a guardian. These stories notwithstanding, some sort of process does exist for making the adjudication. For this reason, if you have a family member who has developed Alzheimer's disease, you ought to know and follow some procedures for determining the loved one's legal competency.

A MATTER OF TERMINOLOGY

Over the years, the term *legally incompetent* has fallen out of favor with the courts, attorneys, and medical practitioners. After all, the term *incompetent* usually connotes a lack of intelligence or skill or even idiocy. When we speak of an incompetent attorney, we mean an attorney who has no clue what she is doing and will most likely lose every case. When we speak of an incompetent physician, we usually mean that the doctor has no clue what he is doing and that you would be better off planning for your funeral than visiting him. An incompetent professor is one who does not have any idea how to teach or do research. To society, then, to be "incompetent" is a bad thing—a very bad thing.

That, however, is not what the term means in the legal sense. What it does mean is that the individual is unable to make reasonable, responsible, legally binding, or legally sound decisions.

Recognizing the difficulties posed by the term, many state legislatures have amended their statutes to replace "legally incompetent" with "mentally incapacitated." This new term suggests that the person in question is not an idiot but that he or she merely suffers from an incapacity, somewhat like the blind or the deaf, the only difference being that the incapacity is of the mental faculties. Hence, this person is ill but is otherwise quite normal.

There are some jurisdictions in the United States where the term "legally incompetent" is still used. However, in keeping with the new trend established in the amended statutes, we shall use the term "mentally incapacitated" throughout the remainder of this book to refer to people who would otherwise be described as being "legally incompetent."

THE ROLE OF THE LAWYER

The question of a person's mental incapacity arises only when a family member or some other party decides to seek a guardianship over the patient. To have the court appoint him or her as guardian of his or her loved one, the family member has to prove to the court that the person is mentally incapacitated. That immediately places a burden on the person seeking guardianship, because the law presumes that every human being possesses all of his or her mental faculties and is therefore not mentally incapacitated. Hence, the one seeking a guardianship must establish to the court's satisfaction that the ailing person is mentally incapacitated.

This requires an attorney. Although the lawyer makes an initial assessment as to whether the proposed ward is mentally incapacitated, that person is not his or her client. The person seeking the guardianship is the client, and the lawyer must serve his or her interests. The lawyer's role is to file the guardianship petition with a court of appropriate jurisdiction and to represent the client in proving that the proposed ward is indeed mentally incapacitated and requires a guardian, most likely the lawyer's client. (For more on guardianship, see Chapter 6.)

THE ROLE OF MEDICAL PRACTITIONERS

The lawyer cannot achieve this goal without nonlegal help. The lawyer must utilize the expertise of medical practitioners: the patient's attending physician, a psychiatrist, a psychologist, and/ or a neurologist. These practitioners collectively possess information that would assist the attorney in presenting sufficient evidence to the court that the proposed ward is indeed mentally incapacitated. For example, the psychologist may have the following: (1) the results of assessment tests; (2) a copy of the patient's psychiatric history (a biography, gathered from as many informants as possible, of relevant details, including the patient's family history, the onset of the patient's forgetfulness, the rate of decline in the patient's cognitive functioning, and the impairments that have developed since the onset of forgetfulness); and (3) a copy of the findings of the patient's mental status examination (a process by which the physician watches for abnormalities in the patient's behavior, listens for disruptions in the coherence of speech, and asks specific questions designed to reveal disturbances in mood and cognition and the presence of delusions and hallucinations). The attending physician and neurologist may be able to testify to their observations of the patient and their findings regarding his or her health and the state of his or her brain.

Working together with medical practitioners, the lawyer would be able to present a convincing case to the court that the proposed ward is indeed mentally incapacitated and would benefit from a guardianship.

THE ROLE OF THE NONPROFESSIONALS

While the lawyer and medical professionals are very important in this process, the nonprofessionals who have cared for the patient and witnessed his or her journey into Alzheimer's disease (usually family members and close friends) have an equally important part to play. First, the family members and friends often are the ones who accompany the patient on visits to the medical practitioners and the attorney. Most likely, without the instigation of these family members and friends, it is doubtful the patient would have ever consulted anyone.

Second, the professionals need the input of family members and close friends. For example, because the psychiatrist needs information from all possible sources in preparing the patient's psychiatric history, he or she turns to the family members and friends for such information. In a sense, then, these family members and friends have a role to play in the process whereby the medical practitioners eventually make a diagnosis.

In the same manner, nonprofessionals have a role to play in the process whereby the attorney decides what to do and executes his or her plan of action. At least initially—and sometimes for the entire duration of the process—the attorney depends on the information provided by the petitioner. Indeed, the attorney draws his or her initial inferences and begins to build his or her case and plot his or her strategy based on the information garnered from the petitioner. It is important, therefore, that the petitioner, in dealing with both the attorney and the medical practitioners, be truthful about the proposed ward's conduct, onset of forgetfulness, and other symptoms and behaviors. To exaggerate or to withhold information would be a great disservice to the patient.

NOTES

1. Leo M. Cooney, Jr., and John M. Keyes, "The Capacity to Decide to Remain Living in the Community," in Marshall B. Kapp, ed., *Ethics, Law, and Aging Review*, Volume 10, December 2004.

2. Loren H. Roth, Alan Meisel, and Charles W. Lidz, "Tests of Competency to Consent to Treatment," *American Journal of Psychiatry*, Volume 134, 1977.

3. Ibid.

4. Paul S. Appelbaum and Thomas Grisso, "Assessing Patients' Capacities to Consent to Treatment," *New England Journal of Medicine*, Volume 319, 1988.

5. Ibid.

CHAPTER 4

BEFORE IT'S TOO LATE: THE ESTATE PLAN

GRANDPA DOESN'T WANT A WILL!

*B*y now, our family has accepted the fact that Grandpa has Alzheimer's. We have no clue what stage he is in, but if his doctor is correct—and we have no reason to doubt that—we do know with 95 percent certainty that he has Alzheimer's.

If the articles and books I have been reading are correct—and I have no doubt they are—Grandpa has at most twenty more years to live. I had always hoped to have Grandpa live long enough to see my children and my children's children, but I also realize that as Grandpa gets into late Stage II of the disease and Stage III, he will be lost to us. I shudder as the thought crosses my mind. And then, I begin to think: Does Grandpa have a will? I know he owns lots of real estate here in America and in the Caribbean, but who will get it when he dies? I am only a grandchild, so I do not expect or desire to *inherit anything from Grandpa. But what about his wife? What about his children—my mom, my aunts, and my uncles?*

I remember the day Uncle Matt talked to Grandpa about preparing a will. Grandpa had become very angry. "So," he had said, "you just want me to die so you can take away all my property? You're just like that prodigal son in the Bible. You want your inheritance before I even die! Well, I am not making any patat *[damn] will!"*

After that incident, I never heard anyone say anything to Grandpa about a will. Still, now that he had Alzheimer's, I began to realize how important it was to have him prepare and sign a will before he lost the ability to do so. I began to hope that Grandpa still had—to use legal lingo—the testamentary capacity to sign a will.

My thoughts next moved on to even less pleasant matters. I couldn't help it. I am, after all, a lawyer and know how important these things are. What if Grandpa was unable to manage his financial affairs? What if he was unable to make personal decisions? What could be done? Surely, Grandpa needed an estate plan.

Estate planning is the process whereby, with the help of a competent attorney, you prepare a plan for:

- The orderly transfer of your assets upon your death
- The transfer of financial and personal decision-making authority to an agent or agents in the event you are adjudicated mentally incapacitated
- The minimization of the transfer tax burden on your estate

- The speedy probate and settlement of your estate and distribution of your assets to your beneficiaries

Although people typically put off estate planning until they experience a health crisis, they should really begin estate planning very early in life. Because of the memory loss and other conditions that accompany Alzheimer's disease, the task of putting together an estate plan is very difficult for someone who has developed the disease.

That said, to the extent the individual has recently begun exhibiting symptoms of Alzheimer's disease—which would indicate that the disease is probably in its early stage—his or her family members, acting on the patient's behalf, should retain a lawyer with training or experience in these matters to assist in the preparation of an estate plan. This plan should contain at least a power of attorney (sometimes called a durable power of attorney), a last will and testament, and a set of medical advance directives (see Chapter 5). Depending on the value and complexity of the patient's assets and the availability of financial resources to pay for it, the plan may also include a revocable living trust. In this chapter, we shall discuss the power of attorney, last will and testament, and revocable living trust.

POWER OF ATTORNEY: WHAT IT IS
AND WHY YOU NEED IT

With a power of attorney, you select a representative—an agent—to make decisions on your behalf. There are two types of powers of attorney: a *financial power of attorney*, which authorizes an agent to make financial decisions on your behalf, and a *medical power of attorney* (see Chapter 5), which authorizes an agent to make medical decisions on your behalf. Financial powers of attorney are of two types: *durable* and *regular*.

A durable power of attorney remains in force even if you are mentally incapacitated. In fact, unless you revoke it, regardless of your health, the durable power of attorney continues in effect until your death. A regular power of attorney, on the other hand, becomes invalid if you ever lose mental capacity. Surely, that is no good: Just when you need the agent to act on your behalf, the power of attorney's legality vanishes! It is no wonder, then, that during the latter half of the twentieth century, the durable power of attorney gained in popularity, and that following the promulgation of the Uniform Durable Power of Attorney Act in 1979, all fifty states and the District of Columbia enacted legislation sanctioning durable powers of attorney. Today, unless you are not concerned about your potential future mental incapacity, you would execute a durable power of attorney rather than a regular one.

A durable power of attorney is a statutory creation; therefore, to create a durable power of attorney, you—through your attorney—must follow the instructions included in the laws of the jurisdiction where you are domiciled. Most states have similar requirements, and a durable power of attorney executed in one state may be readily accepted in another state. (Currently, more than half the states have adopted the Uniform Durable Power of Attorney Act, making the language used in their powers of attorney practically identical.) A few states specifically recognize the validity of a validly executed durable power of attorney executed in another state; however, it is wise to execute a new durable power of attorney if you move to another state.

FUNDAMENTAL REQUIREMENTS OF THE DURABLE POWER OF ATTORNEY

In most states, to be valid, a durable power of attorney must be:

- In writing

- Signed by the principal

- Witnessed

- Dated

Some states also require that the document be notarized. In addition, to be "durable," the document must specifically state that the power is durable and your mental incapacity does not affect the right of the agent to act. The typical wording reads: "This Power of Attorney will not terminate upon the disability of the principal [you]." In a few states, all powers of attorney are legally durable and the document need not contain any language relating to the power's durability. Of course, your death terminates the power and the agent's right to act on your behalf. Hence, the agent may not, for example, distribute your estate or act as its executor, unless your last will and testament or a court of appropriate jurisdiction appoints him or her as the administrator of your estate. Finally, some states require the agent to sign the durable power of attorney and acknowledge the responsibilities of acting as an agent under a durable power of attorney.

Some state statutes, like those in Texas and New York, also provide for two types of durable powers of attorney. The "regular" durable power grants authority to the agent to act as soon as you execute the document. The second type, called a "springing power of attorney," grants the agent authority to act only if you lose the ability to act for yourself.

Whether regular or springing, durable powers of attorney are actually quite simple to create and can be tailored to individual needs and circumstances. Many state statutes detail what powers you can delegate to the agent. In fact, most statutes provide a form called a "statutory durable power of attorney." The form contains a list of the powers you can delegate to the agent. All you need to do is complete the form and initial the line next to each power that you want to delegate to the agent. You can delegate whatever power or powers you believe appropriate or necessary, including general powers to make all decisions you could make, or you can withhold whatever powers you believe you should retain. Generally, though, most state statutes permit you to grant the agent all rights to manage your property and to spend income and principal in whatever manner you might have done if you were not mentally incapacitated.

These powers are certainly broad, and for that reason they present a potential disadvantage: the possibility of abuses by dishonest agents and costly mistakes by inept ones. True, the agent is a fiduciary (that is, a manager), and thus has to perform his or her duties pursuant to the standards of good faith and trustworthiness. Accordingly, under normal circumstances, if you believe your agent is not living up to those standards, you may revoke the power of attorney and sue the agent for restitution of misused funds or other property.

However, Alzheimer's disease is not a normal circumstance. An individual who has developed Alzheimer's and is in an advanced stage of the disease would lack the mental capacity and/ or legal competency to object to the acts of the agent or to challenge the agent. Recognizing that fact, some state statutes permit your legal representative (a successor agent or court-appointed guardian), a family member, or any other interested person to ask the court to have the agent submit an accounting of his or her use of your funds and other property.

In light of what can go wrong with a durable power of attorney, it is important that you choose your agent wisely. Sure, the agent must be someone with some skills or knowledge in asset management. However, he or she must also be someone you trust and believe will act in your best interest.

THE CAPACITY TO CREATE A DURABLE POWER OF ATTORNEY

Ideally, everyone should create a durable power of attorney long before the need for one arises. However, as with the last will and testament and other estate planning documents, most people put off creating a power of attorney until it is "absolutely necessary." For the person who has developed Alzheimer's, that moment arrives when he or she begins exhibiting symptoms of the disease, while he or she still has the mental capacity to execute the document.

Individuals can execute a valid durable power of attorney only if they have the requisite mental capacity to do so. Generally, the mental capacity required for executing a durable power of attorney is similar to that needed to enter into a contract: The principal must have the ability to understand the nature of the document he or she is signing and the significance of signing it. The law demands nothing more. No requirement exists that the attorney who drafts the document, the notary who notarizes it, or anyone else should make a formal determination of the principal's mental capacity or legal competency at the time he or she executes the document.

What all this means for the Alzheimer's patient is that as long as he or she is able to understand the nature of the durable power of attorney and the significance of signing it—that is, the patient is giving authority to an agent to act on his or her behalf—the power is valid. Hence, someone in Stage I Alzheimer's would most likely possess the requisite capacity to execute a durable power of attorney. Yet because the disease progresses at a different pace in each patient and the period of time during which the patient would possess the requisite mental capacity is uncertain, it would do well for all persons to execute durable powers of attorney long before Alzheimer's comes calling.

FORMALITIES OF EXECUTION

As with every other legal document, the durable power of attorney has its unique formalities of execution. State statutes govern these formalities. Generally, the document must be in writing and must include language demonstrating your intent to create an agency that will not terminate should you become disabled or mentally incapacitated (that is, words such as, "This Power of Attorney will not terminate upon the disability of the principal"). Although some states have amended their power of attorney statutes to make all powers of attorney durable, a careful drafter should always include language specifically stating that the power is durable. This ensures that the agent's power to act on your behalf if you become mentally incapacitated will not be challenged by third parties.

The actual formalities of execution vary across the states. For example, in South Carolina, a durable power of attorney must be executed and witnessed in the same manner as a will. In Pennsylvania, the agent must sign the power of attorney attesting to understanding, among other things, that he or she will exercise the powers for the benefit of the principal, keep accurate records, and "exercise reasonable caution and prudence." In Maine, meanwhile, a durable power of attorney can also grant the agent the authority to make healthcare decisions, but if it does, the document must be notarized.

Because of these differences in state statutes and the fact that Americans, including Alzheimer's patients, move often, the drafter should ensure that at the very least the power of attorney is signed, is dated, has two witnesses, and is notarized. That way, the power of attorney will satisfy the requirements of all states and can be used to transfer real property.

The principal, witnesses, and notary should actually sign multiple copies of the power. After all, the agent will need to have an original signed copy when dealing with third parties; some banks and stockbrokers may want to retain an original signed copy; and if the power authorizes the agent to sell any real estate owned by you, the agent may have to file an original signed copy with the registrar of deeds.

THE AGENT

Any person who is not a minor may serve as your agent, regardless of the person's residence. However, it is advisable that you choose an agent who lives near you because it may be difficult for someone who lives far away to perform the duties required of an agent. While it is preferable that the agent possess some knowledge or skills in financial decision making or property management, perhaps the most important qualification is trust: whether you trust that person to act in your best interest.

The document should also name a successor agent. In most cases, married persons name their spouses as agents, with a child named as successor agent should the spouse die, become mentally incapacitated, or otherwise be unable to serve as agent. Most statutes allow you to name joint agents. This, however, poses a problem because both agents will have to agree to any action taken under the terms of the power of attorney. You can alleviate this problem somewhat by naming more than one agent but specifying in the document that any one agent can act individually. Yet third parties may well be wary of acting upon the directives of that one agent, in the event there is a dispute among agents.

Being an agent is an important and serious responsibility and should not be undertaken or assigned lightly. Agents usually serve without compensation, although they can reimburse themselves for "reasonable expenses." They can also "hire themselves" to perform services on your behalf. For example, the agent might pay himself or herself for tax preparation services. However, unless provided for by state law or in the power of attorney itself, agents should not expect payment for carrying out their duties. Moreover, if an agent receives any legally allowed compensation or other payment from your funds, the agent must carefully document such receipts in case he or she is ever challenged about the appropriateness of the compensation or expense reimbursement.

REVOCATION OF THE POWER OF ATTORNEY

You can revoke a power of attorney if you are competent at any time. However, you must notify the agent of the revocation. In fact, several states have added provisions to their durable power of attorney statutes to ensure that the agent and third parties will know when a power of attorney is revoked.

Generally, a power of attorney remains in effect if the agent is unaware that it has been revoked. Until the agent has knowledge of the revocation, his or her acts on your behalf are legally binding on you. Some state statutes even exonerate third parties from liability if they in good faith accept the agent's apparent authority to act on your behalf even if, by then, you had revoked the power but had not yet informed the agent. To minimize the chances of the agent acting on your behalf after you have revoked the power of attorney, you should at the time of revocation inform the agent of the revocation and, to the extent possible, ask him or her to return to you any copies of the power in his or her possession.

THE LAST WILL AND TESTAMENT: WHAT IT IS AND WHY YOU NEED IT

Law school clinics and legal aid societies that conduct will preparation clinics are often surprised—amazed—at the number of people who do not have a last will and testament. These people typically have a variety of excuses for why they have not previously executed a will:

- A will reminds them that they are mortal and will die some day, and they would rather not deal with that eventuality right now.
- Preparing a will reminds them of the poor state of their financial and personal affairs, and they would rather not let anyone know the mess they are in.
- They would have to deal with a lawyer, something they would rather not do.
- Will preparation costs money, something they just do not have.

These excuses notwithstanding, everyone who has any property or even one child should have a will.

As with the durable power of attorney, it is better to prepare and execute your will before the onset of Alzheimer's disease. That way, issues concerning your mental capacity would not be brought to the fore either at the time of will preparation and execution or at a will contest.

MENTAL CAPACITY TO EXECUTE A LAST WILL AND TESTAMENT

As we saw in Chapter 3, for a will to be valid, at the time you (the testator) execute it, you must:

- Understand who constitutes your family members and friends.
- Know what assets you own.
- Know to whom you want to pass these assets.

- Know that you are making or signing a will and the implications thereof.

Someone in late Stage II or Stage III Alzheimer's disease would not possess the requisite capacity to prepare and execute a last will and testament. However, someone who does not have Alzheimer's or is in Stage I or early Stage II would most likely possess this testamentary capacity. For this reason, each of us should take the necessary steps to prepare and execute a will, including retaining a competent attorney to assist with the process. It is possible that the person in Stage I or early Stage II Alzheimer's might need someone to assist in assembling all the necessary documents and information for preparing the will, but this would not preclude that person from executing a will.

TYPES OF WILLS

Among the states, the law recognizes three types of wills: the formal will, the holographic will, and the nuncupative (spoken) will. Not all states recognize all three. Therefore, it is important for you and your family to determine the type or types of wills recognized in the jurisdiction in which you live.

THE FORMAL WILL

The formal will is recognized in every U.S. jurisdiction and is the preferred type of will. An attorney generally prepares it. To be valid, it must:

1. Be dated.
2. Be signed by you.

3. Be signed by at least two witnesses who are fourteen years old or older.

At a minimum, the formal will should contain the following features:

1. The name of an executor who will file the will for probate and distribute your assets

2. The name or names of alternate or successor executors in the event the named executor predeceases you or is otherwise unavailable or unable to serve

3. The identity of the beneficiaries under the will and the names of alternate beneficiaries in the event the first named beneficiaries predecease you, refuse the gift, or are otherwise unable to take the gift

Such a will can also be used for other purposes, such as:

- Appointing a guardian for minor children in the event the other parent predeceases you

- Creating a trust to protect beneficiaries who are minors and their assets

- Reducing or eliminating estate and inheritance taxes

- Providing for your or someone else's pets

- Making gifts to charity

- Specifically excluding someone from receiving a share of your estate

Of course, you should not wait until you are stricken with any disease, including Alzheimer's, to prepare a last will and testament. Rather, you should prepare and sign your will as early as possible in life. You should also either update it as your life situation changes or prepare codicils (amendments to the original will, executed with the same formalities of the original will) when these life-changing situations occur. While it is possible for someone with Alzheimer's disease to possess the necessary capacity to execute a last will and testament, especially if the will execution ceremony takes place in the morning while the patient is lucid, this is not the preferred course of action.

Regardless of when you decide to prepare and execute a formal will, it is essential that you prepare well before meeting with the lawyer who will draft the document. At a minimum, you should:

- Make a list of all family members and friends to whom you wish to pass on property.
- Make a list of all your assets.
- Make a list of all your liabilities.
- Make a list of how you want your assets distributed; in other words, who among the list of family members and friends gets what from the list of assets? This list should also include the names of alternate recipients of these assets.
- Identify the executor and alternate or successor executor. Prior to the meeting with the lawyer, ask the executor and alternate/successor executor about their willingness to serve in their respective capacities.
- If the last will and testament appoints a guardian for minor children, identify that person (and an alternate). Again, verify that these people are willing to serve in these capacities.
- Make a list of persons you do not want to receive a share of your estate.

When you contact an attorney to draft the will, the attorney will most likely ask you to complete a will questionnaire. The information contained in this list will help you complete the questionnaire.

THE HOLOGRAPHIC WILL

A holographic will is a will written entirely in your own handwriting. It is not recognized in all jurisdictions; however, where it is recognized, it can be an important tool for the Alzheimer's patient.

Generally, to be valid a holographic will must:

1. Be written entirely in your own handwriting
2. Contain the date on which it was written
3. Be signed by you

No witnesses are necessary. Note that a holographic will is not the same as the preprinted fill-in-the-blanks forms available at stationery stores like Staples and OfficeMax. When completed, these forms constitute formal wills and must be executed with all the formalities pertaining to that type of will. Why? Because typically, the pertinent parts of these wills are not written entirely in your own handwriting. Having failed to satisfy that requirement, these instruments are not holographic wills.

The holographic will may be an important tool for the Alzheimer's patient in a case like the following, involving a man named Martin:

Martin has begun to exhibit symptoms of Alzheimer's disease. He forgets things. He is quite lucid in the mornings but is irritable and agitated in the afternoons and evenings. Although he owns a significant amount of property, including several acres of land, and has six children, Martin has never executed a last will and testament. Martin and his family are concerned that with his memory problems, he may soon lose both the mental capacity to execute a last will and testament as well as the legal competency to do anything else. What should they do?

What Martin and his family should do is simply this: One morning while Martin is lucid and in possession of all his mental faculties, he should take a blank piece of paper and, in his own handwriting, identify himself, give the date, and describe how he wants his assets distributed when he dies. Martin should then sign the document. After this, he or a family member should call an attorney for an appointment to prepare a formal will.

Essentially, what Martin has is a holographic will. If he loses testamentary capacity or becomes mentally incapacitated prior to the time he signs the formal will, he has a holographic will in place. Barring the presence of fraud or undue influence when he signed the handwritten will (in a jurisdiction that recognizes this type of will), a court would most likely hold that the holographic will is valid.

THE NUNCUPATIVE (OR SPOKEN) WILL

Only a few states recognize the nuncupative, or spoken, will. This type of will dates back to the frontier days, the days of trail drives and gunfights when written documents were not common. Today, although some states recognize this type of will, hardly anybody ever uses it.

SAFEGUARDING THE WILL

If the will is a holographic will or formal will, it is important that you and/or your family members safeguard it after it is signed and witnessed. After all, beneficiaries and non-beneficiaries may want to tamper with the will. This is most important for the person who has developed Alzheimer's disease, since he or she may forget where he or she placed the will or that he or she ever signed a will. If the will is not found soon after the individual's death, his or her estate will be distributed according to the provisions of the state's intestacy statute—a very undesirable outcome.

Several options exist for keeping the will safe. The testator must select the place or method he or she thinks is best. Some of the many options include:

- *At Home.* This is as good a place as any to keep the will. However, if you keep the will at home, you should ensure that it is in a well-protected environment, such as a small fireproof box, which would protect the will from being destroyed by fire or from just being lost.

- *With the Executor.* This is another good choice especially because the executor will administer and distribute the estate after your death, and it makes sense for him or her to keep the will safe until it is needed.

However, there are two problems with this option:

1. You may want to execute either a new will or a codicil naming a new executor. If so, you might not feel comfortable
   asking the executor to turn over or destroy the old will because his or her services are no longer needed.

2. If the executor predeceases you, will your will be safe and
   will you be able to retrieve it in order to turn it over to the
   successor executor?

A possible solution to these problems is to have the testator execute at least three copies of the will. One copy (marked "the
Original") would be given to the executor for safekeeping. This
copy is normally submitted to the probate court upon your
death. Two copies should be clearly marked or stamped "Copy"
on each page; you should keep one copy, and the other should
be kept in your attorney-drafter's file. If the executor predeceases
you and the original will cannot be found in your possession, a
court will normally allow probate of one of the copies if it is
satisfied that the copy is authentic and genuine.

- *With the County Clerk or Clerk of the Court.* Individuals can
  and do give their wills to the office of the county clerk or
  clerk of the probate court for safekeeping. Note, however,
  that safekeeping is not the same as filing the will for probate. All "safekeeping" means is that the clerk's office keeps
  the will in a vault and releases it only to you, to someone
  you specify, to the executor upon your death, or directly to
  the probate court upon your death.

- *In a Safe Deposit Box.* If you choose this option, you should
  hold the box jointly with somebody else. That way, upon

your death the other party can access the box and retrieve the will. If there is no joint renter, the bank may allow an examination of the safe deposit box without a court order by any of the following people: (1) your surviving spouse or parents, (2) any of your adult descendants, or (3) a possible executor who presents a document that looks like a copy of your last will and testament. If the bank agrees to proceed without a court order, the box would be opened and examined in the presence of a bank officer. However, from a purely legal standpoint, if the last will and testament is found in the box, the bank is obligated to deliver it only to the clerk of the probate court and not to some other party.

In this age of computer technology, the question arises whether you could safeguard your will by scanning it onto a flash drive or some other electronic storage device. This is not a good option because third parties may gain access to the storage file and change the will so that by the time it is presented for probate, it does not reflect your intent.

THE REVOCABLE LIVING TRUST: WHAT IT IS AND WHY YOU NEED IT

Over the past few years, the revocable living trust has grown in popularity as a substitute for a will. Essentially, a revocable living trust is a contract you make with yourself to help you while you are alive and then help others after you die. The trust provides mechanisms for managing your assets and protecting your income:

- While you are alive and in full control of your mental faculties
- If you become mentally incapacitated
- When you die

As the name indicates, the trust can be revoked and amended; thus, you can change it if you wish to do so.

Four parties are very important to the establishment of a revocable living trust:

1. The *grantor* (you) is the original owner of the property. You establish the trust, transfer your assets to the trust, and determine the trust's goals. You can amend or revoke the trust unless you give up that right when you first establish the trust (but then, that would make the "revocable" part of the trust meaningless).

2. The *trustee* manages the trust and its assets. In a revocable living trust, you are also the trustee.

3. The *beneficiaries* receive the trust property. During your lifetime, you are typically the *sole beneficiary*. Thus, even after creating the trust, you continue to have access to the trust property. The trust instrument also names certain individuals who will become beneficiaries upon your death. These *secondary beneficiaries* enjoy the same status as beneficiaries under a will, with the significant difference that they do not have to wait for the probate process to be completed before they are able to enjoy the trust property.

4. The *successor trustee* is granted the authority to manage the trust and its assets should you (the original trustee) either become mentally incapacitated or die. Upon the latter occurrence, the successor trustee distributes the trust assets in accordance with the terms of the trust.

REASONS FOR CREATING A
REVOCABLE LIVING TRUST

Generally, creators of revocable living trusts seek one or more of the following three goals:

1. Minimizing, if not avoiding, probate
2. Protecting their assets both while they are alive and healthy and if they become mentally incapacitated
3. Assisting and providing for their loved ones

MINIMIZING OR AVOIDING PROBATE

The primary goal of establishing a revocable living trust is the minimization or avoidance of probate. Probate can be a lengthy process during which the will beneficiaries must wait—sometimes very impatiently—before they may claim their inheritances. A revocable living trust eliminates this waiting period. With a revocable living trust, the successor trustee can transfer the trust property to the secondary beneficiaries one nanosecond after the grantor dies.

This does not necessarily mean, however, that probate will be avoided. Someone who creates a revocable living trust must also execute a will (called a *pour-over will*) to transfer—or pour over into the trust—assets the grantor owns at death that are not included in the trust. The will may also dispose of certain assets outside of the trust. When that happens, these assets become subject to the probate process.

PROTECTING ASSETS

The goal of protecting assets is very important if you are concerned that you might eventually develop Alzheimer's disease. As previously stated, when you create a revocable living trust, you name yourself as the trustee and also name another person as the successor trustee. The trust instrument provides that the successor trustee will succeed to the office of trustee if the original trustee (you, who are also the grantor) either dies or becomes mentally incapacitated. If you develop Alzheimer's disease and become mentally incapacitated, the trust will continue uninterrupted, with the successor trustee now functioning as trustee. As beneficiary of the trust, you will continue to be able to receive all the trust benefits you enjoyed prior to the onset of mental incapacity.

ASSISTING AND PROVIDING FOR LOVED ONES

A revocable living trust can provide for certain beneficiaries while you are still alive. Typically, though, the trust mimics a will and contains instructions for the distribution of your assets upon your death. It can provide that certain assets be distributed to certain beneficiaries immediately upon your death, or it may provide that certain assets be held in trust for the benefit of certain (usually minor) beneficiaries. In essence, you have much flexibility in deciding to whom and how you will distribute your assets.

FUNDING THE REVOCABLE LIVING TRUST

If you decide to create a revocable living trust, you must transfer your assets into the trust. You may accomplish this transfer in one of two ways:

1. Change title to your assets from yourself to the trust at the same time you establish the trust. The trust would then be a *funded trust*.

2. At the time you establish the trust, put only enough assets into the trust to begin the trust's existence (some people put in as little as $1). This is called an *unfunded trust*, sometimes known as a *stand-by trust*.

Of the two options, the unfunded trust is the least desirable. After all, whether your goal in establishing the trust is to minimize or avoid probate, to protect yourself and your assets, or to assist and provide for loved ones, the trust must own the assets at the time of your death. If not, your assets will be subject to probate, and the smooth transition of assets provided for by the revocable living trust will be lost. Delaying trust funding until some future point raises the risks of such an outcome.

With a funded trust, on the other hand, you transfer your assets into the trust at the time you establish it. There is then no risk that you may die or become mentally incapacitated prior to the transfer of assets to the trust.

CHOOSING THE SUCCESSOR TRUSTEE

Establishing a revocable living trust is one thing; having it function successfully is quite another. Of all the factors you should consider, selecting the proper successor trustee is truly the key to a successful revocable living trust. After all, the successor trustee will be the manager of the trust assets and is required to follow the instructions laid out in the trust instrument. In addition, when you create the trust and give it ownership of your assets, the trustee acquires legal title to the assets. This gives the trustee much power—more power than that given to an agent under a durable power of attorney or to an executor appointed under the terms of a last will and testament.

Initially, you are the trustee of the revocable living trust. This is very advantageous for you. As trustee, you hold legal title to the trust assets, and as beneficiary, you hold equitable title (that is, the right to the benefits and enjoyment of the trust property). In effect, although you have transferred the assets to the trust, you retain full control of the trust assets, just as you did before establishing the trust.

If you as the grantor-trustee become mentally incapacitated (as would happen if you develop Alzheimer's disease), the successor trustee would become trustee and would have legal title to the trust assets and the authority to use and distribute the trust assets pursuant to the terms of the trust instrument. For this reason, it is important that you choose a successor trustee (and any alternate successor trustees) very carefully. You should choose people you trust deeply, who have good business sense, and who care about you and want to assist you—people with whom you would be comfortable and who you believe will care for you and act in your best interest should you ever become mentally incapacitated.

MAKING CHOICES

Clearly, estate planning is very important for the Alzheimer's patient. Ideally, it should be embarked upon and completed long before Alzheimer's strikes. If it is not, however, there is still hope: The patient or his or her loved ones should retain an attorney to guide them through the maze of estate planning as soon as the patient begins exhibiting symptoms of Alzheimer's disease.

This, though, is often easier said than done. Many people—like Grandpa in the story at the beginning of this chapter—interpret these pleas from their family members and loved ones as ploys to acquire their property. The family members and loved ones must be prepared to do lots of explaining and guiding if they are to succeed in getting the elderly person to an attorney's office to begin the estate planning process. They have to convince the elderly person (or Alzheimer's patient) somehow that estate planning will be of primary benefit to him or her, and only secondarily of benefit to others.

Once the patient (or his or her loved ones) has decided to embark upon estate planning, the question becomes whether to execute a last will and testament or establish a revocable living trust and execute a pour-over will. I would be untruthful if I were to claim that one path is better than the other. No two people are the same. Hence, no two estate plans are the same. To make an informed decision on what to do, the patient and/or his or her loved ones should discuss the matter with an attorney competent to answer relevant questions and give guidance on the matter.

Another big decision concerns healthcare. The fact is that the patient can decide for him- or herself what he or she wants done in a variety of situations. The patient can achieve this with medical advance directives, which also form part of the individual's estate plan. These directives are the subject of Chapter 5.

CHAPTER 5

BEFORE IT'S TOO LATE: ADVANCE DIRECTIVES

JASMA'S DAD

*B*y now, my family, friends, and even mere acquaintances had heard the news: At least four senior members of my family were suffering from some sort of what they called a "brain disease." The way they said "brain disease" instead of using the term Alzheimer's made me feel that they believed Alzheimer's was a curse. Wherever I went—to the grocery store, the library, the mall, the cricket field—I received sympathetic nods and, at times, I felt like people were staring at me, wondering whether I too was suffering from this dreaded "brain disease." At the same time, I began receiving calls from friends about their own family members who were apparently suffering from the same "brain disease."*

The call from Jasma, my friend from Amarillo, was different. "Vaughn," she said, after hearing my greeting of 'James,

James and James, I'd love to help you,' "remember I told you
my dad has Alzheimer's?"

I clearly remembered our conversations. Her father had developed Alzheimer's disease and had begun to wander the
streets of Amarillo. Sometimes he would leave home without
saying a word and would simply go walking around Amarillo,
not saying anything, not asking anybody any questions, not
troubling anybody. Jasma and her family members were worried about what might happen to him. Their worries proved
justified one day when he wandered onto I-27 and was almost
hit by a semi. Ever since, they'd been keeping close tabs on him.

"What's wrong?" I asked.

"We have a difficult situation here," she answered. "A week
ago, Dad did not get out of bed in the morning. He just lay
there staring into space. He stopped eating. He stopped drinking. No matter what we've tried, he won't touch the food and
drink we bring to him. Yesterday we took Dad to the emergency
room. After ages, a doctor finally looked at him. According to
the doctor, Dad is fine and nothing is wrong with his body. The
doctor said Dad has just lost the will to live. He said we have
two choices: We could either have a feeding tube inserted into
Dad's stomach or through his nostrils so he can receive artificial
nutrition and hydration, or we can simply leave him alone and
let him die. Vaughn, I am so scared. I don't know what to do!"

Jasma began crying. I felt dumb for a minute or two and
then asked, "What do your siblings say?" I knew that Jasma's
mother had died two days after Jasma was born, but that she
had five siblings—two sisters and three brothers. Jasma and
four of her siblings lived in Amarillo; the other lived in Hawaii.

"Kaisha came in from Hawaii yesterday and we held a

family meeting this morning," Jasma replied between sobs. "Three of us are in favor of inserting the feeding tube. The other three are saying that Dad has lived his life and that it's time to let him go. Vaughn," Jasma wailed, "what can we do?"

Advance directives (sometimes called medical advance directives) are documents that tell your family members, caregivers, and medical practitioners about your healthcare and end-of-life choices in the event you suffer from mental incapacity and are unable to act on your own behalf. In such a case, family members, caregivers, and medical practitioners are expected to act in accordance with the wishes expressed by you in the advance directives. Because Alzheimer's patients are certain to become mentally incapacitated (if they live long enough), the issue of advance directives is very important to them.

THE PATIENT'S RIGHT TO MEDICAL SELF-DETERMINATION

Family members, caregivers, and medical practitioners are expected to obey the directives of their patients for one simple reason: The law grants all individuals control of their medical care. Indeed, all patients have a right to autonomy and self-determination.

These rights rest upon two concepts: bodily integrity and personal liberty. According to these concepts, for a person to be truly free, he or she must have control of his or her body. To be autonomous, individuals must be able to control their bodies, which includes controlling their medical care through the right to consent to or refuse medical treatment.

While the common law and some state statutes recognize these rights, only one federal statute—the Patient Self-Determination Act (PSDA)—addresses the matter. The statute applies to any patient receiving care from a facility or care provider covered by Medicare or Medicaid, including hospitals, hospices, nursing homes, and home healthcare agencies. Essentially, whenever you are admitted to a hospital or a nursing home, or when you enroll with an HMO, hospice, or home healthcare agency, the provider must:

- Provide you with written information concerning your rights under state law to participate in decisions concerning your medical care. This includes the right to accept or to refuse medical or surgical treatment and the right to have advance directives.

- Provide you with a written statement of its policy regarding implementation of these rights.

- Document whether you have executed an advance directive. However, healthcare providers are not required to provide the documents needed to make these advance directives.

In addition, the PSDA imposes some uniform standards that all covered providers must follow. For example, they:

- Cannot discriminate when providing medical care based on whether a patient has executed an advance directive.

- Are required to comply with all state laws regarding advance directives.

- Must provide for staff and community education on issues related to advance directives.

While the PSDA governs self-determination for patients cared for by providers receiving federal assistance, the statute does not create a uniform law for all fifty states to follow. Hence, states have had to pass their own statutes regarding advance directives. The basis of these statutes is the legal doctrine of informed consent.

ALZHEIMER'S AND THE DOCTRINE OF INFORMED CONSENT

The basic legal premise relating to medical care is that a *competent* adult is the only person who may give consent to his or her medical treatment. However, to make that choice, the person requires information. After all, decisions cannot be made in a vacuum. Merely having the right to choose whether one should follow through on a proposed course of medical treatment is meaningless if the patient does not have sufficient information to understand the consequences of his or her decision and the possible alternatives to the proposed treatment plan. In addressing that issue, the doctrine of informed consent requires providing a patient with sufficient information to be able to give a meaningful (informed) consent or denial to proposed medical care.

This doctrine of informed consent finds its genesis in a 1914 case in which doctors operated on Mary Schloendorff, a patient, without her consent. In determining whether the patient had a valid claim against the hospital in which the operation was performed, Judge Benjamin Cardozo, writing for the New York Court of Appeals, wrote:

> In the case at hand, the wrong complained of is not merely negligence. It is trespass. Every human being of adult years and sound mind has a right to determine what shall be done with his own body; and a surgeon who performs an operation without his patient's consent commits an assault, for which he is liable in damages.[1]

Just as Mrs. Schloendorff needed the opportunity to exercise informed consent in 1914, today's patients—including those suffering from Alzheimer's disease—need that right.

EXCEPTIONS TO THE RULE

There are, however, three exceptions to the rule of informed consent:

1. *The Emergency Care Exception.* If the patient is unable to communicate, his or her life is threatened by injury or illness, and the time necessary to obtain consent would place the patient in immediate danger, medical practitioners can act without the patient's consent. The law holds that the patient's consent is "implied" in an emergency because it is presumed that the patient would, if able, consent under the circumstances.[2]

2. *The Therapeutic Privilege Exception.* A medical practitioner may also administer treatment without the patient's con-

sent if the practitioner invokes "therapeutic privilege": the belief that the disclosure of the diagnosis or treatment choice would so upset the patient that he or she would be unable to make a rational decision. The physician is freed from the requirement of informed consent to promote his or her primary duty of doing what is beneficial for the patient. In the past (for example, when the diagnosis of cancer was tantamount to a death sentence), physicians invoked the therapeutic privilege exception to justify not telling a patient of a fatal diagnosis. Today, some physicians and psychiatrists invoke it to justify not telling a patient that he or she most likely has Alzheimer's disease or some other form of dementia.

3. *Patient Waiver.* A patient may also waive the right to informed consent. However, to give a valid waiver, the patient must know what rights he or she is giving up. The patient may waive both the right to information (*"Doctor, I've heard enough; please don't tell me anything more."*) and the right to decide (*"Doctor, you are the expert; you know what is best. Just go ahead and decide what must be done."*). Patient waivers are not necessarily bad. They recognize the patient's autonomy, but at the same time they allow the patient to defer to the professionalism of the physician.

INFORMED CONSENT AND
THE ALZHEIMER'S PATIENT

The doctrine of informed consent remains intact even if the patient is mentally incapacitated and is unable to grant consent. In that case, a surrogate decision maker would make the decision for the patient. Therefore, when someone has Alzheimer's disease, this surrogate decision maker gives the necessary consent on the patient's behalf. The big question, though, is how does the physician know the identity of this surrogate decision maker?

This is where an advance directive comes in handy. In the advance directive, the patient would have stated his or her choice of treatment or course of action, or would have appointed a surrogate to make these decisions. In the absence of an advance directive, state law directs the order of persons authorized to make such decisions. A typical statutory order of preference is:

1. The patient's spouse

2. A sole child who has written permission from the other children to act alone

3. The majority of the patient's children

4. The patient's parents

5. Someone the patient "clearly identified" as the surrogate decision maker before he or she became ill

6. Any other living relative

7. Any member of the clergy, whether or not the patient knows that clergyperson

For many reasons—a predeceased spouse, a divorcing spouse, prodigal and uncaring children—an individual may find this statutory list undesirable. Particularly in those instances, then, individuals need to prepare advance directives so that should the need for them arise, these documents will be available and the surrogate decision maker of the patient's choice will be able to act on his or her behalf.

ADVANCE DIRECTIVES FOR THE ALZHEIMER'S PATIENT–AND EVERYONE ELSE!

The advance directives covered here could benefit not only Alzheimer's patients but everyone else as well. After all, young or old, we never know when we might become incapacitated and unable to make decisions on our behalf. For the Alzheimer's patient, however, it is crucial to execute these directives *before* the individual becomes mentally incapacitated.

THE MEDICAL POWER OF ATTORNEY

While the durable power of attorney discussed in Chapter 4 is used for property management purposes, the medical power of attorney is used for making healthcare decisions. Every state has enacted legislation authorizing the use of this device, although the various statutes use different names for the instrument. New York, for example, calls it a Health Care Proxy, Texas calls it a Medical Power of Attorney, and Maine calls it a Durable Health-Care Power of Attorney. Regardless of the name, the purpose of the device is the same: An individual, as principal (you), appoints someone else (an agent) to make healthcare decisions for him or her in the event the person ever lacks the capacity to do so.

The authority given the agent by the document may be as

broad or as narrow as you wish it to be. Either the directive can give away the authority you wish given away, or you could choose from a list of alternatives included in the state's statutory form. Figure 5-1 provides an example from Minnesota that illustrates the choices available on a typical state statutory form.

On matters that are unclear or not covered in the document, most states require the agent to act in a manner consistent with how the patient would have behaved in the circumstances. This is known as the *substituted judgment standard*. A few states permit the surrogate decision maker to use the *best interest standard*, under which the surrogate would do what is best for the patient, particularly if the patient's desires are not known well enough to permit the surrogate to use the substituted judgment standard.

As regards the mechanics of creating and implementing the medical power of attorney, the states vary widely. However, all states require that the document be signed by the principal in the presence of a certain number of witnesses (always more than one). Generally, the principal's healthcare provider, an employee of the healthcare provider, or the residential care provider or an employee thereof are barred from being appointed agent unless that person is related to the principal. In order that the agent begins to exercise his or her authority under the medical power of attorney, the principal or his or her attorney must hand the agent a copy of the document.

Because the agent's authority takes effect only upon a determination that the principal is unable to make his or her own healthcare decisions, the question often arises as to just when the principal is no longer capable of making these decisions. The states are split on this. Some allow the principal's attending physician to make a determination of mental incapacity, others uti-

Figure 5-1. Minnesota Health Care Directive.

I, _____ understand this document allows me to do ONE OR BOTH of the following:

PART I: Name another person (called the health care agent) to make health care decisions for me if I am unable to decide or speak for myself. My health care agent must make both health care decisions for me based on the instructions I provide in this document (Part II), if any, the wishes I have made known to him or her, or must act in my best interest if I have not made my health care wishes known.

AND/OR

PART II: Give health care instructions to guide others making health care decisions for me. If I have named a health care agent, these instructions may also be used by the agent. These instructions may also be used by my health care providers, others assisting with my health care and my family, in the event I cannot make decisions for myself.

THIS IS WHAT I WANT MY HEALTH CARE AGENT
TO BE ABLE TO DO IF I AM UNABLE
TO DECIDE OR SPEAK FOR MYSELF

(I know I can change these choices)

My health care agent is automatically given the powers listed below in (A) through (D). My health care agent must follow my health care instructions in this document or any other instructions I have given to my agent. If I have not given health care instructions, then my agent must act in my best interest.

Whenever I am unable to decide or speak for myself, my health care agent has the power to:

(A) Make any health care decision for me. This includes the power to give, refuse, or withdraw consent to any care, treatment, service, or procedures. This includes deciding whether to stop or not start health care that is keeping me or might keep me alive, and deciding about intrusive mental health treatment.
(B) Choose my health care providers.
(C) Choose where I live and receive care and support when those choices relate to my health care needs.
(D) Review my medical records and have the same rights that I would have to give my medical records to other people.

If I DO NOT want my health care agent to have a power listed above in (A) through (D) OR if I want to LIMIT any power in (A) through (D), I MUST say that here:

_____

_____

_____

lize a committee, while still others require a judge to adjudicate the person mentally incapacitated.

SIGNIFICANCE FOR THE ALZHEIMER'S PATIENT

Ideally, by the time someone develops Alzheimer's disease, he or she would have already created a medical power of attorney. If not, as soon as someone begins exhibiting symptoms of the disease, the person should create the power of attorney, or his or her family members or friends should lead him or her into creating one. Indeed, if the disease runs its course, the time will come when the patient needs a surrogate healthcare decision maker.

THE LIVING WILL

Perhaps the most erroneously named document in the universe is the living will. Contrary to what the name suggests, this document has nothing to do with living, but instead, everything to do with dying! Essentially, a living will is a document by which you attempt to control your medical care in the event you become mentally incapacitated and thus unable to make end-of-life healthcare decisions. The document typically contains treatment instructions in the event the individual becomes either terminally ill or is in a persistent vegetative state (that is, permanently unconscious). The living will details the type of medical care you desire and the conditions under which you want life-sustaining treatment either initiated or discontinued.

Every state has a statute that provides for living wills. Because the statutes vary greatly, it is difficult to generalize about the purposes and requirements of living wills. Accordingly, the following analysis of the provisions commonly found in living will statutes is generally true but does not describe any particular statute.

CONTENTS OF A LIVING WILL

Generally, a living will should contain two elements:

1. A statement that if mental incapacity occurs, the instructions in the document would determine the form of treatment the declarant (you) wishes to receive.

2. A statement of the conditions under which the declarant would like life-sustaining treatment terminated. Usually this is in the case of a terminal illness or persistent vegetative state.

THE TERMINAL ILLNESS REQUIREMENT

Living will statutes permit the patient to authorize the discontinuation or withholding of medical treatment in the event the patient is mentally incapacitated and suffers from a terminal condition or is in a permanent vegetative state. Living wills are effective only for qualified patients, and one such qualification is that the patient be in a terminal condition. If your attending physicians believe you may recover from the illness, the living will is not applicable.

The various state statutes define "terminal condition" in different ways. Several of these statutes define a terminal condition as one in which the patient will die shortly regardless of whether the medical treatment in question is continued. For example, Georgia defines a terminal condition to mean a condition "caused by disease, illness, or injury which, regardless of the application of life-sustaining procedures, would produce death." Wisconsin has a more restrictive definition, requiring that to deem a condition terminal, death must be "imminent" and "the application of life-sustaining procedures [would] serve only to postpone the moment of death." Meanwhile, Oklahoma defines terminal condition to mean that death will occur within six months.

Notwithstanding the different definitions of terminal condition and the fact that these definitions call for the patient's death within a relatively short time, the truth is that no one can give an accurate prognosis of death. Many people who have been "sentenced to death" by their physicians go on to live for months and sometimes years longer than the doctors had indicated. Aware of that fact, the various statutes are written so that they do not prevent mentally incapacitated, terminally ill patients from being sustained by medical technology. Indeed, those statutes defining terminal condition as death being "imminent" or expected to happen "in a short time" severely limit the application of living wills. Under these statutes, even if the mentally incapacitated patient's condition were irreversible and incurable, the directions in the living will could not take effect until almost the moment of death!

Other state statutes provide that a living will is operative only if the patient is expected to die within a certain number of days. Since it is extremely difficult for physicians to predict just when death will occur, in states that allow living wills to take effect only if the patient is expected to die within a few days, living wills have a very limited application.

THE PERSISTENT VEGETATIVE STATE
REQUIREMENT

The requirement that the patient be terminally ill before a living will becomes operative does not cover the situation where the individual is in a persistent vegetative state but is not necessarily terminally ill. After all, people can survive in persistent vegetative states for years.

Unlike the term "terminal condition," a persistent vegetative state has a precise definition. In essence, a persistent vegetative state results from a partial death of the brain—that is, cessation of all upper brain activity, although the brain stem continues to function. With this cessation of upper brain activity, the person loses the ability to think, perceive, use language, or move in a purposeful manner. However, because the brain stem is still functioning, the person is still able to breathe, have blood pressure, react to light, and respond with physical reflexes such as grimacing and yawning.

A persistent vegetative state differs from a coma in that while a patient can awaken from a coma, he or she cannot awaken from a persistent vegetative state. Because brain cells cannot regenerate, someone in a persistent vegetative state will never recover but will remain in that condition until his or her death.

Accordingly, the only relevant issue governing whether the living will should take effect is whether the individual is really in a persistent vegetative state. Generally, several days or even weeks must pass before the physicians can determine that the individual is in a persistent vegetative state. Once the physician is satisfied that the individual is indeed permanently unconscious (i.e., in a persistent vegetative state), the typical living will statute allows the living will to take effect, and no further life-sustaining treatment would be provided if that is what the patient requested in the living will.

Unfortunately, this is not the end of the matter. Termination of life-sustaining treatment for people in a persistent vegetative state usually means removing them from a ventilator or respirator or ending treatment with antibiotics. However, not all patients in a persistent vegetative state require a ventilator or respirator. Many are able to breathe on their own but are unable to feed themselves, so they are fed through tubes inserted either through their nose (a nasogastric tube) or through the wall of the stomach (a gastrostomy tube). If kept on a feeding tube, individuals in a persistent vegetative state could survive for months or even years unaware of their surroundings and feeling no pain whatsoever. Although these individuals are in a persistent vegetative state, their condition is not terminal.

The issue therefore arises of whether you can request in your living will that artificial hydration and nutrition be withheld if you are ever in a persistent vegetative state. The answer depends on state law. Some states say yes, others say no. Before making such a request, therefore, you should determine the provisions of local law. Of course, your lawyer will be able to give guidance here.

THE ALZHEIMER'S PATIENT AND THE LIVING WILL

The Alzheimer's patient is in a unique situation regarding the living will. As an initial matter, if the patient is in an advanced stage of the disease (late Stage II or Stage III), chances are he or she lacks the mental capacity to execute a living will.

Assuming the patient develops Alzheimer's disease after he or she has executed a living will, the question to be answered is whether the onset of late-stage Alzheimer's would trigger the living will and allow the patient's caregivers to withhold treatment. Some patients may favor this. However, although Alzheimer's disease is irreversible, it is not a terminal condition as defined under the living will statutes. Although Alzheimer's is a progressive brain disease, strictly speaking—from a legal perspective, that is—nobody dies from Alzheimer's. Rather, Alzheimer's patients die from other intervening illnesses that are exacerbated because of the presence of Alzheimer's. Further, not only is Alzheimer's not a terminal condition but it does not cause someone to enter a persistent vegetative state. Sure, someone with late-stage Alzheimer's has no memory (short term or long term), but he or she is definitely not permanently unconscious. Hence, the mere presence of Alzheimer's would not trigger the living will.

Accordingly, what some patients in the early stages of Alzheimer's would like to see happen is that if some intervening illness occurred, they would rather not be treated for it. After all, if the patient was irrevocably mentally incapacitated because of Alzheimer's, curing the intervening illness would only prolong his or her life so that he or she may continue living in the dark world of Alzheimer's. Consider this situation:

Angie executed a living will directing her caregivers to terminate all medical treatment if she were ever to suffer from a terminal condition or be in a persistent vegetative state. She specifically mentioned that if she ever developed Alzheimer's disease and subsequently suffered from an intervening illness, she would rather die from this intervening illness, with appropriate pain relief, than be treated for it and then sink deeper into Alzheimer's.

Should Angie come down with an intervening illness such as inoperable cancer, would her doctors allow her to die without having tried therapies like radiation or chemotherapy? In such a case, would the law support the doctors' decision to allow Angie to die rather than treat her? State statutes do not explicitly permit termination of medical treatment under circumstances such as Angie's. What the courts would do is anybody's guess.

TERMINATION OF ARTIFICIAL NUTRITION AND HYDRATION

An issue often arises as to whether a living will can call for the termination of artificial nutrition and hydration. The answer is unclear. As previously discussed, individuals who are in a persistent vegetative state cannot eat or drink and therefore require artificial nutrition and hydration through feeding tubes if they are to survive. Should such an individual's caregivers decide to terminate life support, this would also mean the termination of artificial nutrition and hydration. Indeed, the American Medical Association and the U.S. Supreme Court, in the case of *Cruzan v. Director, Missouri Department of Health*, consider artificial nutrition and hydration to be medical treatment.[3] Accordingly, these bodies say, artificial nutrition and hydration come under the purview of the informed consent doctrine. Just as a patient may refuse chemotherapy for cancer, he or she may refuse artificial nutrition and hydration.

Yet some state statutes do not permit the termination of artificial nutrition and hydration if, at the time the decision must be made, the patient is mentally incapacitated. The rationale for this may be best summed up in the words of one of my students who said that if asked by a client, she would not include that directive in a living will because "this is a cruel way to die."

Notwithstanding the stance taken by some states, most state statutes and court decisions have adopted a middle-of-the-road position: They permit termination of artificial nutrition and hydration if the patient has clearly indicated a desire that it be done. In the absence of a living will, the courts often settle the issue.

In making a decision to terminate artificial nutrition and hydration, a court would require "clear and convincing" evidence that this is the patient's intent. While a living will would provide such clear and convincing evidence and essentially negate the need for a court battle, other forms of evidence exist. These include other written or oral statements made by the patient requiring the termination of artificial nutrition and hydration.

All factors considered, the best approach if you wish to make that choice is to execute a living will. Failing that, you should either create a written document that declares your attitudes toward termination of artificial nutrition and hydration and when and if you would deem it appropriate and necessary, or orally relay this information to someone you trust. If either the written document or the oral declaration clearly shows your intent, it should constitute sufficient evidence to lead the courts to permit your wishes to be carried out.

FORMALITIES OF EXECUTION

A living will is a formal legal document. Accordingly, it must meet certain formal requirements. The requirements vary from state to state. Most state statutes provide that only a competent adult can execute a living will. As to the document itself, at minimum, it must be in writing and signed by the patient. Most statutes require that the document be witnessed (always by two or more witnesses). Many statutes also require that the document be notarized. Almost all statutes preclude people with conflicts of interest—spouses, close relatives, potential heirs, your attending physician, an employee of the healthcare facility where you are a patient—from serving as witnesses.

Many state living will statutes contain a model form that can be used to prepare the document. Some states even require the declarant to use the statutory form. All factors considered, though, optional forms are a better choice because you and your attorney then have the opportunity to create a document that truly expresses your desires. After all, many practitioners have criticized living will forms (both state-sanctioned and privately prepared) as poorly designed, confusing, internally inconsistent, and too reliant upon technical language. Although people often complete these forms in attempts to create living wills, they do so without adequate counsel and consequently end up with documents that do not accurately relay their attitude toward the use of life-sustaining medical care. The results can be disastrous. To avoid disaster, you should have your attorney prepare a unique living will addressing your personal circumstances and addressing your specific desires.

DURATION OF A LIVING WILL

In a few states, living wills automatically terminate after a given number of years. In the great majority of states, however, living wills remain valid until specifically revoked.

REVOCATION OF A LIVING WILL

As with the last will and testament, you can revoke a living will at any time in one of several ways:

- Physical destruction
- Cancellation
- Written revocation
- Verbal revocation

Almost any statement suffices to revoke a living will. Subsequent inconsistent statements or instructions generally supersede the instructions contained in a living will. Whatever method of revocation is used, however, the revocation becomes effective only when your physician becomes aware of it.

VALIDITY OF LIVING WILLS AMONG JURISDICTIONS

Americans are very mobile people. Every few years, we pack our belongings and move from one town to another, one county to another, or one state to another. Most laws are valid throughout the United States. This is not so, however, in the area of living wills. Indeed, it is not always clear whether a living will that is valid in New York is necessarily valid in Louisiana. Furthermore, there is no general reciprocity among the states for recognizing out-of-state living wills. The result in one state can require that for a living will to be valid within its borders, the document must meet the requirements for living wills in that particular state. To prevent having your living will held invalid and your wishes for healthcare treatment disregarded, if you anticipate spending significant amounts of time in more than one state, you should execute separate living wills to satisfy the requirements of each state.

VALIDITY, NOTIFICATION, AND LIABILITY

A living will becomes valid and operative only when its existence is communicated to your attending physician. Although some physicians routinely inquire into the existence of a living will and other advance healthcare directives, the physician is under no duty to do so. It is your responsibility—or that of your family members, if you are suffering from Alzheimer's or some other disease that has left you mentally incapacitated—to notify the attending physician. In practice, if you are mentally incapacitated, your spouse, family members, or friends would present a copy of your living will to the attending physician or the hospital. Many state statutes require that a copy of the living will be placed in the patient's medical record.

The federal Patient Self-Determination Act of 1990 requires all hospitals participating in the Medicaid and Medicare programs to advise patients upon admission of their rights under state law to refuse medical treatment. As a practical matter, while providing such information, hospital authorities typically inquire as to whether the patient has executed a living will or any other healthcare advance directive. If the answer is no, the hospitals provide the necessary forms to their patients so that the patients can prepare the documents if they so desire.

As regards liability issues, all state statutes provide immunity for healthcare personnel who follow the directions contained in a valid, unrevoked living will, so long as they act in accordance with reasonable medical standards. If the attending physician cannot or will not follow the directions of the living will, almost all states require that the patient be transferred to a physician who will follow these directions.

On the other hand, very few states provide any significant penalties for a physician's failure to obey the provisions of a living will. In fact, although these penalties exist on the books, their enforcement is essentially nonexistent. In the same manner, although a physician could incur civil liability for failure to obey the provisions of a living will, my research has not unearthed a single instance where a court held such a doctor liable. In the final analysis, then, living wills are rarely the subject of litigation.

In practice, a living will is used by the spouse, other family members, or friends of a mentally incapacitated patient to determine what course of medical action should be taken regarding continuing medical treatment for the patient. The outside world hardly ever finds out whether a patient's directives were actually followed. If, for example, the relatives and the attending physician decide to ignore a living will and continue life-sustaining treatment contrary to the patient's expressed wishes, no one outside that circle of decision makers would ever know. Essentially, if no one complains about the course of action, these decision makers can have their way. This is indeed a sad state of affairs and one that I hope the law remedies soon.

THE DO NOT RESUSCITATE ORDER

The Do Not Resuscitate (DNR) order is an order not to resuscitate the patient under certain conditions. The DNR comes in two distinct varieties: the *inpatient (or bedside) DNR*, and the *out-of-hospital DNR*. Inpatient DNRs are used, as the name suggests, in hospitals. Out-of-hospital DNRs are used everywhere else: nursing homes, assisted living facilities, hospices, private residences, or the transport vehicles taking patients to the emergency room.

Either DNR, if it is in writing, must be signed by the patient's attending physician. In that sense, it is more like an order from the attending physician to hospital staff and emergency medical services (EMS) workers that they not perform unwanted medical interventions on the patient. The requirement that the physician sign the DNR makes it significantly different from a living will and medical power of attorney. While the patient must sign either of these instruments, there is no requirement that he or she sign a DNR. Still, the DNR expresses the wishes of the patient. Either you or your surrogate decision maker must consent to the physician's signing a DNR.

THE INPATIENT DNR

An inpatient DNR is more limited in scope than a living will. While a living will is valid for the duration of your life (or until the living will is revoked), typically, an inpatient DNR is good for periods from twenty-four hours to one week, or for whatever time period the physician orders. In addition, while the living will is a statutory creation, the inpatient DNR is not; in reality, it is a treatment decision made by you or your surrogate and certified by your physician.

Finally, DNRs and living wills serve different purposes. The living will says, "Don't keep me here! If I would be dead but for these machines, remove the machines and let me go!" The DNR, on the other hand, says, "Don't bring me back! If I am already practically dead—if, for example, I have no pulse or I am not breathing—do not use any heroics whatsoever to bring me back! Leave me as you found me!" In keeping with this latter command, if a DNR order is in a patient's medical file and the patient undergoes an emergency event (such as cardiac arrest), the hospital staff will not resuscitate the patient.

THE OUT-OF-HOSPITAL DNR

The out-of-hospital DNR is a statutory creation. Almost all states have some type of document that tells EMS personnel not to resuscitate (that is, perform CPR or other heroic measures on) a particular patient who has reached the point of medical futility.

The out-of-hospital DNR can take the form of a written order carried around by the patient or his or her representative, a bracelet or necklace worn by the patient, or both a written order and a bracelet or necklace. If in written form, the DNR must be signed by your physician. In the case of a bracelet or necklace, the patient must obtain it in person from the authorities (such as the State Department of Health Services). However, some states (like Pennsylvania) allow for circumstances under which an appropriate representative of an individual who has created a living will may obtain a DNR bracelet or necklace on the individual's behalf. In fact, the representative may even secure an out-of-hospital DNR on that individual's behalf.

REVOCATION OF A DNR

It is actually quite simple to revoke a DNR. Indeed, the verbal wishes of a competent patient always supersede a DNR. Take the case of Debbie, whose physician has signed a DNR. She is lying in the hospital bed dying because the DNR prevents the medical staff from doing anything beyond providing comfort and care. If Debbie opens her eyes and says, "Forget about that DNR nonsense. Do everything you can to save me!" the DNR is thereby revoked and the physicians and nursing staff must do all they can to save her life.

One final note on revocation: In some states, if you are unable to communicate, your attending physician, legal guardian, qualified relative, or agent named in your medical power of attorney can authorize resuscitation.

THE DNR AND THE ALZHEIMER'S PATIENT

We have already seen that individuals who develop Alzheimer's disease eventually get to the stage where all of their memory is gone and they are unable to function without the assistance and care of others. If these individuals develop a debilitating illness that would normally bring about death, barring any intervention by medical personnel, death would surely result.

Now, consider this: If the Alzheimer's patient does not have a DNR (be it inpatient or out-of-hospital) and he or she goes into cardiac arrest, the attending medical personnel are obligated to do their utmost to revive him or her. Let's assume they succeed. They would then have revived a person so that he or she may continue to live in the world of unawareness called Alzheimer's disease. Is that fair? Is that a desirable result?

Some states have addressed this issue by allowing an appropriate representative of a patient who has created a living will to secure a DNR, thus allowing the healthcare team not to resuscitate. But what if the person has not created a living will? Alas, the law has no answer.

The wise thing to do, then, is to promptly create out-of-hospital DNRs and to instruct your physicians regarding your inpatient DNR desires. As an alternative to that—or, indeed, in addition to it— you should execute a medical power of attorney and a living will. Failing that, in the event you begin to exhibit symptoms of Alzheimer's disease, you should immediately execute these documents and, if it is your desire, have your physician sign an out-of-hospital DNR. In states where they are available, the individual should also obtain a DNR bracelet or necklace.

THINGS TO CONSIDER

While advance directives are by no means absolute necessities, they can make decision making easier for family members and loved ones should the need to know an Alzheimer's patient's wishes arise. If your loved one is in an early stage of Alzheimer's disease, you should consider counseling him or her about obtaining one or more advance directives.

Of course, many people view advance directives, particularly DNRs and living wills, from a religious perspective. They maintain that God gave life and that God will take life away when He is ready; hence, they should not interfere with God's plan by obtaining a DNR or executing a living will. Personally, I have lost count of the number of people who have told me in my role as either a minister or an attorney that while they would execute a medical power of attorney, they would certainly never execute a living will or obtain a DNR because these instruments seek to replace God in their lives. If your loved one holds this belief, there is really nothing you can do but, well, pray.

When a person has no advance directive and his or her children disagree on what course to take (or there are no children or loved ones to make a decision), the only legal recourse available is for the court to make the decision. While this might be expedient when there are no living children or other loved ones, in situations where the children or loved ones disagree on the course of action, I do not recommend this step. Litigation could drag on for years while the patient remains in a persistent vegetative state. Worse, the litigation could tear the family apart and eventually do more harm than good. Rather than turn to the courts, I recommend that people in this situation seek counseling from a religious figure, psychologist, family counselor, or attorney who recognizes that a lawyer is actually an "attorney and *counselor* at law."

NOTES

1. *Schloendorff v. Society of N.Y. Hosp.*, 105 N.E. 92, 93 (N.Y. 1914).

2. Alan Meisel, "The 'Exceptions' to the Informed Consent Doctrine: Striking a Balance Between Competing Values in Medical Decisionmaking," *Wisconsin Law Review*, Volume 413, 1979.

3. 497 U.S. 261 (1990). The Court held that the U.S. Constitution "would grant a competent person a constitutionally protected right to refuse lifesaving hydration and nutrition."

CHAPTER 6

CARING FOR A LOVED ONE WITH ALZHEIMER'S: GUARDIANSHIP

AUNTY DAIL AND THE CHECKS

*T*his morning my inbox contained an important e-mail from my cousin Christie:

> I know you are busy and all of that, but I need to talk to you about Mommy. I am getting very worried. I cannot say everything in an e-mail. I called you twice last week but have not heard from you. I guess you are traveling. As soon as you get back, please call me. Thanks, Vaughn. Love you lots, Christie.

I picked up the phone in my hotel room and made the long-distance call. "Christie," I said, "this is Vaughn. I am in Cape Town, South Africa. I just received your e-mail. What's up with Aunty Dail?"

Christie told me her story. Some time after I'd visited Aunty

114

Dail, she began to do a little more than laugh and point. She began misplacing things, getting agitated, and wandering. Some days she would get up early, shower and get dressed, and wander to the old schoolhouse where she was once a student. She would sit on a stone outside the building and smile at everyone who passed.

Concerned, Christie had taken Aunty Dail to the doctor. The doctor confirmed that Aunty Dail was suffering from some form of dementia, but Christie could not remember whether the doctor had mentioned the type of dementia or whether it was Alzheimer's disease. The doctor had prescribed some drugs that, according to Christie, were "costing an arm and a leg."

Christie was also concerned about Aunty Dail's finances. Aunty Dail had saved prudently during her working days and had quite a bit of money in the bank, but her bank accounts were all in her name only. With Aunty Dail ill, Christie had no way of accessing the money to pay the bills. Aunty Dail had been receiving Social Security benefits, but because she was not able to endorse the checks, Christie had no access to that money either. The checks were piling up on the nightstand while Christie was struggling to pay the bills.

"Vaughn," she said, "is there anything I can do? I know you told me to get Mommy to sign a power of attorney, but she can't do that now, can she?"

"No," I responded, "she can't. She lacks the capacity to do any such thing."

"Well," Christie continued, "can I have myself appointed her guardian? Would that help?"

"Let me think about that option, Christie," I replied. "I'll call you tomorrow."

"Thank you, Vaughn," Christie replied, her voice beginning to tremble, "you are an angel."

An angel was the last thing I was feeling like at that moment. What I knew about guardianship was not too good. Would I want my great-aunt to be a ward? If so, would Christie be a good guardian? Were there other options?

Guardianship is a court-supervised procedure for taking away authority from one person and putting it into the hands of another. Guardianship is not a voluntary procedure; rather, it is forced upon a person who is mentally incapacitated.

The law holds that all adults are capable of making decisions on their own behalf. If, however, a person becomes mentally incapacitated, he or she becomes unable to make decisions for him- or herself. Someone—a substitute decision maker—must now make decisions for that person. The process of providing that substitute decision maker is called guardianship.

In some states, the term "guardianship" refers to making decisions about the mentally incapacitated individual's person (that is, his or her body and all that pertains to it, such as healthcare, education, place of residence, and daily routine). In those states, the term "conservatorship" refers to making decisions about the mentally incapacitated person's property (such as his or her home, brokerage accounts, bank accounts, pension plans, certificates of deposit, and other assets). In other states, the term "guardianship" describes decision making for both the mentally incapacitated individual's person and his or her property. The substitute decision maker is known as a *guardian* or *conservator,* and the mentally incapacitated person is generally referred to as the *ward*.

Either type of guardianship is the result of a state judicial proceeding. Only a state court of appropriate jurisdiction can appoint a guardian for another person. Each state's law of guardianship is unique. Hence, any discussion of guardianship in a book such as this is necessarily general in nature and not always applicable to any one particular state. Yet in general, all state guardianship laws subscribe to similar principles, making this general discussion an accurate guide to guardianship in any of the states. However, this is only a guide; you should consult an attorney in the appropriate state for specific details on its statutes.

The sad part about all this is that voluntary, less severe alternatives to guardianship—specifically, powers of attorney and advance directives—do exist. However, through either lack of foresight or lack of competent advice, many people fail to make any provision for managing themselves and their property in the event they become mentally incapacitated. When they do reach that stage, guardianship is the only alternative.

WHO NEEDS A GUARDIAN?

The law presumes that all adult individuals are legally competent. For someone to lose that status, a court with appropriate jurisdiction must decide that the person is mentally incapacitated. Only then will a court appoint a guardian. Although the different states define it differently, the term "mentally incapacitated" generally is used to refer to someone who lacks the capacity to make responsible decisions.

The test is not whether the person's decisions are in fact responsible but whether the person has the capacity to make responsible decisions. After all, a person has the right to make decisions that others may deem foolish and irresponsible without being afraid that a court will declare her mentally incapacitated and appoint a guardian. This is particularly true for people who, because of certain strongly held religious or other convictions, make decisions that seem foolish to others. A Jehovah's Witness should be able to face certain death rather than have a blood transfusion, and a Seventh-day Adventist facing certain death should be able to refuse the implantation of a pig-valve in his heart without either person being declared mentally incapacitated.

Guardianship is for the person who just cannot make a responsible decision. An example is an Alzheimer's patient who, believing it is fifteen years ago when she was well-to-do, writes large checks against accounts that now have negligible balances. Another example is an Alzheimer's patient who has lost his ability to communicate in any way or to voluntarily move his limbs and is thus unable to care for himself or pay his bills, although he saved prudently during his working life and now has huge liquid assets. Such people need protection. They ought not be left alone, unable to act for themselves and perfect targets for victimization by others.

HOW COURTS MAKE THE DETERMINATION

State statutes guide courts when deciding if someone requires a guardian. Increasingly, these statutes use a functional definition of incapacity. They look to the person's behavior to determine whether he or she is mentally incapacitated. Accordingly, a person would not be considered mentally incapacitated merely because of his or her physical or mental status. The mere fact that someone is very old, frail, and/or chronically ill does not in itself mean that the person is mentally incapacitated and in need of a guardian. Instead, the court would have to find that the person has lost the capacity to make decisions. Different tasks require different levels and kinds of mental capacity. Therefore, it is possible that a person has lost only some of his or her capacities, in which case he or she would need a "limited guardianship." If, however, the individual has lost all of his or her mental capacities, he or she would need a "general guardianship."

Among the statutes addressing this distinction, the one from Missouri is enlightening:

> (8) An "incapacitated person" is one who is unable by reason of any physical or mental condition to receive and evaluate information or to communicate decisions to such an extent that he lacks capacity to meet essential requirements for food, clothing, shelter, safety or other care such that serious physical injury, illness, or disease is likely to occur.

> (13) A "partially incapacitated person" is one who is unable by reason of any physical or mental condition to receive and evaluate information or to communicate decisions to the extent that he lacks capacity to meet, in part, essential requirements for food, clothing, shelter, safety, or other care without court-ordered assistance.[1]

By this standard, the court can appoint a limited guardian whenever the mental incapacity of a person is not complete. For example, someone who has lost the capacity to do simple arithmetic and thus pay his or her bills and balance his or her checkbook would have a guardian appointed for the limited purpose of helping that person meet these needs.

In all limited guardianships, the power granted to the limited guardian does not exceed what is required to meet the needs of the mentally incapacitated person; the person retains control of all other aspects of his or her life. Of course, if the individual's capacity declines further, the court will increase the power granted to the limited guardian.

The advantage of a limited guardianship is that it allows the person to retain some autonomy even while he or she gets necessary help in those areas where such help is needed. Yet some people still object to this type of guardianship because limited guardianship[2]:

- Is too complicated to employ, since detailing the contours of the incapacity and creating an appropriate, individualized guardianship is not feasible.
- Is too time-consuming and expensive to be of much practical significance.
- Denies the guardian the necessary authority to handle the ward's assets.

For these reasons, the limited guardianship is not often used. Nevertheless, limited guardianship appears to be a good option for the person experiencing early-stage Alzheimer's disease. The person can retain authority over those things he or she can control, and a limited guardian can manage those matters he or she cannot deal with because of the disease.

PROCEDURAL ISSUES

Only a court of appropriate jurisdiction can appoint a guardian for someone else. Although the potential ward, if able to, may consent to the guardianship and agree to the appointment of a particular person as his or her guardian, the law treats the parties to a guardianship proceeding as adversaries.

THE PETITION

Accordingly, the first step toward the appointment of a guardian for someone is the filing of a guardianship petition. The person who files the petition is known as the *petitioner*; the potential ward is known as the *respondent*. In most states, any interested person may file a guardianship petition requesting that the court find the respondent mentally incapacitated and appoint a guardian for him or her. In most cases, though, guardianship petitions are filed by spouses, children, other relatives, friends, or concerned neighbors of the potential ward. If no family member or friend is willing or available to file the petition, institutions such as service agencies and hospitals may file it.

The petitioner will undoubtedly retain an attorney to assist in preparing the petition and to represent the petitioner during the guardianship proceeding. This attorney prepares the petition, following the requirements of state law and local court rules. The petitioner names the proposed guardian. In fact, some courts will not accept a guardianship petition unless it identifies a proposed guardian or guardians.

The petition must be filed in a court of appropriate jurisdiction, which means:

- Normally, that the petition be filed in a court having jurisdiction over probate matters.

- That the petition be filed in the county where the proposed ward lives or in which he or she is "present."

Consider this case:

Fred owns a home in Poughkeepsie, which is located in Dutchess County, New York. After he begins exhibiting symptoms of Alzheimer's disease, he moves in with his daughter, Alisha, who lives in Newburgh, New York, in Orange County. Alisha wishes to file a guardianship petition naming her as her father's guardian. Where may Alisha file the guardianship petition?

Most states would permit the petitioner to file the guardianship petition in either county: Dutchess County, where Fred is domiciled, or Orange County, where he is now physically present. If Fred also owns property in Texas, someone would also have to file a guardianship petition in Texas in order to take any action concerning Fred's property in that state.

The law requires that the proposed ward receive timely notification that someone has filed a petition for guardianship. Remember, the law considers this an adversarial procedure, so the person must be able to defend against the petition. The number of days' notice varies from state to state, but from three to ten days is common. Most states require that the petitioner serve notice of the filing on all appropriate parties, such as the respondent's family members, creditors, and the person or persons with whom the respondent lives.

THE HEARING

After the court receives the petition, it schedules a hearing. Before the hearing, most courts send a representative (called a *court visitor*) to visit the alleged mentally incapacitated person in his or her place of residence. On that visit, the court visitor gauges the person's physical and mental condition, his or her reaction to the possibility of having a guardian, and whether the person's physical or mental condition precludes him or her from making a personal appearance at the hearing.

The court visitor also interviews the petitioner and the individual nominated to act as guardian to gain an understanding of why the petitioner filed the petition and whether the proposed guardian is capable of carrying out the responsibilities of the position. The court visitor then reports his or her findings to the court. Although the court visitor's report does not determine whether the court will hold that the proposed ward is mentally incapacitated, it often plays a significant role in determining whether the court will appoint a guardian, whom it will name as guardian, the powers that it will grant the guardian, and what it will order the guardian to do as it relates to the ward and his or her property.

As far as the actual hearing is concerned, state law usually permits but does not compel the presence of the proposed ward. While the person may waive his or her right to attend, the law does provide him or her with this right. In fact, to encourage and permit the presence of the person, some courts hold the hearing at the person's place of residence. For example, if the person is bedridden but communicative and is living in a nursing home, the court may hold the guardianship hearing at the nursing home. This has two benefits:

1. The court is able to observe the proposed ward and thus determine his or her level of mental incapacity, if any.

2. The court protects the person from the physical burden of traveling to the courthouse for the hearing.

Many states require that an attorney represent the proposed ward. If the person cannot afford an attorney, the state provides one. Some states use a "guardian ad litem" (a person—not necessarily an attorney—vested with the legal authority to care for the personal and property interests of the proposed ward) either to represent the person or to determine whether the court should provide the person with an attorney. For example, a guardian ad litem who finds that the proposed ward is in an advanced stage of Alzheimer's disease, noncommunicative, and unable to do anything for herself might well inform the court that it has no need to appoint an attorney because the person clearly is mentally incapacitated. On the other hand, the guardian ad litem might recommend that the court appoint an attorney if the person strongly denies being mentally incapacitated or if no apparent reason for appointing a guardian exists. A few states do not require the appointment of an attorney; many permit the person to waive the right to counsel and attempt to represent himself.

CHOICE OF GUARDIAN

All states require that the petition nominate a potential guardian. Unless the court finds some reason not to do so, it appoints the nominee as guardian. Reasons for not appointing the nominee include a finding that the nominee lacks the ability to assume the responsibilities of a guardian or that the nominee has been abusive toward the mentally incapacitated person or other similarly situated persons. Should the court decide against appointing the nominee as guardian, most state statutes provide a preference list of persons the court may appoint instead, giving priority to spouses followed by children, other relatives, friends, members of the clergy, and so forth. Notwithstanding the statutory priority list, the court is free to select the person who or institution that will best serve the interests of the mentally incapacitated person.

Realistically, though, the court's choice of whom to appoint as guardian is limited to those persons who or entities that are willing and able to serve as guardian. After all, the court has no power to compel anyone to accept appointment as guardian. Because courts are limited to selecting guardians who are willing and able to serve, in most cases the court simply appoints the person or entity nominated in the petition. The court may also appoint a guardian who will be paid by the state. These individuals are typically lawyers trained in these matters. Some states also have "public guardians" to act as the guardian of last resort when no private individual or entity is available. Public guardians are agencies, offices, or public officials whose job is to act as guardian of the estate or person of a mentally incapacitated person. Some are employed by the state or county; others are hired on an as-needed basis. Most states charge the cost of the public guardian to the estate of the mentally incapacitated person; if the estate cannot afford to pay, the state bears the cost. Most states expect a public guardian to work closely with social service agencies in an attempt to meet the needs of the mentally incapacitated person.

The rules regarding the choice of guardian present opportunities for the family of the mentally incapacitated person to choose the guardian. Because family members file most guardianship petitions and the petitioner gets to nominate the guardian, the mentally incapacitated person's family members can indeed decide among themselves just which family member would be the best guardian for their loved one. Not only that, but even the mentally incapacitated person can have a say in the matter. If Laurel begins exhibiting symptoms of Alzheimer's disease, she and her family members can meet to discuss her options as the disease progresses. If they see guardianship as an option, they—in Laurel's presence—can discuss just who Laurel's guardian should be if the need arises. In fact, Laurel can name the person *she* would like to serve as her guardian in the event she ever needs one.

COST OF GUARDIANSHIP

One of the drawbacks to guardianship is its cost. To put it bluntly, guardianships are expensive.

To begin the guardianship process, the petitioner must retain an attorney. The attorney prepares and files the guardianship petition and represents the petitioner at the guardianship hearing. Typically, the attorney's fees run from $500 to $3,000, going even higher if the ward resists the guardianship and hires opposing counsel to represent him or her. Other costs include court fees (usually a modest amount); fees to a physician or other qualified professional who will prepare an affidavit affirming the potential ward's mental incapacity (these costs are higher if the physician or other professional must testify in person, in which case the fees could be $500 to $2,000 a day); fees to a social worker to prepare a plan of how the alleged mentally incapacitated person will be cared for; investigatory expenses; and witness fees. In addition, if the court uses a court visitor or guardian ad litem, that person will also receive a fee. If the case is appealed, additional costs will be incurred.

If the guardianship petition is successful, the ward's estate bears all costs of the proceeding. This, of course, decreases the size of the estate. In addition, the guardian may also charge a fee for guardianship services. Banks and attorneys who serve as guardians are paid for their efforts, usually an hourly fee. A bank that acts as guardian of the estate may be paid an annual fee equal to a percentage of the value of the estate. Nonprofit entities that serve as guardian usually receive a flat sum, often several hundred dollars, or else an hourly fee. Family members or friends who serve as guardian usually are not paid for their time. However, as is true of other guardians, any out-of-pocket expenses they incur are reimbursed from the ward's assets. Public guardians are paid by the state, which may then seek reimbursement from the ward's estate.

THE ROLE OF A GUARDIAN

Some family members who have a close relationship with the mentally incapacitated person are often disappointed that the person did not select them to serve as guardian. They should not be. Serving as guardian is a difficult and sometimes burdensome task, even if the guardian is being paid for the effort. Being someone's guardian carries great responsibility, and you should not seek or accept this responsibility if you do not believe you can thus serve.

The nature and extent of a guardian's powers depend upon the nature of the guardianship (that is, whether guardianship of the person, guardianship of the property, or a plenary guardianship, meaning that the guardian holds full power), the type of guardianship (that is, limited or general), the applicable state law, local court rules and customs, and any specific orders given by the court. Typically, guardians receive a general grant of authority from the court and carry out their duties without ongoing court supervision. While the guardian must periodically report to the court, on a day-to-day basis the guardian is free to act within the limits of his or her delegated power.

In most states, guardians of the person or plenary guardians have the power to determine where the ward will live. For example, the guardian may decide that the person can no longer live alone and should relocate (or rather, be relocated) to someplace like an assisted living facility or a nursing home. Indeed, sometimes the petitioner seeks the guardianship in order to move the person into such a living arrangement if, for example, the mentally incapacitated person lacks the mental capacity to sign the admission agreement with the facility. Through the creation of a guardianship, the guardian obtains the authority to sign the documents on the mentally incapacitated person's behalf, permitting the person to move into the nursing home. The law is not clear on whether a guardian may move the ward into a nursing home without the court's approval. It is therefore wise, when seeking approval of the guardianship, to inform the court of the intent to move the person into a nursing home. In that way, you obtain the court's approval at the same time that it approves the guardianship.

As guardian of the property of a mentally incapacitated person, you have extensive powers over the person's assets. You must take control of the person's assets, collect any income the person may receive, and pay for the person's maintenance and support. Unless specifically ordered by the court, state statute governs how you may invest the person's assets. With all of this, you have a great deal of power over the person, but problems can develop. If, for example, Jack serves as guardian of the person's property and Jill serves as guardian of the person, and Jack and Jill disagree about placing the person in a nursing home or other assisted living facility, Jack can block the move by simply refusing to pay for the cost of the facility. If the two guardians cannot agree about the best course of action, a court might have to make the ultimate decision. Because of this potential for conflict, some people might choose to appoint a plenary guardian—someone with authority over both the person and property of the mentally incapacitated person.

Although guardians of the person and plenary guardians have wide latitude to act, they face some limitations in just what they may do. For example, under normal circumstances, a guardian cannot vote for the ward or consent to the person's marriage. In most states, the guardian also cannot consent to a divorce on behalf of the ward, and in a few states, the guardian cannot consent to the termination of the person's life-sustaining treatment without a prior court order.

Even with these restrictions, the guardian has great authority—and responsibility. It is important, therefore, that the court appoint the best available and willing person to the position. Yet when you consider the importance of individual autonomy, it would be good if the now mentally incapacitated person had had a say in who the eventual guardian would be. Therefore, if it is not done before the onset of symptoms of Alzheimer's disease, the individual should discuss the matter of guardianship with his or her loved ones as soon as the symptoms appear and identify just who he or she wants to serve as his or her guardian if it becomes necessary.

GUARDING THE GUARDIAN

Guardians, especially guardians of the person's property, may be tempted to misuse the ward's assets or to use the assets for their personal gain. Indeed, there have been instances where guardians have been prosecuted for such conduct. To avoid or at least minimize this tendency, state statutes provide that guardians be supervised by a court of appropriate jurisdiction.

Once appointed, the guardian is accountable to the court. Soon after the appointment, the guardian of the property is required to inventory the person's assets. Thereafter, the guardian submits financial accountings to the court. The frequency of these submissions varies from state to state. Many states require annual or periodic accounting by the guardian of the property. All states require a final accounting at the end of the guardianship, be it because of the termination of the guardianship by the court, the resignation of the guardian, or the death of the ward. In these accountings, the guardian must account for all income received on behalf of the ward and for all expenditures from the ward's assets.

We see, then, that the guardian of the property must maintain accurate financial records. Any mistakes or misuse of funds may give rise to liability to the ward, or the court may assess penalties. If the guardian is an attorney, such conduct could also lead to disciplinary action by the jurisdiction's attorney disciplinary committee, with penalties ranging from a "letter of education" to disbarment. It is no wonder, then, that to avoid such occurrences, some jurisdictions favor appointing banks as guardians of larger estates and individuals as guardians of the person.

Like the guardian of the estate (or property) of the mentally incapacitated person, the guardian of the person must also report to the supervising court. Here, too, the frequency of the reports varies from state to state. In part as a reaction to cases where the guardian has abused his or her discretion and has mistreated or neglected the mentally incapacitated person, many state laws mandate regular judicial review of all guardianships. This court supervision can take many forms. It might be as simple as requiring the guardian to make regular written reports to the court, or it might be as complex as having court visitors visiting the ward and making findings to the court. Many jurisdictions require that a guardian of the person make a preliminary report to the court, describing the person's living conditions, presenting a plan for promoting the person's welfare, and explaining how the guardian expects to deal with the problems that gave rise to the guardianship. Thereafter, the guardian must make annual reports to the court, describing any changes in the person's mental and physical condition and any of the person's unmet needs. The report should also advise the court on whether the guardianship should be continued or if the powers of the guardian should be modified.

In carrying out their responsibilities, guardians are expected to act in the best interests of the ward. At the same time, the guardian must make decisions in a manner consistent with the values, aspirations, and lifestyle of the mentally incapacitated person. To do this successfully, the guardian either should ask the ward what he or she would like or, if such communication is not possible, attempt to carry out the preferences the ward expressed before the onset of the mental incapacity. If the ward has no preference or never expressed one, the guardian can act in the way a "reasonable person" would act under similar circumstances. If the guardian fails to carry out the fiduciary obligations of the position, the supervising court can either remove the guardian from the position or order him or her to act in a more appropriate manner.

Regardless of the type of guardianship, other parties may request that the court replace the guardian. Generally, state law permits any interested person (including the mentally incapacitated person) to petition the court to make it aware of any guardian who transgresses his or her obligations or in any way acts against the best interests of the ward. The interested person may ask the court to remove the guardian.

TERMINATION OF THE GUARDIANSHIP

Guardianships automatically terminate upon the death of the ward. However, the death, incapacity, or resignation of the guardian does not terminate the guardianship. Should any of these events occur, the supervising court would simply appoint a successor guardian. However, no guardian may resign unless a successor guardian is available. After all, it would not be right for the ward, who is already unable to make his or her own decisions, to be left without someone to make those decisions.

If the ward regains mental capacity, the court should terminate the guardianship. However, the ward must first petition the court to terminate the guardianship. Under the traditional model, the burden of proof is on the ward to prove that he or she has regained mental capacity. If the guardian agrees that the guardianship is no longer needed, the petition for termination will be uncontested and the court will terminate the guardianship. If, however, the guardian opposes the termination, the ward will have to prove to the court that he or she is no longer mentally incapacitated. As you can imagine, this is difficult for the ward to do because, with the guardian having control of his or her assets, the ward would lack the financial resources to pay for a medical opinion or to produce evidence of his or her restoration. Moreover, because someone in an advanced stage of Alzheimer's lacks the mental capacity to petition the court for termination of the guardianship, it is unlikely that such a person would ever be able to get out of the guardianship.

Recognizing the great burden placed upon the ward under the traditional model, many states have reformed their guardianship statutes to reverse the burden of proof in guardianship termination proceedings and to place it on those who wish to continue the guardianship. In other words, those who wish to continue the guardianship must prove that the ward has not regained legal capacity. In addition, many states permit the ward to request termination of guardianship by an informal request to the court rather than through a formal petition with its accompanying requirements of notice.

Regardless of the formal or informal requirements, though, no guardianship should be allowed to continue if the ward has regained legal capacity or if the guardianship is not promoting the person's best interests. When the guardianship is not serving the ward's best interests, the court has three options: (1) it can remove and replace the guardian, (2) it can terminate the guardianship, or (3) it can limit the guardian's power to reflect a partial restoration of capacity.

WHEN FAMILIES CAN'T AGREE: MEDIATION IN GUARDIANSHIP

An individual's mental incapacity can precipitate intense disagreements among family members. Either because family members do not understand what is happening to their loved one, are in denial about their loved one's loss of capacity, or are too confident that they and only they know what is right for their loved one, they often become so embroiled in arguments about what to do and who should do it that they neglect the needs of the person, allowing these needs to remain largely unmet. In addition, sometimes mentally incapacitated people do not believe that there is a problem and interpret the family's efforts to assist them as hostile acts designed to rob them of their freedom, their assets, or both. Should either of these things happen, rather than rushing to the courts for resolution, families should consider seeking mediation.

Mediation is a voluntary process in which the parties to a dispute, with the assistance of a neutral third-party facilitator, explore their options and attempt to reach agreement. Unlike a judge sitting on a trial or hearing, the mediator does not render a judgment. In fact, the mediator does not even recommend a solution! Although it is important that mediators in guardianship cases understand guardianship procedure, they do not provide legal advice to the parties but instead encourage them to get independent legal advice.

Mediation can be used at any point in the guardianship dispute: before the petitioner files a guardianship petition, after the petition is filed but before the hearing, or after the court has appointed a guardian, such as when someone challenges the need for a continuation of the guardianship or disputes the guardian's action or inaction. In mediation, the parties talk to each other directly rather than through their attorneys, and thus they have the opportunity to listen to each other and to understand each other's interests and positions.

An agreement arrived at through mediation does not necessarily have to be approved by a court, although an agreement to appoint a guardian must be approved by a court of appropriate jurisdiction. However, if the parties agree to a solution other than guardianship, they may simply agree to adhere to whatever satisfactory solution they arrived at. If a guardianship petition has already been filed, the petitioner may simply withdraw it. If the dispute arose after the court already appointed a guardian, the agreement between the parties may take the form of a stipulated proposed order (a writing that reflects the parties' agreement), which is then approved by the court.

The parties to the mediation share the costs, often on a 50–50 basis. This is one of the reasons why mediation is typically less costly than a full-blown guardianship proceeding. Also, because mediation often eliminates the need for protracted litigation, it is a less stressful process.

Still, mediation is not always the best solution. If, for example, the proposed ward already has advanced to late-stage Alzheimer's disease, the person will most likely not be able to understand the mediation process sufficiently to participate meaningfully. In such a case, mediation may not be appropriate.

NOTES

1. Mo. Rev. Stat. § 475.010(8), (13).

2. These objections are identified in and taken from Lawrence A. Frolik and Richard L. Kaplan, *Elder Law in a Nutshell*, 4th ed. (St. Paul, Minn.: Thomson/West, 2006).

CHAPTER 7

WHEN AN ALZHEIMER'S PATIENT DOES SOMETHING WRONG: LEGAL LIABILITY

What Do We Do with Aunty Arlette?

*V*ilna and I set about cleaning up the mess caused by Aunty Arlette's purchase of the car that she couldn't afford and that she no longer had the mental capacity to purchase. After several phone calls from Vilna and me to the car dealership and a short trip by me to the dealer, we convinced him that Aunty Arlette was mentally incapacitated and that her contract to purchase the car was null and void. Because Aunty Arlette had only driven the car from the dealership to her home on the day she made the purchase, the dealer agreed to take the car back and refund the total amount. We breathed a collective sigh of relief and thanked the Lord for our good fortune—or rather, mighty blessing.

The blessing was not to last. Not long after, I again visited

Aunty Arlette and Vilna. We had a normal breakfast, after which I began cleaning up the yard and helping Vilna "put the house in order" for another winter. We worked through the morning. Shortly before noon, Vilna left me to prepare lunch and to check on Aunty Arlette, who had been asleep in her bedroom when we began cleaning. Less than five minutes later, Vilna shouted, "Vaughn, have you seen Mommy? She's not in her bedroom, and I've searched the house and can't find her!"

"I'll look in the yard," I replied, heading out the back door. No sign of Aunty Arlette. No sign of her at the front of the house, either. I returned to the house. In the kitchen, I looked at the board where we hung our car keys and noticed that the keys to Vilna's car were missing. "Strange," I thought. "I didn't hear Vilna's car leaving." I shouted, "Vilna, are you there?"

"Yes," came the response from the laundry room, where she was looking for Aunty Arlette. "Where would I be?"

"I thought maybe you'd gone out looking for Aunty Arlette without telling me you were leaving. The keys to your car are missing."

"My keys are missing?" asked Vilna incredulously. "I put them on the nail on that board after I came in from the store last night!"

We looked at each other. We knew what had happened to Aunty Arlette. Vilna immediately got on the phone and called the police to report a missing person. It did no good. Although she told the police officer about her mother's memory problems and our fear that something might happen to her, the officer just repeated the same refrain: Aunty Arlette was an adult and unless she had been missing for seventy-two hours, the police could not do anything.

We decided that I would stay home in case Aunty Arlette returned and that Vilna would use my car to drive around town looking for her mother. Before Vilna even left the house, the phone rang. Vilna picked up the phone, furrowed her brow, and then looked at me. "Let's go," she said. "Walgreens at 82nd and University."

As we drove, Vilna told me that the call was from the Walgreens manager. He had recognized her car, which was at the store. The manager wanted her to come to the store immediately. He would not say more on the phone.

When we got to the store, we were completely unprepared for what we saw. Vilna's car was there, all right. It was slammed into one of the columns that held up the store's awning. A small crowd had gathered. Standing on the fringes of the crowd was Aunty Arlette, shaking her head and muttering, "They moved the ice cream shop. They moved the ice cream shop." Aunty Arlette was right; the ice cream shop that had been there for decades had closed years ago.

The police arrived shortly after we did. Officers took measurements and asked questions. No matter what they asked Aunty Arlette, all she said was, "They moved the ice cream shop. They moved the ice cream shop." After about an hour—by which time a tow truck had taken Vilna's car to a repair shop—an officer handed us a police report and told us that the whole mess would be a matter for the insurance companies. In light of Aunty Arlette's "distressed" condition, he said, he would not issue her a citation. "But," he said in parting, "you guys must keep that old lady off the road. She is nuts!"

I opened my mouth to tell him that the "old lady" wasn't

nuts, she was ill, suffering from a disease I hoped he would
suffer from some day, but I decided to say nothing. Instead, I
stood in the parking lot looking at the column; six of its bricks
were missing. Vilna's car had also been badly damaged. Aunty
Arlette had definitely caused the damage to both, and my law-
yer's mind wondered: Who was liable? Did liability end with
Aunty Arlette? Was Vilna liable too? And what would happen
if tonight, somebody who had been in the store at the time
Aunty Arlette struck the column suffered from an acid reflux
attack or even cardiac arrest and blamed it on the stress of what
he had seen? Would Aunty Arlette be liable for this? Would
Vilna be liable?

Put simply, the word *tort* is a legal term used in common law
jurisdictions to mean a civil wrong that can be grounds for a
lawsuit. Unlike the obligations you voluntarily assume when
you enter into a contract, the duties imposed under tort law are
mandatory for everyone within a certain jurisdiction. They cover
harm done to another's body, property, or legal rights, or a
breach of a duty owed to another person under statutory law.

Someone who is harmed by another's tort is entitled to redress in a court of appropriate jurisdiction. Typically, the court
orders the person who commits the tort to pay compensation to
the person who or entity that was wronged. Courts sometimes
order an extra payment simply as punishment for the wrongdoing. The total amount paid is known as damages. Damages paid
as compensation are labeled "compensatory damages," and
damages paid as punishment for wrongdoing are called "punitive damages."

Under U.S. law, torts are divided into two broad categories: intentional torts and unintentional torts.

INTENTIONAL TORTS

All jurisdictions define "intent" as an act done with the purpose of bringing about harm or with substantial certainty that the harm will occur. Intentional torts are intentional, voluntary misdeeds that one person commits against another (called the *plaintiff*). Intentional torts include assault, battery, false imprisonment, intentional infliction of emotional distress, invasion of privacy, fraud, defamation of character (which includes libel, which is written defamation of character, and slander, which is nonwritten defamation of character), malicious prosecution, abuse of process, trespass to land, conversion, and trespass to chattels.

In the context of Alzheimer's disease, two intentional torts have great significance: *assault* and *battery*.

ASSAULT

Under the common law, *assault* is an intentional and voluntary act that causes the reasonable apprehension of an immediate harmful or offensive contact, coupled with the ability to carry it out. Assault need not involve actual contact between the person and the plaintiff. All it requires is the intention of the person to inflict harm and the plaintiff's resulting apprehension of harm.

For example, if Ricky races her car toward Gulrez, causing him to fear that she would knock him down, yet she brakes two inches from Gulrez, leaving him trembling but very much alive and unharmed, she would most likely have committed the tort of assault. If, however, Ricky is an Alzheimer's patient who is unaware of what she is doing, the intent element is lacking, and if Gulrez sues to recover damages for assault, he would most likely lose.

In summary, then, assault is committed:

- When a person makes a harmful threat or offer of contact
- In a situation that creates fear
- Where the person could carry out the act if he or she is not prevented from so doing

Assault does not always lead to liability on the part of the alleged perpetrator. Indeed, assault can be justified in situations of self-defense or defense of a third party where the act was reasonable. It can also be justified in the context of a sport, like football or boxing, where consent is implicit.

BATTERY

Battery is the tort of intentionally and volitionally bringing about a harmful or offensive contact with a person or to something closely associated with a person such as someone's hat, walking stick, or pocketbook. Whether the contact is offensive is judged by the reasonable person standard—that is, looking at the incident objectively, as a reasonable person would see it—would it be offensive? For example, an elderly man who is pushed and shoved a little by fellow passengers on a rush-hour subway heading from Manhattan to Brooklyn would not prevail if he brought a battery action against them because a reasonable person expects to be pushed and shoved a little on the rush-hour subway in any city.

The contact is "harmful" if it results in any physical damage to the body. The contact need not necessarily be between the person and the plaintiff; rather, the person may bring about contact with something else. Hence, if Ricky in our previous discussion of assault intentionally runs over Gulrez's foot with her car, she has committed battery although she never personally touched Gulrez.

As stated previously, to commit battery, a person does not necessarily have to come into direct contact with the other person. In fact, battery need not require person-to-person contact. Any volitional movement, such as throwing an object toward another, can constitute battery. Touching an object "intimately connected" to a person can also be battery. For example, if Melissa, a very disagreeable elderly woman, takes her walking stick and strikes the two back legs of the chair on which Michael is sitting, causing the chair to collapse and Michael to fall, Melissa has committed battery although she never used any part of her body to commit the act and neither she nor her walking stick ever came into contact with Michael.

Finally, it is also battery if you intended to harm one person and in the process harm a different person. Hence, if Baden, an eccentric and elderly individual, swings at Amelia with his walking stick as she passes him on the sidewalk, intending to hit her, but misses her completely and instead hits her companion, Amoy, Baden is still liable for battery.

There are two defenses to a claim of battery: *necessity* and *consent*. Necessity is a valid defense when an emergency exists and the situation can be alleviated or eliminated only by unauthorized contact. For example, if Jackie—an elderly individual in Stage I Alzheimer's disease who has no living will, DNR, or medical power of attorney—is brought to the hospital unconscious and in need of life-saving surgery, the surgeon would not be committing battery if she performed the operation without Jackie's consent.

As to consent, people often expressly give or imply their consent to harmful contact. This is the case with certain sports. If, for example, an elderly person playing badminton at a retirement home is hit by another player's racquet and suffers a cut to the forehead, he cannot claim battery against the other elderly player who swung the racquet because the contact—though injury-causing—is permitted by the rules of the sport and by participating therein. Thus, the elderly player has expressly given or implied consent to the contact, as harmful as it may turn out to be.

UNINTENTIONAL TORTS

As the name suggests, a person does not necessarily have to intend to harm another person to commit an unintentional tort. In such cases, the mere failure to perform, or not perform, a certain act is sufficient. In the United States, unintentional torts come in two types: *negligence* and *strict liability.*

NEGLIGENCE

Negligence claims are the most common tort claims in the United States. Yet the modern law of negligence actually found its genesis in Scotland in the early twentieth century with the tale of a decomposed snail. In the 1932 case of *Donoghue v. Stevenson*, Mrs. Donoghue was enjoying a drink of ginger beer at a bar in Paisley, Scotland, when, after having consumed some of the liquid, she discovered that a decomposed snail was inside the opaque bottle. Mrs. Donoghue subsequently became ill; no one can tell whether this was from having consumed ginger beer contaminated with a decomposed snail or from the realization that she had consumed a decomposed snail. She sued the manufacturer of the ginger beer, Mr. Stevenson, for having caused her illness.

The case went to the British House of Lords. The members agreed that Mrs. Donoghue had a valid claim but could not agree on just why such a valid claim existed. It was left to Lord Atkin to devise the reason. He argued that the law should recognize the principle that we all owe a duty of reasonable care to our neighbors. He quoted the Bible in support of his argument, leaning particularly on the principle "thou shalt love thy neighbor." Using this principle, Lord Atkin created a new legal doctrine: We should not harm our neighbors. This doctrine forms the bedrock for modern negligence law.

There are four elements of negligence: (1) duty of care, (2) breach of the duty of care, (3) breach causing actual harm, and (4) breach as the proximate or not too remote cause of the harm. Let's examine each of them using hypothetical situations involving our world: the Alzheimer's patient and his or her family members and caregivers.

DUTY OF CARE

The first element that a person who has been harmed by another has to prove in a negligence lawsuit is that the person who allegedly caused the harm owed him or her a duty of reasonable care. Various circumstances can give rise to a person having a duty of care for someone else or even for multiple persons. In addition to the duty not to harm our neighbors, we owe a duty of care (1) when someone contractually assumes this duty of care for someone else, and (2) where the parties are related. The law imposes upon a spouse the duty to care for his or her spouse and upon parents a duty of care for their minor children.

These scenarios can arise in the context of Alzheimer's disease. In the contractual context, the caregiver is the one most likely with a duty to care for the patient. If, for example, New Horizons Assisted Living Facility enters into a contract to care for Marie, an elderly woman stricken with Alzheimer's, no one would deny that New Horizons has assumed a duty to care for her. Similarly, if Kelleb, an eighty-year-old Alzheimer's patient, is married to sixty-six-year-old Edith, the law holds that unless Kelleb named someone else to care for him (through a durable power of attorney or medical power of attorney), then Edith has a duty to care for him.

As for the general duty of care we owe each other, Lindsay,

Kelleb's neighbor and the owner of a ferocious pit bull, may not allow Rover to attack and injure Kelleb. Similarly, Kelleb has a duty to not drive his car into Lindsay's wall or throw his baseball through the front window of her house. As we shall see later in this chapter, Kelleb's Alzheimer's disease does not allow him to escape liability.

BREACH OF THE DUTY OF CARE

Once we have established that the defendant owed the plaintiff a duty of care, we must determine whether the defendant breached that duty. While *breach* may sound like a "fancy" legal word, all it means is that a person did not live up to his or her responsibility to provide reasonable care for another person. For example, if, after having contracted to care for Marie, New Horizons Assisted Living Facility continually allows her to wander the streets of Chicago at night, Marie's relatives may well claim that New Horizons has breached its duty of care. Likewise, if Edith becomes addicted to watching television and cannot be drawn away from the television set to attend to Kelleb's needs, Kelleb's children from his first marriage may well claim that Edith breached her duty of care.

Under the general responsibility established in *Donoghue*, we could find three different sets of breaches:

1. The Alzheimer's patient could be in breach. If Kelleb, knowing he is an early Stage I Alzheimer's patient who should not be driving, takes the keys to his car and drives across Lindsay's front lawn and slams into the wall of her house, he might have breached his duty of care to Lindsay.

2. The neighbor could be in breach. For example, suppose Lindsay knows that Kelleb is stricken with Alzheimer's and cannot walk quickly, and that Rover, if allowed to roam loose, will bite every human being in sight. Yet she allows Rover to run loose in Kelleb's backyard. If Rover bites Kelleb, no one would deny that Lindsay is in breach of her duty to care.

3. If the Alzheimer's patient injures or harms someone, his or her caregiver could be in breach of the duty of care. Imagine that Edith knows that Kelleb has developed Alzheimer's disease and should not be driving, yet she makes no effort to take the car keys from him or prevent him from driving. One day, Kelleb takes the keys and drives to the mall, where he slams into the glass windows at Sears. Sears may well claim that not only Kelleb but also Edith has breached the duty of reasonable care.

BREACH CAUSING HARM IN FACT

Proving that a person had a duty of care toward another and that he or she breached that duty does not necessarily entitle the claimant to damages. Rather, the claimant needs to show that the breach caused him or her some type of harm. Hence, Marie (or her family filing suit on her behalf) would have to demonstrate to the court that she endured some form of injury during her nocturnal wanderings before she may succeed in a claim against New Horizons Assisted Living Facility.

BREACH AS A PROXIMATE CAUSE OF THE HARM

The next step is for the plaintiff to prove that the breach of the duty of reasonable care caused the harm from which the person suffered. Marie would have to prove, for example, that if it were not for New Horizons' breach in allowing her to roam the streets of Chicago, she would not have been hit by a car and left half-dead on Garfield Boulevard. This "not too remote" element of the negligence claim leads to the question: Was it foreseeable that the breach of someone's duty of care would have caused the harm that was indeed caused?

What if Kelleb, who should not be driving, takes the keys to Edith's car from the board on the kitchen wall where the family has always kept the keys to their cars? Edith has no idea that Kelleb has taken the keys. Kelleb drives to the ExxonMobil service station, where he proceeds to pump some gasoline into the car's tank. For some reason unknown to anyone (maybe not even to Kelleb himself), he allows about a gallon of gas to spill on the ground. Kelleb uses a credit card to pay at the pump and then gets into the car and returns home. Five minutes later, Max pulls into the service station to buy gas. Seeing the "No Smoking" sign on the columns, he drops the cigarette he was smoking on what he believes to be the safest place: the ground. Alas, the gas that Kelleb spilled has settled into a pothole and formed a puddle there. As fate would have it, Max's cigarette falls into the puddle. A fire erupts, severely burning Max and two other service station patrons. Who—if anyone—is liable for the accident? In other words, whose negligent act caused the accident?

We have a number of candidates. First, there is Kelleb. After all, he was the one who spilled the gas. Moreover, he knows or should know that he has Alzheimer's disease and therefore should not be driving or pumping his own gas at service stations.

Next, we have Edith. She is Kelleb's wife and is well aware that her husband has Alzheimer's disease. While she did not know that Kelleb had taken the keys to the car, she should not have left them where Kelleb (or anyone else, for that matter) would have such easy access to them.

Next, there is Max. Is he a moron? Doesn't he know that nobody smokes at a gas station? To make matters worse, he simply dropped the cigarette on the ground! Couldn't he have looked first? After all, being at a service station, wouldn't it be reasonable for him to assume the possibility that someone spilled gas on the ground?

What about the owner of the service station? Didn't he or she see the pothole? If the pothole was big enough so that the gas spilling into it formed a puddle that caused all these injuries, it must have been a rather large or deep pothole. In that case, shouldn't the service station owner have assumed that this could have happened and thus taken precautionary steps by filling the pothole?

While these questions are all good ones, liability may fall only upon the shoulders of the person or persons whose actions were the proximate cause of the fire.

STRICT LIABILITY

People bring legal actions for strict liability torts when the harm they have suffered results from injuries caused by inherently dangerous activities (activities that are so dangerous that a court will hold the person liable even if he or she had not been negligent).

LEGAL LIABILITY OF DEFENDANTS WITH ALZHEIMER'S

Of the situations discussed thus far, only negligence holds significance for the Alzheimer's patient. Since an Alzheimer's patient would most likely not have the requisite mental capacity to possess the intent to commit a tort, such a patient may not be found liable for an intentional tort. The same is true for strict liability torts. Negligence, however, presents fertile ground for holding patients liable for torts they commit against their caregivers (both formal and informal) and third parties (as in car accidents caused by Alzheimer's patients).

Because Alzheimer's disease affects the patient's cognitive functions, much of the existing jurisprudence on their tort liability is built on insanity defense models. Under the common law, the general rule holds mentally disabled or incapacitated persons liable for their torts. This means that they are held to the same objective standards as those who have no mental disability. Thus, in cases where a mentally disabled person commits a tort, the court will hold him or her liable to the injured party regardless of any mental deficiency.

EXCEPTION: WHEN INSTITUTIONALIZED PEOPLE INJURE THEIR CAREGIVERS

Many jurisdictions have carved out an exception to this rule based on the nature of the care relationship between institutionalized patients and their caregivers. The exception holds that Alzheimer's patients in nursing homes or convalescent centers owe no duty to their caregivers for injuries sustained by these caregivers while caring for these patients. (Other jurisdictions have adopted a narrower version of the exception, declining to impose liability upon institutionalized individuals with mental disabilities for injuries they inflict on their caregivers *if* these individuals do not have the capacity to control or appreciate their conduct.)

The reason for this exception lies in public policy justifications and the nature of the relationship between caregivers and their institutionalized patients. Some courts have held that the public policy reasons for holding mentally disabled persons liable for their torts are not applicable to institutionalized individuals and that it would be a grave injustice to hold institutionalized persons liable in these cases. Regarding the relationship between the institutionalized patient and his or her caregiver, some courts have held that because a caregiver in an institutionalized setting is not a member of the public, he or she is able to foresee harm from Alzheimer's patients who are usually combative by the time they are institutionalized. One court went further and gave the following reasons for excusing the torts committed by Alzheimer's patients against their caregivers:

- A caregiver is not an innocent party on whom it would be unfair to place the burden of expecting the type of harm encountered.
- The inducement of family members to prevent the harm rendered is immaterial because by placing the patient in an institution, they have fulfilled their responsibility as best they can.
- It is unlikely that a person with Alzheimer's disease has or would feign the disease to escape liability.
- A person diagnosed with Alzheimer's disease who is institutionalized for the disease alleviates the administrative difficulties of determining mental disability.

- Holding an Alzheimer's patient responsible for his or her torts would place "too great a burden on him because of his disorientation and potential for violence [which] is the very reason he was institutionalized and needed the aid of employed caretakers."[1]

Thus, although the traditional common law rule provides no excuse for mentally disabled persons who injure others, the courts view institutionalized patients differently and are therefore more willing to excuse such conduct. However, even in excusing this conduct, the courts consider each patient's medical and behavioral history and the training received by the nursing home employee involved. That way, the courts can determine whether the employee was sufficiently aware of the hazard involved in caring for the patient who committed the injury.

In summary, then, although mental disability is not typically an excuse for negligence torts committed by individuals against their caregivers or third parties, if the patient is institutionalized, the courts will not impose liability on that person. But do any circumstances exist whereby a noninstitutionalized Alzheimer's patient may have his or her conduct involving torts excused by the courts?

EXCEPTION: SUDDEN INCAPACITATION

At least one jurisdiction—North Carolina—has carved out another exception to the general rule. This time, it exempts patients who are not in nursing homes or convalescent centers. In the case of *Word v. Jones*, an Alzheimer's patient was driving a car that was involved in an accident. The person driving the other car sued the patient, alleging that it was negligence on the patient's part to be driving the car. The patient pled the affirmative defense (that is, an excuse or justification) of sudden incapacitation, a defense that, under North Carolina law, requires the following elements:

- The defendant was stricken by a sudden incapacitation.
- This incapacitation was unforeseeable.
- The defendant was unable to control the vehicle as a result of the incapacitation.
- The sudden incapacitation was the cause of the accident.

In this case, at trial, the defendant's medical experts testified that the mental condition causing the incapacitation was (1) an Alzheimer's disease sensory overload, (2) a transient ischemic attack, or (3) a heart arrhythmia. After the other driver lost and appealed to the North Carolina Supreme Court, the court upheld the trial court's decision, explaining that the medical conditions presented to the trial court by the Alzheimer's patient's medical experts went directly to the elements of sudden incapacitation. Thus, at least in North Carolina, if the presence of Alzheimer's disease causes a sudden, unforeseen incapacitation such as sensory overload regardless of ultimate unconsciousness, an Alzheimer's patient causing a car accident has an established affirmative defense to a tort action brought against him or her upon the ground of negligence.

Several other jurisdictions have rules similar to North Carolina's rule concerning sudden incapacitation, although no other courts have specifically ruled on the matter with reference to Alzheimer's patients. However, one California court has refused to extend the rule barring a negligence claim against a person suddenly stricken by a physical illness to one who suffers a sudden mental illness. According to this court, then, for the Alzheimer's patient, the key to determining whether sudden incapacitation is a viable defense to a negligence suit is whether the court sees the disease as a physical or a mental illness.

It is clear that the unique nature of Alzheimer's disease has led to varying results in cases involving direct liability of Alzheimer's patients for their negligent acts. In general, though, when Alzheimer's patients are the defendants, most jurisdictions have relaxed the common law rule of not excusing such conduct of mentally disabled individuals.

LIABILITY OF OTHERS FOR INJURIES COMMITTED BY AN ALZHEIMER'S PATIENT

Unlike suits brought directly against Alzheimer's patients, negligence suits brought against their caregivers enjoy a fair measure of success. Generally, a caregiver has a duty to protect others from harm inflicted by the patient if the caregiver:

- Has prior knowledge of the patient's potential to cause harm.
- Undertakes measures to prevent the patient from causing harm and such measures fail.
- A third party is injured.

One California court has amended this rule somewhat, holding that the caregiver's duty arises only under certain circumstances. According to the court, a jury could find on certain facts that the caregiver acted reasonably despite the failure of the preventive measures he or she instituted.

THE CAREGIVER'S DUTY OF CARE

The above rules most often come into focus when an Alzheimer's patient causes an accident while driving a car. Instead of filing suit against the patient, the injured party may sue the patient's caregiver under a tort called *negligent entrustment*, in this case entrusting an Alzheimer's patient with a motor vehicle. Liability for negligent entrustment is predicated on the:

- Mental incapacity of the person entrusted with the vehicle or other instrument
- Caregiver's knowledge of the person's condition
- Fact that the instrument involved was dangerous and created an appreciable risk of harm
- Causation

If Dominique, knowing that his mother, Marina, suffers from Alzheimer's disease, allows her to drive the family car, whereupon she drives the car to the mall and strikes and injures Edward, a shopper, Edward would most likely be successful in a negligent entrustment suit brought against Dominique even if Dominique had taken measures to ensure that his mother did not find the keys to the family car. In California, however, Dominique's liability would depend upon the reasonableness of the measures he took to prevent his mother from ever driving the family car.

A 1985 Florida case (*Garrison Retirement Home Corp.* v. *Hancock*) illustrates the issues involved in such a circumstance. In that case, a resident of a retirement home had repeatedly attempted to drive his car. Concerned about the resident's potential use of the car, the home administrator made inquiries to various authorities as to the legal measures the home could take to prevent the retiree from using his car. The authorities informed the administrator that the retirement home had no authority to take the man's car away. In response, staff members began immobilizing the car so that the resident would not be able to drive it. Despite these efforts, the resident was always able to return the car to operational condition. On one occasion, the resident accidentally drove the car into someone who was visiting the retirement home. The individual sued the retirement home, claiming that the home owed a duty to individuals injured by residents in similar circumstances.

Concluding that the retirement home did in fact owe a duty to the injured person, the appellate court first acknowledged the general rule that no one owes a duty to anyone else to control the conduct of a third party. The court then recognized that exceptions exist and that, once the retirement home became aware that the resident was likely to cause bodily harm to a third person, it had a duty to exercise reasonable care to control the resident's conduct and activities. Although the court distinguished the duty of a retirement home from that of a hospital for the mentally ill, it specifically noted the home's attempts to disengage the car prior to the accident, which, it concluded, demonstrated the retirement home's ability to control the resident's activities.

The court also looked to the theory of premises liability and held that because the injured individual was an invitee on the premises, the home had a duty to warn the visitor of the resident's potentially dangerous conduct. The court then remanded the case to the trial court for a determination of whether the home's breach of its duty to the visitor was the proximate cause of his injuries, and whether the visitor was himself contributorily negligent.

Other jurisdictions have begun to recognize the duty established in the Florida case, although none have had the opportunity to decide whether to apply it to Alzheimer's patients. This is important for caregivers of Alzheimer's patients. In jurisdictions that adopt the Florida rule, courts will rule that caregivers of Alzheimer's patients have a duty to use reasonable care to control the activities of patients under their care, and the caregivers will be held liable for injuries caused by these patients if they breach this duty.

CONTROL OF PREMISES

As noted earlier, the Florida court based its decision partly on the theory of premises liability. Indeed, even where no special relationship like caregiver-patient exists to give rise to the duty to control, a court may still find liability where a defendant exercises control of the premises on which another party harms someone. The law in some jurisdictions (like Connecticut and Rhode Island) also holds that owners of property have a duty to control the dangerous conditions on their property caused by the presence of dangerous adults who may be there. Even then, however, a court would have to decide whether the owner of the premises could have foreseen that the adult would have acted as he or she did, based either on previous dangerous acts committed by the person or the person's violent history.

As applied to Alzheimer's patients, their caregivers or family members could be held liable for injuries arising from a patient's use of a car if the car is located on premises controlled by the family member or caregiver and such family member or caregiver was knowledgeable about the nature and effects of Alzheimer's disease. In jurisdictions that have followed Connecticut and Rhode Island, therefore, caregivers and family members should be wary about allowing their Alzheimer's-stricken relatives to drive.

Although it is difficult to convince an Alzheimer's patient to stop driving, if necessary, the caregiver should take the patient's keys away. Typically, patients complain incessantly and go so far as to accuse their caregivers of attempting to take away their independence or of treating them like children. Yet if only to avoid liability, the time comes when the caregiver has to be firm and take away the patient's driving privileges. (More on this issue is found in Chapter 10.)

PROTECT THE PATIENT, PROTECT THE CAREGIVER

While it is difficult—maybe improbable—for a court to hold Alzheimer's patients liable for intentional torts like assault and battery, in some circumstances, courts may hold them liable for unintentional torts, like negligence, that they commit. Moreover, the injury resulting to third parties may leave caregivers of Alzheimer's patients liable. This liability arises based on:

- The family member or caregiver's ability to control the premises where either the patient committed the act or where the instrument (such as a car) was located prior to the patient using it to commit the injury to the plaintiff
- The presence of a special relationship, such as caregiver-patient, between the caregiver and the Alzheimer's patient

In essence, where direct liability against the patient is unlikely to succeed, most courts will fill the void by holding the patient's caregiver responsible. Even when an Alzheimer's patient unsuccessfully invokes the sudden incapacitation defense for driving, the court may hold the caregiver liable for allowing the patient access to the car.

Because Alzheimer's patients eventually need the services and assistance of informal caregivers, and because public policy shies away from always holding these patients directly liable for the harm they inflict on others, caregivers are likely to bear the brunt of liability for not controlling the patient. Indeed, the key for caregivers is to control their patients' activities. That way, both they and the patients will eliminate the problem before it occurs.

NOTE

1. *Creasy v. Rusk*, 730 N.E.2d.

CHAPTER 8

WHEN AN ALZHEIMER'S PATIENT MOVES: LEGAL ISSUES

UNCLE'S COMING TO AMERICA!

*S*ince I was writing a book about the legal aspects of Alzheimer's disease, I was now "the expert" in the eyes of my family. I was not surprised, therefore, when I received a call from Francis, my eldest brother. "Vaughn," he said, "It's time we met as a family to discuss what to do about our aging family members and their medical conditions. I am calling a meeting of all "The Grandchildren" living in the United States. Do you think you can make it?" ("The Grandchildren" was a term we used to describe all of our grandparents' children. I can't remember who gave us this title or why.) Not long after, Francis picked me up at New York's LaGuardia Airport and we headed for Poughkeepsie. Two days later, the U.S. contingent of The Grandchildren gathered for our meeting. We were an impressive bunch: three professional caregivers, three accountants, one *pilot, one social worker, one medical technologist, and one law-yer/law professor.*

The problem we faced was twofold. First, Uncle Andy and Aunty June, both U.S. citizens who were currently living in Dominica, had decided to return to the United States, at least temporarily. We all knew that Uncle Andy was exhibiting symptoms of Alzheimer's disease. We also knew that, upon my advice, he had retained an attorney in Dominica to help him prepare various estate planning documents. What we did not know was whether these documents would be valid in the United States.

Second, Vilna—who couldn't come to the meeting because she couldn't leave Aunty Arlette—was having a difficult time caring for her mother. We were all sympathetic. Everyone had heard about Aunty Arlette's driving Vilna's car into the column at Walgreen's. Fortunately, the insurance company had covered most of the cost of the repairs to the column and the car, and we had pooled our resources to help Vilna cover the rest. Under-standably, Vilna needed a break. She had asked us to consider moving Aunty Arlette, even for just a year, to New York where other family members could help care for her. We readily agreed to move Aunty Arlette to New York and asked ourselves the same questions we asked about Uncle Andy's case: What about her estate planning documents? Would they be valid in New York? Would her advance directives—assuming she had any—be recognized in New York?

Americans typically change their place of residence every five years. It is inevitable, therefore, that some Alzheimer's patients will move during the course of their illness. They may move to the United States from other countries, or they may move from the United States to another country. More likely, they will move from town to town or from state to state.

What happens to these mobile patients if they:

- Prepared advance directives in anticipation of developing a disease like Alzheimer's, moved prior to the onset of the disease, and then developed the disease in their new place of residence.

- Prepared advance directives after they began to exhibit symptoms of Alzheimer's disease, and then moved to find better healthcare or to be with family.

Will the state where the patient is now domiciled recognize the advance directives? Will a foreign country recognize an advance directive executed in the United States? Will the United States recognize an advance directive executed in a foreign country?

VALIDITY OF OUT-OF-STATE ADVANCE DIRECTIVES IN THE UNITED STATES

Most Americans who change their places of residence move, not from the United States to some foreign country, but from one state to another. When an individual with an advance directive relocates, will the new state of domicile recognize the validity of that advance directive?

No uniform national law exists that governs advance directives. In fact, the states vary widely on how these directives are created, the requirements for their execution, and how they must be applied. Accordingly, an advance directive may be prepared and executed in one way in New York, but the preparation and execution requirements in Florida may be quite different.

Notwithstanding these varied requirements, several states have enacted statutes instructing medical practitioners and providers to accept out-of-state advance directives where they were validly executed in another state. Accordingly, the directive need not meet all the requirements for validity in the new state of domicile. Rather, all that is required is that at the time of execution, the directive met the requirements for validity in the state of execution.

There is an exception. Generally, an out-of-state advance directive given effect in another state is henceforth governed by the laws of that new state. Texas law provides an example of how and why this is important. Texas law prohibits an agent under a medical power of attorney from consenting to voluntary inpatient mental health services on the patient's behalf. Therefore, if an individual arrives in Texas with a medical power of attorney that allows the agent to consent to voluntary inpatient mental health services on the individual's behalf, Texas law would override the agent's authority to make such a decision. The out-of-state medical power of attorney would remain valid, but its scope and operation would be limited to conform to Texas law.

For advance directives naming surrogate decision makers such as the medical power of attorney, once the directive is given effect, the medical provider should attempt to locate the agent or agents and alternate agent or agents named in it. That should not be difficult because the names and addresses (and sometimes telephone numbers) of all agents and alternate agents are typically listed on the medical power of attorney. After contacting the agent or agents, the medical provider should inform the agent(s) that the power is now effective. The agent(s) would then be able to either commence or continue making necessary decisions.

This, however, may pose a problem when someone moves across the country. It would be difficult, for example, for an agent residing in California to effectively make medical decisions for the now mentally incapacitated individual who has moved to Maine. This is just one of the reasons, notwithstanding the validity of out-of-state advance directives in a new state of residence, why people should seriously consider executing new directives when they relocate.

The same advice applies to individuals who frequently move between locations, such as a person with a summer home in Big Rapids, Michigan; a fall home in Cape May, New Jersey; and a winter home in St. John, Virgin Islands. It would be wise for such a person to execute advance directives in each of these jurisdictions so that regardless of where he or she may be if mental incapacity strikes, an advance directive valid in that location is readily available.

THE IMPACT OF RELOCATION ON THE ALZHEIMER'S PATIENT AND GUARDIAN

It is sometimes necessary to appoint a guardian for a person with Alzheimer's disease. If the patient subsequently moves to another state, would the guardian—who still lives in the state where the guardianship petition was granted—still be able to transact the ward's business, and if both the ward and the guardian move, what court would then oversee the guardianship? In the event guardianship proceedings began in one state and the proposed ward moved to another state before the matter was concluded, what court has jurisdiction over the guardianship proceeding? Assuming the court grants the guardianship petition, may the guardian place the ward in a nursing home or other facility in another state?

FILING THE GUARDIANSHIP PETITION

Consider this scenario:

Annie, who lives in New Jersey, has developed Alzheimer's disease. Annie owns real property in New Jersey. Her son, Geoma, a resident of New Jersey, files a petition in the appropriate New Jersey court to have the court appoint him as his mother's plenary guardian. One month later–and before the court has even heard the matter–Annie moves to Buffalo, New York, to be with her other son, Swales, so that she may receive medical treatment at a Buffalo facility. While Annie is in Buffalo, Swales files a petition with the appropriate court to have the court name him her plenary guardian.

In this case, both the New Jersey and the New York courts have the authority to act on the respective guardianship petitions. Since Annie has real property in New Jersey and the basic rule of law is that state courts have jurisdiction over real property within the state's borders, the appropriate New Jersey court would have jurisdiction over Annie's real estate. However, at the time Swales filed the guardianship petition, Annie was living or present in New York. The basic rule of law is that a state court has jurisdiction over the person of anyone present in that state. Hence, the appropriate New York court would have jurisdiction over Annie's person, a subject of the guardianship petition.

Should both courts proceed, the result would be years of litigation while Annie languishes in the dark world of Alzheimer's disease. To avoid this, the Uniform Probate Code, the Uniform Guardianship and Protective Proceedings Act (UGPPA), and some state statutes provide that the court where the guardianship proceeding was first filed would determine the jurisdictional issues.

Five states—Arizona, Indiana, Kansas, North Dakota, and Oregon—have enacted statutes addressing the matter. Among these jurisdictions, Kansas states that if the mentally incapacitated person is not a resident of the state, the court has the option to dismiss the petition or postpone the matter for sixty days to allow for a petition to be filed in the person's home state. In Indiana, the court may transfer the guardianship proceeding to an out-of-state court, but only if the other state has assumed jurisdiction.

In an effort to provide a uniform treatment of these issues throughout the nation, the UGPPA provides that if a proceeding is pending in another state when a petition is filed in the local court, the second-in-time court must consult with the original court where the guardianship proceeding is pending before it assumes or declines jurisdiction, whichever is in the best interest of the ward.

The determination of what is in the ward's best interest is left to the presiding judge. Some judges do make a conscientious effort to determine the answer to this issue and make their decisions based on their analysis—and their analysis only. For example, in explaining the reasoning for its decision, one Massachusetts court stated that it was not obligated to give full faith and credit to a foreign guardianship if the best interests of the ward indicated otherwise.

PLACING THE WARD IN A FACILITY ACROSS STATE LINES

Consider this case:

Wayne, a resident of Arkansas, has developed Alzheimer's disease. His daughter, Dournalyne, has successfully petitioned the court to be his guardian. Dournalyne (who also lives in Arkansas) has determined that her father would be better served if she moved him to a rehabilitative center located in neighboring Tennessee in order to receive therapy. Following several months of therapy, Wayne will return to Arkansas. Can Dournalyne continue to serve as her father's guardian after he arrives at the Tennessee facility?

Whether Dournalyne can continue in her role as guardian after she transfers her father to the Tennessee facility depends on the law of Arkansas, where she and her father reside, and that of Tennessee, to which she is moving her father.

Only twelve states—California, Colorado, Delaware, Florida,

Kentucky, New Hampshire, New Mexico, Ohio, South Dakota, Vermont, West Virginia, and Wyoming—extend some recognition to guardians from another state to make personal care decisions for a ward located within their borders. The Delaware statute on the matter is illustrative of what pertains among these twelve states. According to that statute: If no guardianship proceeding for a person is pending before a Delaware court, and that person is brought to Delaware either for medical treatment or to take up residence, and the person already has a guardian appointed by an out-of-state court, then that guardian may continue to have all the powers granted him or her by the out-of-state court and could conduct the guardianship pursuant to those powers.

The other thirty-eight states fall into two groups: those that have adopted the UGPPA and those that have not. In states that have adopted the UGPPA, the guardian could make personal decisions for a ward receiving care at an out-of-state facility. However, the guardian has to petition the appropriate court in the new state for appointment as a local guardian. The guardian has to furnish to the new court proof of appointment and a certified copy of the appointing court's record and has to provide notice of the petition to the ward and other persons entitled to such notice. No hearing is necessary. The court must make the appointment unless doing so would be adverse to the best interest of the ward.

In states that have not adopted the UGPPA, the law is unclear. These states have not yet addressed the issue of whether or how to recognize an out-of-state guardian's authority to make personal care decisions when a ward temporarily relocates to the state. With such uncertainty, it would be wise for someone who is planning such a move to consult an elder law attorney in either of the states involved before making the move.

MOBILE GUARDIAN AND MOBILE WARD

Sometimes it is necessary for a guardian to move out of the state where the ward is domiciled. At other times, both the guardian and the ward relocate to another state. In either instance, two questions arise: (1) Can the guardian, who now lives in a different state, make decisions concerning the ward's property located in the original state? (2) When both the guardian and the ward move to a different state and the ward still owns property in the original state, which jurisdiction has authority over the guardianship?

THE OUT-OF-STATE GUARDIAN

Consider the following case:

Ignatius lives in Montana. A court in Montana appoints him guardian of the property of his mentally incapacitated father, Ian, who also lives in Montana. Ignatius is offered a job in Nebraska and relocates to that state. Can he continue to serve as guardian of Ian's property, making business decisions and transactions on his behalf?

Ignatius will most likely be able to continue as guardian of Ian's property until such time that a court in Montana appoints a new guardian resident in that state. Montana is one of thirty-nine states that have some process allowing an out-of-state guardian of the property to act when the ward does not have a local person available to fulfill that role.

Even among those states, however, the process varies for recognizing an individual—resident or nonresident—as guardian of another's property. Most states require that the guardian file copies of the guardianship order and bond. Eleven states— Florida, Michigan, Montana, Nebraska, Nevada, New Jersey, North Dakota, Oregon, South Carolina, South Dakota, and Utah—allow the guardian to collect debts and receive money or property on the ward's behalf only after the guardian (or someone acting on his or her behalf) demonstrates proof of the appointment and files an affidavit attesting to the appointment. Eight states—Colorado, Connecticut, Iowa, Mississippi, New York, Texas, West Virginia, and Wyoming—require an out-of-state guardian of the property to petition to be appointed as a local guardian. This requires the formalities of notice and a hearing and may be unduly cumbersome, particularly if the guardian needs to conduct only a single transaction in the state.

Ohio, Arkansas, and New Hampshire take different approaches. Ohio prefers a resident guardian of the property. Hence, even if the ward already has an out-of-state guardian, an Ohio court could well appoint a resident guardian to have authority over any property the ward may have in that state. In Arkansas, meanwhile, if the ward has both a local guardian and an out-of-state guardian, the court may terminate the local guardianship and order payment, transfer, or delivery of the ward's property to the out-of-state guardian. Alternatively, the court could order the local guardian to take the action the out-of-state guardian was seeking or deny the out-of-state guardian's petition. New Hampshire is not any friendlier to out-of-state guardians of the property. An out-of-state guardian of the property must petition an appropriate court to be appointed as a New Hampshire guardian, post bond, and account to the New Hampshire court.

The states are also not uniform in the authority they grant guardians of the property. Some states limit the authority of the guardian to remove the ward's personal property, sell real property, or maintain pending legal actions. Taking a different approach, California grants the out-of-state guardian all the powers that would be given to a local guardian. In some cases, this authority may well exceed that given to the guardian in the original state.

These varied rules make one thing clear: When the ward resides in one state and has property there but the guardian of the property resides in a different state, the guardian should either learn the rules as they pertain to the state where the property is located or retain a competent attorney in that state to represent him or her. Of course, if the guardian—like Ignatius in our hypothetical case—had been serving as guardian in the state of the ward's residence before relocating to another state, he would most likely have some knowledge of the rules pertaining to out-of-state guardians of the property.

WHEN THE WARD RELOCATES

It may sometimes be necessary for the ward to move permanently from his or her original state of residence. This relocation raises a host of issues. Consider this:

Jorge, a resident of one state, has developed Alzheimer's disease. Both Jorge's physician and his plenary guardian, Esther, agree that Jorge would be better cared for if he relocated to a nursing home in a neighboring state. This would be a permanent move; Jorge will not return to his original state of residence. Esther has family and employment commitments in that state and cannot relocate to Jorge's new state of residence or anywhere else. Can Esther retain her position as Jorge's guardian?

Very few states would allow Esther to transfer the guardianship of Jorge. Only fourteen states—Alabama, Alaska, Arizona, Idaho, Indiana, Kansas, Missouri, New Hampshire, Oregon, South Carolina, South Dakota, Tennessee, Vermont, and West Virginia—have established procedures to transfer a guardianship to a new jurisdiction where the ward has relocated. Both the UGPPA and the National College of Probate Judges (NCPJ) model law offer similar recommendations for transfer procedures.

These statutes and guidelines all try to smooth the transfer of the guardianship to another state, eliminate unnecessary litigation costs, and ensure that an appropriate court in the new state takes over monitoring responsibilities. The UGPPA allows the original court to transfer the guardianship to an out-of-state court if it is in the best interest of the ward to do so; however, it sets forth no specific procedural steps to accomplish this transfer. The NCPJ model law sets out a more elaborate process that requires that the "transferring court" and the "accepting court" take specific steps to make the transfer. Under this model, the guardian must file a notice of transfer and a final report with the transferring court and notify the ward and interested parties of the intent to transfer the guardianship, their right to object, and their right to request a hearing. The receiving court must then notify the transferring court that it accepts the transfer and has imposed a new bond. Although the ward's mental capacity and the extent of the guardian's powers do not need to be re-litigated as part of the transfer proceedings, the ward can request such a hearing and the accepting court must hold a review hearing shortly after acceptance.

Other states have taken various approaches to the transfer or nontransfer of cases out of the state. Missouri specifies that even if the ward or guardian moves out of state, the guardianship is not terminated. Tennessee's transfer section applies if both the ward and the guardian relocate out of the state or if the ward moves and a new guardian is appointed in the new state of domicile. Kansas has a highly detailed process to petition the court to give full faith and credit to the prior adjudication, appoint a guardian, and terminate the other state's proceeding. Indiana specifically gives an Indiana guardian the authority to place the ward in another state, with court approval.

Considering the varied rules governing this matter, Esther in our hypothetical case may be lucky and not have to re-litigate the entire guardianship case if she is moving Jorge to one of the states that has transfer provisions. If Jorge is moved to a state that does not have transfer provisions, she may have to initiate the proceeding as an original guardianship petition in the new state.

THE VALIDITY OF FOREIGN ADVANCE DIRECTIVES IN THE UNITED STATES

When someone executes an advance directive in a foreign country and then moves to the United States and becomes mentally incapacitated, the question arises: Will the U.S. jurisdiction in which the person now resides recognize the foreign advance directive?

At first glance, you might be tempted to say "no." After all, the now mentally incapacitated person executed the advance directive in a foreign country, under a foreign set of laws, and the United States should not be expected to recognize such an instrument. However, a 2007 letter of advice issued by the Maryland Attorney General suggests otherwise. Answering a query seeking clarification of the validity in Maryland of a durable power of attorney for healthcare, a living will, or a similar advance directive executed in a foreign country, the Office of the Attorney General stated:

> . . . if such an advance directive satisfies Maryland's procedural requirements–that is, it is signed and dated by the individual and two witnesses–it is legally valid in Maryland and should be honored by Maryland health care facilities. . . . I advise that a foreign advance directive is valid. Maryland health care providers who rely in good faith on a foreign advance directive enjoy the immunity afforded under [Maryland law].[1]

The letter also indicates that Maryland would give full force and effect only to those advance directives or parts thereof that agree with Maryland law. Hence, if an advance directive executed in the Netherlands (where euthanasia is legal) provides for euthanasia, this portion of the directive would not be valid in Maryland (where euthanasia is not legal).

As this book went to press, no other state had issued a statement or letter of advice similar to Maryland's; no state or federal court has spoken on the matter. However, the Maryland approach appears reasonable and wise and could easily be adopted by the other states.

Until other states speak on this issue, an immigrant or long-term resident with an advance directive from a foreign country should execute a new directive in the state where he or she is now domiciled.

THE VALIDITY OF U.S. ADVANCE DIRECTIVES IN FOREIGN COUNTRIES

No clear rule exists as to the validity of U.S. advance directives in foreign jurisdictions. Two significant reasons exist for this. First, while end-of-life care in the United States focuses primarily on patient autonomy and the doctrine of informed consent (discussed in Chapter 5), in most foreign countries, the focus is on providing adequate services to as many people as possible. Hence, unlike their foreign counterparts, medical practitioners in the United States look to the patients' (or their surrogates') wishes in determining the level of care and life-saving or life-prolonging technologies to employ. Second, in many foreign countries, individuals are not hospitalized or placed in hospices at the end of their lives. Rather, they remain at home where practitioner-nurse teams care for them. In this setting, these patients get to know and trust their healthcare providers. It is easy, then, for the medical practitioners and the patient's family members to agree on what is best for the patient. Advance directives become moot, regardless of where they are prepared.

Thus, if an individual prepares an advance directive in the United States and then moves to a foreign country, the issue of whether that country will give credence to the provisions of the directive usually is a nonissue—at least when the individual possesses mental capacity on arrival in the foreign country. No case law or statute exists to provide guidance on the matter.

In light of this, a person residing in the United States who executes an advance directive while in the United States and then moves to a foreign country should execute a new directive shortly after arriving in the foreign country, if he or she has strong feelings about physicians following the provisions of the directive exactly. Even then, because medical practitioners in many foreign countries do not honor advance directives, the person could not be certain that his or her wishes for end-of-life care would be followed.

BEFORE ANYONE MOVES, PREPARE

Many issues arise when Alzheimer's patients or their guardians relocate to different states or countries. While some answers do exist to these issues and questions, none is simple and many are state- or country-specific. Although efforts are currently under way to resolve the differences in these laws and rules, many obstacles remain to the development of a uniform system. Meanwhile, the Alzheimer's patient (if able) and his or her family, friends, and other loved ones should recognize the many problems that may arise if the patient and/or the guardian relocates. They should also be prepared to seek the assistance of an attorney trained in these matters to unravel these rules and guide them in the process.

NOTE

1. Letter from the Office of the State of Maryland Attorney General to Sunil Bangali (July 18, 2007), available at www.oag.state.md.us/ Healthpol/Bangali.pdf (last visited November 22, 2007).

CHAPTER 9

THE COST OF CARE: WHERE IT GOES, WHERE IT COMES FROM

WOULD MY FAMILY HAVE TO FILE FOR BANKRUPTCY?

*A*fter Francis called the very successful meeting to discuss the issues involved in relocating Uncle Andy, Aunty June, and Aunty Arlette to New York, we decided to hold conference calls at least once a month to discuss family matters, particularly Grandpa, Uncle Andy, Aunty Arlette, and Aunty Dail, all of whom had Alzheimer's disease. One meeting early on concerned an extremely important question: How would we pay for the care of our loved ones?

Sure, we were not exactly "poor." We had worked hard over the years, saved some money, and invested some. We would never be included in the Forbes list of the country's wealthiest people, but we had enough to get by. At the same time, we all had families. Some of us had children attending college; others

179

had children entering the final stages of high school and preparing for college. As for me, my eldest son was attending a private college in Atlanta, Georgia; my four-year-old was attending church school in Lubbock, Texas; and my wife and I were expecting our third child, a girl. I, for one, did not have too much money to spare. I suspected my siblings and the rest of The Grandchildren were in a similar situation. The way I saw it, if we had to foot the bill for the care of our stricken relatives, sooner or later, we would have to seek bankruptcy protection.

Although Alzheimer's disease sometimes develops in people under the age of fifty, most Alzheimer's patients are elderly. Although the elderly represent less than one-fifth of the population of the United States, about one-third of all health services in the country are provided to them. In addition, an elderly person is twice as likely as his or her younger counterpart to enter a hospital, and once admitted, is likely to need care for a significantly longer period than a young person would.

The services provided the elderly come at a cost—a huge cost. When we consider that the United States spends more of its gross domestic product on healthcare than any other nation and that one-third of this spending goes to providing healthcare services to the elderly, we can understand why healthcare services for the elderly come at such a great cost. Indeed, an elderly person in the United States may receive highly skilled healthcare to meet his or her every need—provided he or she is able to offer some form of payment.

In satisfying this payment requirement, the elderly either pay out of their own pockets or depend on health insurance. Many are unable to pay for adequate healthcare. To assist in satisfying the payment requirement, the United States provides universal government-subsidized healthcare coverage through the Medicare social insurance program for persons age 65 and older and persons with long-term disabilities. Medicare's companion program, Medicaid, provides somewhat different, broader coverage for a segment of the poor, including the elderly poor. Together, these programs provide hospital and outpatient coverage with limited out-of-pocket costs to 97 percent of the elderly population. In light of the rising cost of health insurance and limited retirement incomes, many of the nation's elderly would be uninsured or underinsured but for the government programs.

Included among the vast number of elderly Americans needing healthcare are the millions suffering from Alzheimer's disease. Their healthcare needs are unique in that they are tied to housing issues: Where will the Alzheimer's patient live once he or she has been diagnosed? For this reason, this chapter examines the issue of the cost of caring for an Alzheimer's patient by first looking at the patient's housing options and then discussing payment options, not only for housing, if necessary, but also for healthcare.

HOUSING AND THE ALZHEIMER'S PATIENT

The Alzheimer's patient and his or her family members have several options regarding where the patient will be housed. Because Alzheimer's patients in the early phases of the disease are prone to wander and those in the later phases are unable to care for themselves, no Alzheimer's patient should live or be allowed to live alone. While many Alzheimer's patients, like many elderly people, would like to "age in place" (that is, continue to live in their own homes), this option is not always feasible. Because of their physical and/or mental condition, some of these patients may require housing where they can receive adequate care and be safe.

Sometimes, that place may be the home of a family member—a son, a daughter, a sibling, or some other relative. After all, family members are typically the primary providers of assistance to Alzheimer's patients. Indeed, if the person has a very capable caregiver or younger relatives willing to care for him or her, he or she can stay at home or move in with a family member. However, because of changes in work patterns and family size and the trend toward decreased family stability, fewer family members are available or able to care for their Alzheimer's-stricken relatives. Because people live much longer today, a growing number of adult children are in their sixties or seventies and have parents in the nineties. These adult children may themselves have health problems and be in need of care or, because they had their own children late in life, may be providing financial assistance (such as college tuition) to their children. Thus, they may not be able to provide the care or financial support their parents need.

Another factor affecting the availability of family members to care for a parent with Alzheimer's is that providing care—especially personal, in-home services—still usually falls on daughters. With a large number of women now working full time, many adult daughters do not have the time to provide the care that daughter-homemakers have provided in the past. Many have to balance the demands of work, their children, and the needs of their elderly parents. Meanwhile, adult sons who in the past helped in the caregiving process by running errands or assisting with home repairs now find their lives too busy to offer much help. Further, even if adult children would like to help, their careers may have caused them to move away from their parents. For all these reasons, the government and the private sector have become more involved in providing housing and help for the elderly, including those with Alzheimer's disease. Among the available housing options are aging in place (that is, staying at home), moving in with adult children, moving to assisted living facilities, and moving to nursing homes.

STAYING AT HOME

Many older people want to remain where they have lived when they were younger. They have emotional ties to the house and town where they grew up or spent years of their lives, and now that they are older, they do not want to move. Some of them get their children to agree that they will never move them out of their homes. If the elderly people develop Alzheimer's disease, however, the children may not be able to keep these promises. Yet staying at home may be the best option for people who have developed Alzheimer's disease. Because they are familiar with the surroundings, they would most likely be less disoriented at home than if they were moved elsewhere. Some studies suggest that this decreased disorientation may slow the disease's progress.

If the Alzheimer's patient has a capable caregiver available at home, such as a spouse or younger relatives or friends willing to move into the house to care for him or her, the patient can indeed be cared for at home for the rest of his or her days. Healthcare providers can provide services to the patient in his or her own home, with the patient visiting the doctor or staying in the hospital when necessary.

MOVING IN WITH ADULT CHILDREN

Parents who have developed Alzheimer's disease may also move in with their adult children. Admittedly, this may be a cause of severe emotional strain for the children. Many of them have great difficulty accepting the fact that their parents are stricken with a disease that has changed them in many ways and that the fun-loving, witty, and sharp parents they once knew no longer exist. In addition, if the parent moves in with the child during an early stage of the disease, the parent may still have enough of his or her mental faculties to resent having to depend on a child for care.

Yet moving in with an adult child can be beneficial on many levels. First, the child would have peace of mind knowing that the parent is being cared for by someone he or she knows and loves. Second, the parent—to the extent to which he or she can understand anything—might be less upset to have a child rather than a stranger as caregiver. Third, the cost of such care is significantly less than other options.

On the negative side, the child-parent caregiving relationship might result in emotional strain for the child. One such caregiver told me that she was often tempted to strike her mother because of the strain and tension she was experiencing. In addition, some Alzheimer's patients can be very aggressive, exacerbating the already tension-filled relationship between the parent and child.

ASSISTED LIVING

Assisted living is a private sector creation designed to house the elderly (not just those suffering from Alzheimer's) in nonmedical residences while providing them with the assurance of available assistance. Assisted living is quite expensive. Hence, it is an option typically considered only by those who have either sufficient financial resources or long-term care insurance to cover this eventuality. Even with long-term care insurance, the cost can be prohibitive because not all long-term care insurance policies cover a person indefinitely; some policies also restrict the types of long-term care facilities for which they provide benefits. For those who can afford it, assisted living is geared toward individuals who need help in their life activities but do not need the degree of healthcare provided in a nursing home, and therefore, it is useful for those in the earlier stages of Alzheimer's disease.

Law Professors Lawrence A. Frolik and Alison McChrystal Barnes describe it this way:

> [Assisted living] combines individualized support services with modest health care services to help people live as independently as possible. Assisted living facilities also provide recreation, social activities, and meals in common areas. The essence of assisted living is custodial care in the form of assistance with bathing, grooming, and dressing. The facility will almost certainly have 24-hour nursing oversight as well as other licensed staff, such as dieticians. Health care needs are monitored to prevent medical problems that might require care in a hospital or nursing home. In particular, the facility will ensure that the residents take all of their prescribed medications.[1]

Approximately 90 percent of individuals who live in assisted living facilities are single. After all, if the individual has a spouse, that spouse would most likely provide home care for his or her loved one. Because women generally outlive men, more than 70 percent of residents at such facilities are women.

About 25 percent of assisted living residents are diagnosed with Alzheimer's disease or related disorders. Because of the unique nature of Alzheimer's disease, such as the tendency of Alzheimer's patients to wander, many assisted living facilities have separate wings or floors to house these patients and others with severe forms of dementia.

Most state laws prohibit assisted living facilities from admitting bedridden individuals. Such people typically require a level of healthcare best provided in a licensed nursing home, especially because they typically are unable to help themselves in the event of an emergency that would require them to leave the room or building. Such patients are definitely not good candidates for assisted living, although some states do permit assisted living facilities to continue to house residents who become confined to bed if a physician certifies that these residents are not in need of skilled nursing care. However, the assisted living facility must meet state requirements for a level of care that will meet the resident's daily needs and provide adequate protection and assistance in the event of an emergency.

If you can afford it, assisted living facilities present a good option for housing the Alzheimer's patient.

NURSING HOMES

Currently, more than 1.7 million elderly Americans reside in the more than 18,000 nursing homes in the United States, the majority of which are private, profit-making facilities, often owned by a chain. Ninety percent of nursing home residents are age 65 or older. Under federal law, a nursing home is an institution that provides skilled nursing care or rehabilitation services for injured, disabled, or sick persons. The federal definitions of "nursing facility" are found in the Medicare and Medicaid laws. Although these programs are similar, they provide coverage for different levels of care. They also define the facilities in which their beneficiaries may be housed differently.

The Medicare law speaks of a "skilled nursing facility," defined as an institution that is primarily engaged in providing skilled nursing care and rehabilitation services for injured, sick, or disabled persons and *not providing* services primarily for the care and treatment of mental diseases. The Medicaid law refers to a "nursing facility," which it defines in terms similar to Medicare's skilled nursing facility, but includes institutions that provide "on a regular basis, health-related care and services to individuals who because of their mental or physical condition require care and services." Because of the inclusion of this "health-related care" clause, Medicaid is much more inclusive than Medicare in its definition of what we know as nursing homes.

Combining the definitions provided in both laws, we can say that nursing homes provide medical care to their residents (unlike assisted living facilities), as well as room and board and other custodial care (including assistance in the activities of daily living such as eating, bathing, and other personal care needs).

Though more costly than home care or home nursing care (particularly where the home care provider is unpaid), nursing homes are less expensive than hospitals. They can also offer specialized care such as dieticians, rehabilitation specialists, and social service providers that a caregiver may not be able to provide in a home setting. The price tag for a nursing home today is anywhere from $4,000 to $7,000 a month, depending on the facility and its location.

Notwithstanding all the positive attributes of nursing home care, these institutions do have negative characteristics. The high cost tops the list. In addition, for the resident, living in a nursing home means a loss of privacy, autonomy, and personal freedom. The resident must rise at an appointed time, eat at specified mealtimes, dine with others, and accept what the home provides. Many nursing home residents share a room, and even those who can afford private rooms have rooms that are so small they have little space to place their lifetime of collections that, for them, hold such precious memories. In light of this, for many nursing home residents, life can be lonely.

ADMISSIONS ISSUES

Before being admitted to a nursing home, an individual must sign an admissions agreement or contract. This contract covers the conditions under which the home will provide care for the resident, the type of care, and the terms of payment. Although these contracts are often signed at times of great physical and emotional distress for the person and his or her family members, it is important that someone pay careful attention to the terms of the contract, ask questions about provisions that are not clear, and seek legal advice, if necessary, before signing the contract.

State and federal laws prohibit nursing home contracts from including certain things. These include third-party guarantees, solicitation of contributions, duration-of-stay clauses, waivers of liability, and unfair trade practices.

Third-Party Guarantees

Some nursing homes require that a "responsible party" sign the admissions contract and assume responsibility for payment. The nursing home reforms of the Omnibus Budget Reconciliation Act of 1987 (OBRA 1987) prohibit the inclusion of such clauses in any contract with a facility that participates in Medicare or Medicaid. In fact, barring certain circumstances, the nursing home cannot legally require the third party to sign, even if the contract does include a promise of payment by this third party. Federal regulations governing the delegation of resident rights preclude anyone from signing an admissions contract on behalf of the resident unless a court has adjudicated the resident mentally incapacitated or a physician certifies that he or she is incapable of understanding the rights and responsibilities listed in the contract. Indeed, the resident has an express right, pursuant to the federal Residents' Bill of Rights, to participate in treatment decisions and manage his or her own financial affairs. The prohibition on delegation of rights should eliminate such practices as consulting a third party for treatment decisions and financial matters. Alas, it does not always do that, and family members must be wary about provisions sneaked into the admissions contract that are contrary to federal law.

Of course, because an Alzheimer's patient would most likely be adjudicated mentally incapacitated by the time he or she is admitted to a nursing home, his or her guardian or agent under a durable power of attorney and/or a medical power of attorney would be authorized to sign the contract and make personal and financial decisions on his or her behalf—but not be personally liable for the cost.

Solicitation of Contributions

Although no prohibition exists against genuine voluntary financial contributions from a nursing home resident or his or her family to the nursing home, it is illegal under the Medicaid and Medicare antifraud and anti-abuse act for a nursing home to require a "gift, money, donation, or other contribution" as a condition for admission or continued stay. Family members of an Alzheimer's patient or the patient's guardian or agent under a durable power of attorney must be wary of such requests and must report them to the relevant authorities.

Duration-of-Stay Clauses

Duration-of-stay clauses require the prospective resident and his or her family to assure the facility that the resident will stay a certain number of months at the private pay rate before attempting to qualify for Medicaid assistance. The nursing home reform provisions of OBRA 1987 prohibit such clauses. The law also prohibits nursing homes from requiring any additional payment for the care of a Medicaid resident. Some facilities still attempt to enter into oral agreements with family members to make such payments, and some even refuse admission based on financial information.

Waivers of Liability

Many nursing home contracts include waivers, or limitations, of liability. These provisions, often scattered throughout the document, attempt to waive the facility's liability for the loss of or damage to the resident's personal property. The contract may also attempt to waive responsibility for the resident's personal injuries, whether these are caused by the negligence of the facility, its staff, or another resident, or may set a limit on the amount the resident can recover for his or her injuries or the length of time within which the resident may file suit. These provisions all violate federal and state laws.

Some clauses also seek to give the nursing home broad advance consent to the resident's medical treatment. Such clauses deprive the resident of his or her right to give informed consent to medical treatment. As long as the resident possesses mental capacity, he or she should be allowed to give informed consent to medical treatment. If the resident is suffering from Alzheimer's disease and is mentally incapacitated, his or her guardian or agent under a medical power of attorney must be allowed to give such consent.

Unfair Trade Practices

Many nursing home contract provisions that are not expressly prohibited by state or federal law can be challenged as unfair trade practices under state unfair and deceptive acts and practices laws. Every state has such laws. Some call them "deceptive trade practices acts," while others call them "fair trade acts."

As defined under these statutes, unfair trade practices include the use of any contract terms that are vague or misleading and the use of print that is difficult to read. Unfortunately, nursing home contracts, whether deliberately or inadvertently, sometimes contain these vague and misleading terms and/or very tiny print that is difficult for the resident and guardian to read. When they do, the aggrieved party or parties may file suit to recover actual damages, punitive damages for the nursing home's intentional violations, injunctive relief and other equitable relief as appropriate, court costs, and attorney's fees.

RESIDENTS' BILL OF RIGHTS

The law also protects individuals after they have become residents of a nursing home. Standards for nursing home care are set by statutory law, industry practice, and the courts. The federal government has gone one step further and has developed a statutory Residents' Bill of Rights. Pursuant to the provisions of this Bill of Rights, nursing home residents have several rights, including:

Autonomy

- To choose a personal physician
- To participate in planning care and treatment, based on full information from their caregivers
- To reasonable accommodation of individual needs and preferences
- To voice grievances and to receive a response promptly and without reprisal
- To organize with other residents and family groups

Information

- To be informed of resident rights upon admission and on request and to receive a written copy of rights and grievance procedures

- To be informed of the latest facility inspection results and any plan of correction
- To be informed in advance of any changes in room or roommate
- To be informed of any rates and extra charges for services
- To be informed regarding Medicaid benefits and applications

Privacy and Communication

- To participate or decline to participate in social, religious, and community activities
- To bodily and personal privacy in medical examination and treatment
- To privacy in personal visiting, written and telephone communication, and meetings of resident and family (i.e., advocacy) groups
- To confidentiality in personal records
- To give consent to ombudsman access to personal records
- To immediate access by a personal physician, representative of the health department, and the long-term care ombudsman
- To immediate access by relatives, if desired
- To access to other visitors, including organizations and individuals providing health, social, legal, or other services, subject to the resident's consent and to "reasonable restrictions"

Limitations on Transfers and Discharges

- No transfers unless the facility cannot meet the resident's medical needs; the resident has improved so that nursing home care no longer is necessary; continued residence threatens the health and safety of others; or the resident has failed, after reasonable notice, to pay for continued residence in the facility

- Notice of transfer at least thirty days in advance, or as soon as possible if transfer is required for health reasons, including reasons for transfer, information regarding rights to appeal, and the name, address, and phone number of the long-term care ombudsman or other advocacy program

- Notice of bed-hold (that is, bed reservation if the resident is hospitalized so that upon release from the hospital, the resident can return to a bed in the nursing home) policies and Medicaid bed-hold coverage

Personal Financial Protection and Access

- To keep funds of more than $50 in a separate interest-bearing account

- To keep other funds in a separate account or petty cash

- To a complete, individual written accounting of transactions, available for review

In addition to these rights, the Residents' Bill of Rights provides nursing home residents with the right to freedom from discrimination based on their Medicaid status, if any, and freedom from abuse and the use of restraints without a physician's authorization.

As you can see, nursing home residents are not left unprotected under the law. Although many stories of nursing home abuse and failures abound, these failures and abuses are the result, not necessarily of a general failure of the legal system, but of individual occurrences where nursing home employees and administrators inadvertently, negligently, or deliberately have failed to provide the necessary level of care. When these failures or abuses occur, the legal system provides the resident and his or her family with an avenue to seek redress.

WHERE WILL THE MONEY COME FROM? (PAYING FOR CARE)

Now that we have explored the various options Alzheimer's patients have at their disposal for obtaining care, we come to the important question of whether they can pay for such care. These patients and their family members essentially have four payment options: personal funding, long-term care insurance, Medicare, and Medicaid. Whatever option the individual and his or her family chooses, they can be assured of one thing: The cost of care is expensive.

It is difficult to obtain data on national spending on providing care for Alzheimer's patients and other elderly ill individuals. The most recent figure, reported in December 2002 by the Congressional Research Service, estimated the annual cost of nursing home and home care services for people of all ages (not just the elderly) at $140 billion, with $86 billion (about 61 percent) paid from government programs. Just over 10 percent of the costs are paid by long-term care insurance. The rest is met by care recipients and their families. These figures do not include the cost of the informal care provided by patients' family and friends.

The Alzheimer's patient and his or her family members may incur out-of-pocket costs only when the patient needs to visit a doctor, purchase prescription drugs, obtain at-home help, or be admitted to an assisted living facility, nursing home, or hospital. Hospitalization is generally the most expensive. Nursing home care is not far behind, at $4,000 to $7,000 per month, with a monthly average of $5,000 in 2007. Assisted living facilities cost about two-thirds as much ($70 to $150 a day).

How can Alzheimer's patients (really their estates and/or family members) afford to pay for the patients' care? Next, we'll examine the available funding options.

PERSONAL FUNDING

Family members can indeed attempt to fund the Alzheimer's patient's care from their own and the person's resources. However, unless the patient and/or the family members are extremely wealthy, this is a daunting proposition. Failing that, the individual could sell his or her home (assuming the person owns it) to pay for care or to pay for the cost of moving into an assisted living facility or a nursing home. In fact, many do sell their homes to finance such a move. However, the sale of the home sometimes poses emotional problems for many elderly people. In addition, the sale might generate undesirable tax consequences if the taxable gain upon the home's disposition exceeds certain limits (currently $250,000 gain for an individual, $500,000 for a married couple).

THE REVERSE MORTGAGE

For the Alzheimer's patient who does not intend to move into an assisted living facility or nursing home (at least not in the near future) and envisages having in-home care, the patient and/ or his or her guardian or agent under a durable power of attorney may consider a reverse mortgage. This is a financial instrument whereby the lender pays the homeowner a fixed sum each month or allows the person to draw down on a line of credit as needed. The lender collects the total of such payments, plus interest, at the end of the loan term, typically when the home is sold or the elderly person dies. These monthly payments supplement other sources of income. The funds can be used for any purpose, including meeting the cost of in-home care, long-term care insurance, and other medical needs.

Several national companies as well as the federal government and state and local governments offer reverse mortgages. The Federal National Mortgage Association ("Fannie Mae") supports reverse mortgages. Fannie Mae bases the loan limit amount on the homeowner's age and the appraised value of the house. In 2007, the maximum Fannie Mae–backed loan, depending upon location, ranged from $200,000 to more than $350,000. Applicants seeking amounts in excess of these limits must depend on state programs and private financial arrangements for the excess funds.

Under the typical reverse mortgage contract, the lender can require full and immediate payment if certain events occur, including:

- When the last borrower dies
- If the borrower transfers title of the home to a third party and, if there had been more than one borrower, no other borrower retains title to the property or a long leasehold thereon

- If the property is not the borrower's principal residence
- If the borrower fails to occupy the premises for more than twelve consecutive months because of physical or mental illness

Of course, the features of any specific reverse mortgage depend in large part upon the program under which the mortgage is made—state, local, or federal government program, or private contract between the financial institution and the borrower. The more salient features concern loan duration and payback schedules, borrower eligibility, loan size, and disclosure requirements.

- ***Loan Duration.*** Reverse mortgages come in different types. Some are simply lines of credit secured by a home's equity; the homeowner draws down funds as required. Others are fixed-term agreements that provide a series of monthly payments for a specified period, with the total amount paid out, plus interest, repayable at the end of the term unless the mortgage is extended or refinanced. Yet another type of reverse mortgage provides monthly payments as long as the homeowner occupies the home as his or her principal residence. The homeowner makes no repayment until he or she moves or dies, such payment presumably coming from the proceeds of the sale of the house. Upon the homeowner's death, however, the owner's heirs—usually his or her children—can choose to pay off the reverse mortgage or to refinance it and keep the home in the family.

  This last type of reverse mortgage holds a distinct advantage for the elderly homeowner because, as long as the person lives in the home, the elderly homeowner does not need to pay off the loan and does not have to fear outliving the equity in the home and being forced to leave the home prematurely. Instead, the owner has "life tenure" in the property. In exchange for this assurance, life tenure comes at a high cost. Homeowners with life tenure reverse mortgages receive smaller monthly payments than homeowners with fixed-term reverse mortgages. Lenders justify this by saying that the homeowner with a life tenure contract could live for several years after entering into the agreement.

Even with this additional cost, the life tenure reverse mortgage remains a good choice for the elderly Alzheimer's-stricken homeowner. Such a homeowner need never fear being forced out of his or her home to pay off a loan. In addition, the borrower never owes more than the home brings when it is sold. Even if the sum of the monthly payments received by the homeowner during his or her life plus the interest thereon exceeds the value of the home when it is eventually sold, the homeowner's liability is limited to the home's value. He or she owes nothing more. Under the federal government program, the federal government makes up the deficiency to the lending institution. This encourages financial institutions to make these loans without fear of incurring financial losses.

- *Borrower Eligibility.* Age is definitely an eligibility requirement for a reverse mortgage. Under the federal government program, the homeowner must be at least sixty-two years old. In some states, the minimum age is sixty years old, while in others, it is sixty-five; in Florida, it is seventy.

Note, however, that the older the homeowner is on the date he or she enters into the reverse mortgage agreement, the higher the monthly payment he or she will receive because such a loan is assumed to have a short duration, giving the homeowner less time to consume the equity in the home.

In addition to age, homeowners also face restrictions on the types of residences eligible for reverse mortgages. Under the federal government program, for example, the homeowner must reside in a single-family dwelling (which would include a condominium but not a shareholder-owned cooperative).

- *Interest Rate and Loan Size.* Some states cap the interest rates that may be charged on reverse mortgages. Some of these states (California is a good example) compensate a lender for this limitation by allowing the lender to receive a portion of the price appreciation on the residence that accrues over the period of the loan. The loan amounts are also limited. Most states limit the loan to a percentage—typically 80 percent—of the home's appraised value. The federal government program and the Fannie Mae program also have limits (in the form of maximum amounts) that may change from year to year. Individuals requiring loans larger than those amounts would necessarily have to consider other loan programs.

- *Disclosure Requirements.* It is true that the reverse mortgage is a strange "creature." Someone pays the elderly homeowner to stay in his or her own home, while deferring repayment until some often unspecified future date. To protect the lender, these mortgages come with special disclosure requirements. In addition to these requirements, the federally insured reverse mortgage program requires that prospective borrowers receive financial counseling prior to obtaining a reverse mortgage. This counseling covers topics like budgeting, general financial planning, tax implications of the reverse mortgage, and Medicaid/public assistance ramifications.

Income Tax Considerations

Generally, reverse mortgages generate few income tax consequences. The proceeds of the loan are not taxable. The interest paid is not deductible to most homeowners, who typically report on a cash basis and thus have no deduction until the entire loan is paid off. Even when the interest may be deducted, interest expenses on reverse mortgages are deductible only as "home equity indebtedness," which is limited to loan principal amounts not exceeding $100,000. Most reverse mortgages exceed that amount.

While a reverse mortgage does not have immediate income tax consequences, it can affect the taxation of the home's appreciation. When a reverse mortgage becomes due, either because its fixed term has expired or the homeowner has moved out of the home or has died, the home is usually sold to pay off the mortgage. The gain realized at that time will be shielded by the $250,000 residential gain ($500,000 for a couple); however, any gain in excess of this amount would be taxable as a capital gain. For example, let's assume the following:

Akashi's home has an unrealized gain; the difference between the home's current value and its purchase price is $400,000. If Akashi holds the home until he dies, none of that gain will be subject to federal income tax.

If, however, Akashi obtains a reverse mortgage on the home and then moves out of the home into a nursing home, the mortgage would be payable upon his departure from the home. Akashi (or his guardian or agent under a durable power of attorney) will most likely sell the home to repay the funds he received from the reverse mortgage lender and to pay for the nursing home. Assuming the home sells for $400,000, Akashi will be taxed on $150,000 of the gain (after applying the $250,000 exclusion).

Essentially, the reverse mortgage prevented Akashi's heirs from obtaining the unlimited gain exclusion that would apply if he held the property until his death when the mortgage would have been paid off and the entire gain would have been exempt from federal income tax.

Because of the tax implications of the reverse mortgage, it is advisable that someone doing tax planning with Alzheimer's disease in mind consult with a tax attorney before opting for a reverse mortgage. Similarly, it would appear that the reverse mortgage is a tool best suited to the Alzheimer's patient who intends (or whose guardian or power of attorney agents intend) to always receive at-home care and not be moved to a nursing home or assisted living facility.

Public Assistance Implications

A reverse mortgage also carries public assistance implications. Many elderly people who receive reverse mortgages would otherwise be eligible for means-tested public assistance benefits such as Supplemental Security Income, Medicaid, and food stamps. The federal government and many state governments have determined that payments received from a reverse mortgage are not income for the purpose of determining eligibility under these public assistance programs. However, if these payments are not spent at the end of any one month, they are counted among the beneficiary's qualifying resources and, if the total amount exceeds the limits, the person will be disqualified from receiving public assistance for at least a short while. Therefore, it is important that someone in this situation (or his or her family members or guardian or agent under a durable power of attorney) ensure that reverse mortgage payments are completely spent before each month's end. Because there are no restrictions on how someone may use the proceeds of a reverse mortgage, it should not be too difficult to use up all available funds by month's end.

LONG-TERM CARE INSURANCE

Long-term care insurance describes a wide variety of private contracts between insurance companies and policyholders. Long-term care insurance is quite expensive. As of October 2007, an individual who is sixty-five years old and in good health can expect to pay between $2,000 and $3,000 a year for a policy that covers nursing home care and home care, with premiums adjusted annually for inflation. People who have health problems like diabetes, cancer, or arthritis pay higher premiums. In addition, some rates can go up, sometimes by as much as 40 percent or more in a given year.

No nationwide rules exist regarding long-term care insurance. Regulation is left to the individual states. Further, no standardization of long-term care insurance policies exists. Accordingly, it is very difficult to compare these policies. Indeed, the contracts themselves can vary with the particular issuer. In general, though, a long-term care insurance policy covers the cost of long-term care for the insured individual under various scenarios, with coverage beginning after an "elimination period" has expired.

COVERAGE

Most long-term care insurance policies pay for care whether such care is provided in a nursing home, in an assisted living facility, or in the insured person's home. Hence, individuals who wish to stay at home and never relocate into a nursing home or assisted living facility can have the cost of their care paid for by their long-term care insurance policy.

FINANCIAL LIMITS ON COVERED COSTS

Long-term care insurance policies do not typically pay the entire cost of long-term care. Rather, policies pay a fixed per diem dollar benefit, which is less than the actual daily cost of care. For example, while the actual daily cost of care for an Alzheimer's patient might be $200, the long-term care insurance policy might pay only $160. Further, the daily payment benefit for home healthcare is usually one-half that paid for institutionalized care.

In addition to the daily benefit limit, policies also limit the duration of coverage. Typically, policies limit the number of days for which they will pay benefits. Generally, duration periods go from one to five years, but the premiums increase as the number of years of possible benefits increases. Some policies do pay benefits for an indefinite period, but their premiums are quite high. In addition, some policies that offer benefits for both home healthcare and institutionalized care tend to have separate daily limits for each kind of care, or pay for a set number of days regardless of the type of care the patient uses during that period.

As a final financial limitation, long-term care insurance contracts contain a waiting or elimination period. Policies typically require that the beneficiary pay for some care before the policy benefit begins. This waiting period is selected by the beneficiary when he or she first obtains the policy. This entire arrangement functions like the deductible amounts we come across in other types of insurance: No insurance benefits are paid to the beneficiary during the first thirty to 120 days ("the deductible period") of an otherwise covered care situation. The longer the elimination period, the greater the out-of-pocket expenses the insured will face, and accordingly, the lower the cost of the insurance premium. Moreover, the longer the elimination period, the less the chance that the beneficiary will actually collect benefits; hence, the premiums are lower. The elimination period does not begin until the preexisting condition limitation (discussed below) has been satisfied.

PAYMENT OF BENEFITS

Long-term care insurance policies strictly define when benefits may be paid. Typically, these policies pay benefits when the insured person's mental or physical condition meets certain defined standards and when the insured either resides in an assisted living facility or a nursing home or is receiving home healthcare from an authorized provider. Policies also spell out the conditions that would trigger the payment of benefits. These include:

- A medical necessity such as a stroke that leaves the insured in need of long-term care

- Severe cognitive impairments, such as Alzheimer's disease, that require daily care and supervision

- The inability to perform a specified number of activities of daily living, as defined in the policy

With no standard definition available, policies vary widely in their definitions of "activities of daily living." The following are typical:

- The ability to dress oneself

- The ability to feed oneself

- The ability to move about the living unit with or without an assistive device such as a wheelchair

- The ability to get in and out of bed and chair without assistance

- The ability to control the bowel and bladder voluntarily (continence) and the ability to use the toilet

Generally, policies pay benefits upon a physician's certification that the person is unable to perform a certain number (usually two or more) of the five defined activities of daily living. Before paying benefits, the policy may require that the person be examined by the insurance company's physician. If the policy pays greater benefits for institutionalized care, it typically requires that the person prove that he or she resides in a facility that meets the policy's definition of an "institution" and is receiving the level and kind of care required by the policy.

If the policy pays for home healthcare, the person may be required to prove that he or she is receiving such care from a licensed home healthcare provider.

MEDICAL LIMITS ON COVERAGE

Long-term care insurance policies also contain some medical limitations.

Preexisting Conditions

The most significant of these medical limitations is that placed on so-called preexisting conditions—medical conditions that already existed when the insured first purchased the policy. In fact, some preexisting conditions are deemed so severe that an insurance company would not issue a policy to a person with any of these conditions. Indeed, denial of insurance or lack of access to long-term care insurance is not unusual for persons with certain medical conditions. The phrase *preexisting condition* is usually defined in the policy itself, subject to state law or regulation. A typical definition might include any medical condition for which the policyholder sought treatment—or should have sought treatment—within some period (usually six months) preceding the policy's effective date.

If the policyholder needs long-term care after the policy takes effect but the need is attributable to a preexisting condition, the insurance company may deny coverage for a certain specified period *beyond* the customary elimination period. Six months is typical, although in some cases, particularly group policies where all group members are automatically accepted by the insurance company, the denial period may be much longer—sometimes indefinite.

Some conditions do not preclude issuance of a policy; instead, they are excluded from its coverage. These conditions include alcoholism, drug addiction, illnesses caused by an act of war, attempted suicide or other intentionally self-inflicted injuries, or nervous disorders other than Alzheimer's disease.

Still, Alzheimer's patients and their family members should be wary about purchasing long-term care insurance. Indeed, if a physician has already diagnosed the individual with Alzheimer's, the disease will no doubt be viewed as a preexisting condition subject to the policy's exclusionary provisions governing these conditions. Ideally, with 20/20 hindsight, the patient would have purchased long-term care insurance *before* the disease strikes. However, some question the wisdom and cost-effectiveness of making such a purchase, essentially because the purchaser may never need long-term care or because, should the need for such care arise, the insurance policy may be inadequate or insufficient because of inflation and rising healthcare costs.

Case Management

A second medical limitation on covered costs is the case manager provision found in the policies. This provision calls for an insured person needing long-term care to be examined by a caseworker (who is frequently an employee of the insurance company). This caseworker assesses the insured person's condition and determines whether he or she can be best cared for in a nursing home or in some less intensive setting. This assessment process occurs when the person first needs long-term care and may be repeated regularly thereafter to monitor the person's progress—or lack thereof—and ongoing needs. The insurance company typically denies coverage for any treatment plan at variance with the caseworker's assessment.

Prior Hospitalization Requirement

Yet another medical limitation on covered costs is a requirement in some policies of prior hospitalization in order for the policy to cover the cost of care. This prior hospitalization requirement typically mimics Medicare's rule that a minimum of three days in a hospital must precede the patient's admission to a nursing home or assisted living facility. This rule holds significant implications for Alzheimer's patients. After all, many Alzheimer's patients go to a nursing home or assisted living facility directly from home without first going to a hospital. A prior hospitalization provision included in the policy would severely limit the policy's usefulness. To prevent this outcome, three-quarters of the states currently prohibit the inclusion of such clauses in policies sold to their residents.

Eligible Facilities

Long-term care insurance policies sometimes restrict the number and type of facilities from which a policyholder may receive care. Some policies dictate that care must be provided in a nursing home, even if all the policyholder needs is custodial care. Some other policies limit coverage to "licensed" facilities or exclude specific institutions or categories of institutions. These restrictions place severe limits on the policyholder's ability to choose his or her care facility—a choice private long-term care insurance should indeed provide!

TO BUY OR NOT TO BUY

The decision on whether to purchase long-term care insurance is an individual one. Long-term care insurance provides significant benefits but also comes with significant risks, particularly the risk that the policyholder may never need long-term care. When thinking of Alzheimer's disease, however, one should weigh the benefits and risks of holding a long-term care insurance policy versus the risks of developing Alzheimer's disease with insufficient funds to pay for adequate care. If you are contemplating purchasing long-term care insurance, you should consult an attorney or family financial planner and discuss the matter with family members and loved ones.

MEDICARE

Succinctly put, Medicare is the federal government's health insurance program for people sixty-five years of age and older. The program pays for healthcare for these elderly citizens without regard to their health status or financial resources. It consists of four major programs: (1) Part A ("Hospital Insurance") covers hospitalization, short-term nursing home care, and some home health services; (2) Part B ("Supplemental Medical Insurance") mainly covers physician fees; (3) Part C ("Medicare Advantage") is a managed care program; and (4) Part D covers prescription drugs. Even with all this coverage, Medicare does not cover all of an elderly person's medical costs, leaving him or her to pay for the uncovered costs. In response, private insurance companies have developed "Medigap" policies to cover the costs Medicare does not.

MEDICARE ELIGIBILITY

Eligibility for all aspects of Medicare depends on eligibility for Part A benefits. Accordingly, individuals are eligible for Medicare Part A hospital coverage provided they fulfill any of the following:

1. Are over age 65 and have paid Federal Insurance Contributions Act (FICA) or Self-Employment Contributions Act (SECA) taxes through employment for a minimum number of quarters (currently forty).

2. Are disabled, as determined under the Social Security Act, for at least twenty-four months (regardless of age).

3. Have end-stage renal disease and require dialysis treatment or a kidney transplant.

4. Are over age 65 but ineligible for Social Security benefits because they have not worked the requisite number of quarters, but elect to purchase Part A at a monthly premium.

Eligibility for Part B supplemental medical insurance is distinct from but is related to eligibility for Part A benefits. The big difference is that persons eligible for Part B must pay a monthly premium in order to receive the insurance benefits. Generally, individuals are eligible for Part B coverage if they meet any of the following:

1. Are eligible for Part A.
2. Are over age 65, regardless of employment history.
3. Are disabled persons eligible for Part A.
4. Are persons with end-stage renal disease who are eligible for Part A.

Persons who have other retirement programs, such as railroad or Federal government pension plans, may sign up for Part B coverage, but they would have to pay a larger-than-minimum premium.

To be eligible for Part C coverage, an individual must be eligible for Part A and enrolled in Part B. Persons with end-stage renal disease cannot enroll in Part C, but an enrollee who develops the condition can continue coverage.

As with the other parts, to be eligible for Part D coverage, an individual must first be eligible for Part A. As with Parts B and C, Part D enrollment is voluntary and takes place during December of the preceding year.

MEDICARE BENEFITS

The Medicare program does not directly provide medical care. Instead, the program reimburses providers of healthcare services to program beneficiaries. Each part of the program provides a different type of healthcare benefit. For example, Part A provides coverage for inpatient hospital services including room and board; routine nursing care; diagnostic and therapeutic services such as laboratory, radiology, and physical therapy; supplies and equipment where Part A services are provided; and prescription and nonprescription drugs.

Part B covers a wide range of noninstitutional services not covered by Part A, including physician services (whether provided in a hospital, nursing home, or physician's office); diagnostic studies performed in the physician's office; outpatient hospital diagnostic, therapeutic, or surgical services; dialysis services (whether provided at home or in an institution); rural health services; and durable medical equipment such as walkers and wheelchairs for which Part B pays a rental fee.

Part C is a managed care system (such as an HMO or PPO) designed by the same types of organizations that design other managed care plans. As this book goes to press, Medicare Part D is still relatively new, having taken effect on January 1, 2006. Part D covers out-of-hospital prescription medications. (Prescription drugs used during a hospital stay are covered by Medicare Part A.)

MEDICARE AND THE ALZHEIMER'S PATIENT

As an insurance program for all individuals sixty-five years of age and older, Medicare covers persons who have developed Alzheimer's disease. Also, because people who have received Social Security disability payments for at least twenty-four months are eligible for Medicare coverage, those who develop Alzheimer's disease prior to age 65 and are able to obtain Social Security disability benefits are also eligible for Medicare coverage beginning twenty-four months after they begin receiving Social Security benefits.

Most Alzheimer's patients receive care at home, in an assisted living facility, or in a nursing home. Because of the prior hospitalization requirements, an Alzheimer's patient who is not hospitalized prior to being treated at a skilled nursing facility or at home would not be eligible for Part A benefits. Moreover, even when the Alzheimer's patient is first hospitalized and then released either to a skilled nursing facility or to his or her home, Medicare's coverage of healthcare costs does not last indefinitely. Coverage in a skilled nursing facility ceases after one hundred days, while coverage for home visits ends after the one hundredth day of a "home health spell of illness" period.

Some of the services not covered by Part A are covered by Part B. Among these are home health services that were not preceded by a hospital or skilled nursing facility stay or that have extended beyond one hundred home visits during a "home health spell of illness" period. Hence, the Alzheimer's patient who has run out of Part A benefits may receive Part B benefits.

Medicare Part C is also an option for the patient who is comfortable with a managed care plan run by a private entity. Medicare Part D is also available to the Alzheimer's patient, although depending on the extent of the patient's illness, a guardian or agent under a power of attorney would have to complete the enrollment forms on the patient's behalf.

MEDICAID

Medicaid is a federal program designed to pay for the medical expenses of low-income individuals who are aged, blind, or disabled. Medicaid does not provide medical services directly to beneficiaries, nor does it reimburse individuals directly for their out-of-pocket medical expenses. Rather, Medicaid, acting through state agencies, reimburses providers of medical care for services they provide to Medicaid beneficiaries. Although each state has its individual approach to Medicaid, because the program is federally governed and states must follow federal law as to eligibility and what services they provide, it can be described in general terms.

AVAILABLE BENEFITS

The Medicaid statute guarantees certain medical services for eligible individuals. States, at their expense, may expand benefits, and many states have done so. Pursuant to federal law, state Medicaid programs must provide the following services:

- Inpatient hospital services (other than in a mental hospital)
- Inpatient hospital services and nursing facility services for individuals age 65 or older in an institution for mental diseases
- Outpatient hospital services
- Rural health clinic services
- Laboratory and X-ray services
- Nursing facility services for individuals age 21 or older
- Physicians' services, medical and surgical services furnished by a dentist, midwife services, and medical care furnished by practitioners licensed under state law
- Home healthcare services
- Private duty nursing services

- Nurse practitioner services
- Clinic services furnished on- or off-site under the directions of a physician
- Dental services
- Physical therapy services
- Prescribed drugs, dentures, prosthetic devices, and eyeglasses prescribed by a physician or optometrist
- Diagnostic, screening, preventive, and rehabilitative services
- Intermediate care facility services for the mentally retarded other than in an institution for mental diseases
- Hospice care
- Case-management services
- Respiratory care services and any other medical care recognized under state law as specified by the Secretary of Health and Human Services

Medicaid also provides significant benefits to elderly persons—those persons most likely to be suffering from Alzheimer's disease. Among these benefits are reimbursement for the costs of nursing home care and the provision of limited home and community care for functionally disabled elderly individuals. The latter is limited in the sense that Medicaid mandates home healthcare only for the "categorically needy," not the "medically needy" (we shall discover the meanings of these terms shortly), except for those persons who are entitled to skilled nursing care. However, some states, acting beyond what is required by the federal Medicaid program, provide home health services for the medically needy. If, however, a state chooses to provide home health services, such services must include nursing services, home health aide services, and medical supplies and equipment. Some states also provide personal care services in a recipient's home.

Because of the high cost of institutionalization in a hospital or nursing home, many states, known as *waiver states,* receive special federal funds (called *waivers*) to provide Medicaid services to individuals who live at home or with a relative or friend. These services include homemaker services, home health aides, personal care services, adult day care services, habilitative services for the mentally retarded, respite care, and case management.

Medicaid Eligibility Requirements: The Categorically Needy

State Medicaid programs must provide benefits for financially needy individuals, known as categorically needy individuals. They are defined as individuals who are aged, blind, or disabled, and are eligible for Social Security Income (SSI). Some states (Connecticut, Hawaii, Illinois, Indiana, Minnesota, Missouri, Nebraska, New Hampshire, North Dakota, Ohio, Oklahoma, Utah, and Virginia) have adopted eligibility standards that are generally stricter than those under SSI.

- *Income Requirements.* Except in strict eligibility states, individuals are eligible for Medicaid benefits if their income is low enough to qualify for SSI. In 2007, this was $7,479.50 annually or $623 a month for an individual, and $13,690 per year or $1,140.83 per month for a couple.

- *Resources Requirements.* Medicaid recipients must have

very limited resources. An individual may have no more than $2,000 in countable resources; if both spouses apply for benefits, the couple may not have countable resources with a value in excess of $3,000. Strict eligibility states may use a lower dollar amount. Not all resources are countable toward determining SSI and Medicaid eligibility. Some assets are excluded. Among them are:

- The personal residence, if the individual's equity interest in it is $500,000 or less (a state may elect $750,000) and the individual lives in it, intends to return to it, or has a spouse living in it (the $500,000 and $750,000 figures will be indexed for inflation beginning in 2011)

- The value of household and personal belongings

- An automobile necessary for transportation of the individual or a member of the individual's household

- The cash surrender value of life insurance if the face value of the policies does not exceed $1,500

- The value of burial plots and up to $1,500 specifically set aside for burial expenses

Medicaid Eligibility Requirements: The Medically Needy

Many of the states (Arizona, Arkansas, California, Connecticut, Florida, Georgia, Hawaii, Illinois, Iowa, Kentucky, Louisiana, Maine, Maryland, Massachusetts, New Hampshire, New Jersey, New York, North Carolina, North Dakota, Oklahoma, Oregon, Pennsylvania, Rhode Island, South Carolina, Tennessee, Vermont, Virginia, Washington, West Virginia, and Wisconsin) and the District of Columbia extend Medicaid assistance to so-called medically needy individuals. These people can qualify for Medicaid assistance even if their income exceeds SSI eligibility if they meet the applicable SSI resource test. If their income is insufficient to pay for the cost of their nursing home or other medical care, they would receive Medicaid assistance to pay those bills.

States in which the medically needy are eligible may use either "spend-down" or "income cap" tests to determine whether Medicaid applicants satisfy the requirements for assistance. In spend-down states (Arizona, Arkansas, Florida, Iowa, Louisiana, Oklahoma, and Oregon), individuals become eligible for Medicaid assistance by spending down their income on medical expenses—excluding nursing home costs—until their income is less than a standard of income eligibility determined by the state. In income cap states, to be considered medically needy, an individual's income may not exceed 300 percent of the SSI monthly benefit for a single person. For example, the SSI monthly benefit for an individual in 2007 was $623; hence, the income cap was three times that amount, or $1,869. The cap is the same for individuals and couples. No spend-down is allowed; an individual or couple is ineligible for Medicaid assistance even if their income is only $1 above the cap.

Medicaid Assistance and the Personal Residence

Before applying for Medicaid assistance, a person should consider the effect receipt of such assistance would have on what may be his or her most precious possession: the personal residence. Under the Medicaid regulations, the home is an exempt asset. It is not taken into account when calculating the value of one's resources to determine whether a person qualifies for Medicaid assistance. That is not so, however, in the area of estate recovery.

In 1993, Congress passed a little debated law that requires states to try to recover the value of Medicaid payments made to nursing home residents after these residents die. This process is referred to as *estate recovery*. In essence, the state is recovering from the person's estate the amount it spent on the person's nursing home care.

Although the home is an exempt asset for purposes of qualifying for Medicaid, it is not exempt from estate recovery. That is why the home is the asset most frequently sought by the state in Medicaid estate recovery. Medicaid administrators typically place a lien on the home, such lien being limited to the person's interest therein. The release of such liens and their eventual disposition depend on state law. Generally, states allow the deceased person's family members to either sell the home to satisfy the Medicaid claim or to satisfy it using their personal funds, thus keeping the home in the family.

Medicaid and the Alzheimer's Patient

With the cost of healthcare continuing to spiral, it is quite possible that Alzheimer's patients—even those with higher than average fixed incomes—would someday need Medicaid assistance. Individuals should consider planning ahead, preparing themselves and their loved ones just in case they do develop Alzheimer's disease and might someday need Medicaid assistance.

This type of preparation is known as Medicaid planning. Contrary to what some people think, Medicaid planning is legal. Moreover, all it entails is the wise use of funds (that is, the spending down of funds) so that the individual's remaining resources would not disqualify him or her from receiving Medicaid assistance. The following is a brief list of ways in which a person could spend down his or her funds:

- Obtaining a thorough dental examination and dental work

- Purchasing new glasses

- Attending to medical needs that government benefits do not cover

- Paying off debt on the personal residence

- Making necessary repairs to the home

- Purchasing life insurance that does not have cash value

- Purchasing a burial plot, casket, and tombstone or setting up a burial account

PLAN AHEAD AND AVOID BANKRUPTCY

With all the available options, there is no need for an Alzheimer's patient or his or her family members to be forced into bankruptcy to pay for the patient's care. Several programs exist whereby the patient, regardless of his or her income or social standing, can procure the necessary funds to pay for his or her care. It is important that individuals begin planning early for the possibility that Alzheimer's disease will come calling. With this in mind, worthwhile options are saving toward paying part of one's healthcare when necessary, purchasing long-term care insurance, and engaging in Medicaid planning. Which one or ones you select is a matter of personal choice. However, everyone should do something.

NOTE

1. Lawrence A. Frolik and Alison McChrystal Barnes, *Elder Law: Cases and Materials*, 4th ed. (Newark, N.J.: LexisNexis, 2007).

CHAPTER 10

CARING FOR THE CAREGIVERS

"I CAN'T TAKE IT ANYMORE!"

*B*ack in Amarillo, Jasma's dad had made a miraculous recovery—well, sort of. His children had not come to an agreement on the issue of inserting a feeding tube. Because he had never executed advance directives and had never discussed the matter with any of his children or other relatives (or anyone else, for that matter), no one knew what his wishes were, and so his children remained deadlocked while their father lay dying.

Well, not really. Just as suddenly as he had stopped eating and drinking and had taken to simply lying in bed, Jasma's dad woke up one morning, spoke with his children, and then had a hearty meal. Shortly thereafter, his children met and decided that Jasma would petition the Potter County Court to be appointed her father's guardian. After a judge adjudicated the man mentally incapacitated, Jasma began her role as plenary guardian of her father.

Not long after that, Jasma's dad went from being a relatively quiet and peaceful man to being very combative and aggressive, especially in the afternoon. His language also changed. He swore often. It got so bad that his other children decided that they would no longer bring their young children to visit their grandfather. To make matters worse for Jasma, he called her some of the worst names imaginable and accused her of being a "loose woman." If she so much as spoke to a male friend passing by, he would accuse her of being a "harlot" who had no right to call herself his daughter.

Alas, his preoccupation with sex did not end there. One morning Jasma found him in the corridor masturbating and groaning.

Taking her father to doctors' visits was a nightmare for Jasma. Her father routinely protested, cursing the doctors. When one doctor attempted to check his prostate, he accused the doctor of being gay. Somehow, the doctors always smiled and did their best to tend to him. However, poor Jasma just wanted the earth to open up and swallow her.

His illness progressed, and each time he misplaced something, he accused Jasma of stealing it to give to one of her "men." He also began accusing Jasma of beating him and of generally being cruel to him.

"Vaughn," she said to me on the phone one day, "I can't take it anymore. I've done my best. I've worked myself to the bone for the man, but I can give no more! I need a break! I love my dad, but sometimes I hate him!"

If someone were to ask me which job I least desired, I would respond without a moment's hesitation: "Being the caregiver of an Alzheimer's patient." Truly, no task on earth is as difficult as caring for an Alzheimer's patient. Yet some people have the responsibility thrust upon them. They are faced with a difficult task that gets increasingly difficult as the patient's condition worsens.

During Stage I of the disease, the caregiving responsibility may be *merely* mentally exhausting. The caregiver is coming to terms with the dreaded disease, learning to accept the fact that a loved one has developed Alzheimer's, and juggling the day-to-day logistics of caring for the person. As the disease progresses, the caregiver may take on more financial and legal responsibilities on the patient's behalf. Over time, as the person's physical abilities diminish and his or her cognitive skills erode even further, caregiving becomes more physically taxing. Eventually, the caregiver becomes fully responsible for the patient's health, safety, and well-being. This is an awesome responsibility.

Not only that, but throughout the years of caring for a loved one, the caregiver may experience a variety of emotions. As the spouse or child watches the person undergoing personality changes and sees his or her cognitive and then physical abilities disintegrate, the caregiver may well experience feelings of sadness and loss. The caregiver may also experience anger over what has become of his or her loved one as well as moments of intense frustration over dealing with the day-to-day changes in the patient's personality and behavior. The caregiver may also feel extremely isolated and overcome with stress as he or she struggles daily to give the best care possible. If the caregiver has a full-time job outside the home and cares for other elderly parents, children, or other family members, the task is even greater.

Caring for someone who has Alzheimer's disease is a life-altering responsibility, and it is not unusual for a caregiver to develop some stress-related condition. There are, however, ways to minimize the negative effects and accentuate the positive.

WHO ARE THE CAREGIVERS?

Some Alzheimer's patients wind up in nursing homes where they remain until they die. They are cared for by professionals trained in caring for those with Alzheimer's disease and other types of dementia. However, family members care for the majority of Alzheimer's patients. The majority of these caregivers are spouses; however, daughters, daughters-in-law, sons, siblings, and grandchildren often play a role in providing care for the Alzheimer's patient. Friends, neighbors, and members of the patient's faith community may also be involved in caregiving.

No two people react the same way to being a caregiver of an Alzheimer's patient. While some caregivers may suffer family conflict, isolation, and tremendous emotional distress, others may experience a renewed sense of purpose or meaning in life. Research undertaken by the National Institute on Aging indicates that male spouses, those having a preexisting illness, and those getting few breaks from the responsibilities of caregiving are more vulnerable to the physical and emotional stresses of caring for someone with dementia. Often adding to the emotional distress is the necessity for the caregiver to make significant changes in his or her daily routine.[1]

THE PHYSICAL IMPACT OF CARING FOR AN ALZHEIMER'S PATIENT

The caregiver of an Alzheimer's patient has more health problems than other people of his or her age who are not providing such care. Caregivers report 46 percent more doctors' visits, use 70 percent more prescription drugs, and are three times more likely to become clinically depressed than non-caregivers.[2] Moreover, a study published in the *Journal of the American Medical Association* reports that caregivers between the ages of 66 and 96 have a 63 percent higher risk of dying than people the same age who are not caregivers.[3] Yet as bad as these physical effects are for the caregiver, the emotional effects are even worse.

THE EMOTIONAL IMPACT OF CARING FOR AN ALZHEIMER'S PATIENT

Since most caregivers are close relatives of the patient—usually a spouse, sometimes a child or sibling—their lives can indeed be quite miserable. Imagine that the caregiver has to look on for years—as many as twenty years, in some cases—as his or her loved one becomes sicker and needier as Alzheimer's robs the person of memory, cognitive functions, and eventually basic physical functioning. Imagine also that this caregiver must provide twenty-four hours of care for that loved one, 365 days a year. Under these circumstances, it is no wonder that caregivers experience an array of negative emotions, including depression, loneliness, anger, and frustration, with sometimes devastating effects.

DEPRESSION

Many caregivers of Alzheimer's patients become mildly or moderately depressed. Indeed, someone who is caring for a loved one with Alzheimer's disease is twice as likely to develop depression as someone caring for a loved one not suffering from Alzheimer's. That should not be surprising. After all, the caregiver of an Alzheimer's patient is more likely to devote more time and energy to caregiving, to miss work often (and thus develop problems on the job), and to have less time to devote to other family members or to doing things he or she enjoys. The caregiver may also experience family conflicts. Family members who are not providing care often have no idea what it takes to give such care, and they may criticize the caregiver unnecessarily, increasing the caregiver's stress levels and hastening the onset of depression. Caregivers of Alzheimer's patients may also be sleep-deprived, a condition that can bring on depression.

Finally, the caregiver, who must helplessly watch a loved one slipping away, will inevitably feel sad. Sometimes this sadness can be so intense that even if the Alzheimer's patient is placed in a nursing home or dies, the caregiver remains sad and may begin or continue to experience symptoms of depression.

LONELINESS

There can be no doubt about it: Caring for an Alzheimer's patient is a lonely task. As the demands of caregiving increase, the caregiver often becomes cut off from the once active social life he or she led. His or her circle of friends may diminish as the caregiver's world begins to revolve around the Alzheimer's patient. The sense of increasing isolation that results often leads to depression.

ANGER AND FRUSTRATION

Maybe because of feelings of inadequacy, or maybe because of a growing sense of hopelessness, caregivers sometimes experience feelings of anger and frustration. The anger is sometimes directed toward the patient and is expressed in harsh words ("You idiot! You burned the bagel again!"). Sometimes the anger is directed inward and is expressed in words of regret ("I raised all my children by myself; now I have to raise my mother, too!"). Sometimes the anger is directed at others, and the caregiver may explode over the simplest missteps of others ("When will you nincompoops realize you've got to leave your muddy shoes at the door?").

THE IMPACT OF CHANGES IN ROLE AND ROUTINE

As Alzheimer's disease progresses, the sufferer's cognitive abilities continue to decline. As this happens, the caregiver is required to make significant changes in his or her daily routine in order to provide the level of care needed. These changes are even more drastic if the caregiver is a spouse unaccustomed to managing the affairs of the home. The caregiver—particularly if the caregiver is a spouse—now has to undergo many changes.

DOING MORE–AND PERHAPS
UNFAMILIAR–CHORES

In most households, spouses have a routine. Susan, for example, does the grocery shopping, mows the lawn, and plans the family vacations. Marty prepares the monthly budget, writes the checks, and balances the checkbook. Now imagine that Marty develops Alzheimer's. Suddenly, Susan, who has rarely written checks and never balanced the checkbook, has this responsibility. In another family, imagine that Zindzhi, who always mowed the lawn, develops Alzheimer's disease. Having her continue mowing the lawn puts her (and maybe the neighbors and the neighbors' dog) in great danger. To avoid this, Runako, who had done the cooking, now has to learn to mow the lawn. Sure, he could hire someone to do it, but with the cost of Zindzhi's care escalating each day and with the family desperately short of finances, Runako must bite the bullet and learn to mow.

Such adjustments are not always easy, particularly for older persons who have become used to their routines, and the transition often increases the caregiver's level of desperation, anxiety, and stress.

Adjusting to Reduced Income

Imagine that Benjamin and Ruth have been married for forty years. Throughout those years, both worked hard to maintain a middle class standard of living. Benjamin has now developed Alzheimer's disease and has had to stop working. In order to care for her husband, Ruth has to first work fewer hours a month and, as Benjamin's disease progresses, quit working altogether.

The family has lost not only Benjamin's wages but also Ruth's. The middle-class lifestyle they were used to is now history. While Benjamin is too sick to know of the adjustments the family has to make, Ruth is acutely aware of them.

TAKING THE WHEEL

While a person in early Stage I Alzheimer's may still be able to drive, as the disease progresses, there comes a time when the person has to stop. This presents several dilemmas to the caregiver. Believing that he or she is still able to drive, the person may not be willing to give up the keys and will initially resist attempts to relieve him or her of driving privileges. He or she might complain about being held captive in the house or that the caregiver is treating him or her like a child. Yet the caregiver has to do the right thing: At some point, the keys have to be taken. Eventually, the patient will forget the incident.

A daughter of an Alzheimer's patient shared this story:

After the family had determined that Daddy should no longer be driving, we took away his car keys. He fussed and fumed, telling us that we were treating him like a child. We relented and let him have the keys back. But we were concerned and knew that he should not be driving, so we told him the car needed to go to the repair shop. Instead of taking the car to the shop, however, we drove the car to my house and left it there. Whenever Daddy asked about the car, we told him that it was still at the repair shop. As the days turned into weeks, Daddy apparently forgot all about his car and stopped asking about it.

Several months later, the family went on a trip. Because Daddy's car was big, we used it. Daddy didn't seem to notice, but when we arrived at our destination, Daddy looked at the car lovingly and said, "You know, I used to have a car just like this one."

Until the person forgets about the car, however, the caregiver should expect complaints.

LEARNING TO COPE WHEN CARING FOR AN ALZHEIMER'S PATIENT

Thus far, we have painted a rather bleak picture of the life of a caregiver of an Alzheimer's patient. Still, there are ways to cope with the new realities.

LEARN ABOUT THE DISEASE

When it comes to Alzheimer's disease, ignorance is not bliss, and denial is not wise. You need to learn as much as you can. Reading this book is a good beginning, and by all means, do read as many other books as are available. The Internet is another good source of information. Many experts have written articles about the disease and have posted them on the Internet. Caregivers should avail themselves of this wealth of information. Finally, the Alzheimer's Association's website, *www.alz.org*, contains much information about the disease and almost everything related to it.

JOIN A SUPPORT GROUP

Apart from reading about the disease, you can also join support groups for family members and caregivers of Alzheimer's patients. At support group meetings, people share their experiences about their loved ones who have the disease. Caregivers can learn much from each other and develop strategies for dealing with the daily challenges of caring for their loved ones. Support groups are also a good source of information about community resources.

FIND A CARING AND COMMUNICATIVE DOCTOR

When an individual develops Alzheimer's disease, he or she needs a doctor whom he or she likes, someone who will be gentle and kind. At the same time, the doctor must be willing to communicate with the patient's caregiver or caregivers.

Often, a major communication gap exists between caregivers and the doctors attending to their loved ones. While many doctors say they provide the caregivers with information on what to expect as the disease progresses, medications, recommendations on caregiving, and advice on helping the patients on a day-to-day basis, the majority of caregivers claim that doctors do not provide such information. Certainly, the doctors believe they are providing the desired information, but the sad fact is that many doctors engage in "doctorspeak," using terminology nondoctors do not understand. (I'll admit that many lawyers do the same, using legal terms and Latin phrases that no one else—sometimes even the lawyers themselves—can understand.) The poor caregivers leave the doctor's office numb and bewildered, not having any idea what the good doctor just said.

The cure for this is to ask questions. You should ask as many questions as you feel necessary so that you know what to expect and how to best care for your loved one. If the doctor is unwilling or unable to answer the questions and/or provide the requested information, find a doctor who will—and who is also someone the patient likes.

FIND OTHER SOURCES OF INFORMATION AND SUPPORT

In preparing to write this book, I spoke to many people who either have cared for or are currently caring for someone with Alzheimer's disease. One message rang clear: Taking care of someone with Alzheimer's disease requires the caregiver to develop some measure of knowledge about various things—the law, medicine, finance, and psychology, among others. Yet it is difficult for one person, no matter how intelligent, to possess all this knowledge.

Instead of feeling overwhelmed, get help. Delegate tasks to family members and close friends who are willing to help. Ask the financial expert in the family to render advice on financial matters. Ask the nurse to help with the medical matters. Consult a lawyer friend about estate planning and powers of attorney.

SELF-CARE FOR THE CAREGIVER

Beyond the shadow of a doubt, the responsibilities laid upon the shoulders of a caregiver of an Alzheimer's patient are enormous.

The caregiving task is a twenty-four hour, seven-day-a-week unpaid job. Not surprisingly, the caregiver often is so involved in providing care to the patient that in the process he or she overlooks his or her own needs—physical and emotional. Yet neglecting these needs is counterproductive. After all, if the caregiver is to provide the best care possible, it is important to maintain good physical and emotional health.

Moreover, it is important to begin this health maintenance emphasis as early as possible—in fact, as soon as a loved one begins exhibiting Alzheimer's symptoms. During the early stages of the disease, the person may be relatively self-sufficient. The person may still be able to drive, prepare a meal, take a shower, or perform many other everyday tasks. As the disease progresses, however, the patient will be able to do less and less, until the time comes when the person will be unable to do anything for him- or herself.

Knowing what is to come in the stressful days ahead, you should create habits and routines that help you maintain good health during the long, lonely days (make that years) of caregiving. Indeed, it is vital that even at that early stage, you learn to minimize your stress, get adequate exercise, maintain a healthy diet, get sufficient sleep, and develop or improve your caregiving skills. You might also join a support group at this early point.

MINIMIZE STRESS

External events often precipitate stress: Every traffic light in town may be red on the day you are late for work; a crazy, uncaring, uncouth driver may cut in front of you, causing you to stamp down hard on your brake pedal; and on the day you just have to make that bank deposit during your lunch hour, everyone in town has the same idea and the line in front of each teller at the bank is interminable. Yet people react differently to these stressors. Some may swear, rant, and rave, while others smile and hum, seemingly oblivious to the stressful events.

The difference is how they perceive these stressful events. The stress brought on by any situation is a function of both the situation itself and how you perceive it. The same principle applies to caregivers of Alzheimer's patients: The stressfulness of the caregiving process is largely a function of both the process itself and the way in which the caregiver perceives it.

Of course, the level of the stressfulness of the caregiving process is affected by other factors, including the relationship between the caregiver and the patient, the caregiver's ability to cope with stress in the past, whether the caregiver has support from others (siblings, children, or friends), and whether the caregiver voluntarily chose to become the caregiver. Those who volunteer to be caregivers are less likely to suffer from stress than those who take on the job because of some obligation.

In either case, caregivers need to keep their stress levels in check. Following are six recommendations for achieving this goal:

1. *Be on the lookout for warning signs.* You should be concerned if you are suffering from sleep problems, forgetfulness, or irritability. If you are, chances are that the cause is stress, and you should take steps to relieve the stress before it gets out of hand.

2. *Identify stressors.* You should identify—pinpoint—the source of your stress and devise ways to overcome it (or them).

3. *Figure out what you can and cannot do.* You cannot control certain situations, like forcing a sibling to come over and help take care of a parent. However, you can change and control the angry feelings that might arise.

4. *Do something about it.* Rather than sitting back and being angry about a particular situation, take action. For example, instead of sitting around waiting for a sibling to help take care of your parent, if you can afford it, hire someone. (Your local Alzheimer's Association can guide you to sources of respite care.) To help alleviate stress, pursue a hobby, go for a walk, or call a friend.

5. *Take a break.* Notwithstanding the hectic schedule of caring for an Alzheimer's patient, you should find time to do something just for yourself. It could be as simple as taking a ten-minute walk three times a week, going to the mall for an hour, or just sitting down to watch a sitcom. Knowing that you have that "special" time can help get you through the more difficult moments.

6. *Ask for help.* Caregivers must be prepared to ask for help. They should not expect others to read their minds, know what help they need, and volunteer their help. If caregivers need help, they should ask for it. Moreover, if someone volunteers to help, you should accept the offer and give the person a specific task to perform.[4]

Following these principles will do much to reduce your stress levels and make the caregiving experience easier to endure.

GET ADEQUATE EXERCISE

Many people allow life's hustle and bustle to curtail or completely wipe out their exercise routines. This may be tempting to the caregiver of an Alzheimer's patient. After all, with the 24/7 caregiving schedule, you might be tempted to give up on exercise.

Do not yield to this temptation. Physical activity has many benefits, especially for the caregiver of an Alzheimer's patient. Exercise can help relieve stress. It also helps fight weight gain (and helps maintain weight loss), staves off disease, leads to better sleep, maintains your strength and endurance, reduces tension and anxiety, boosts your energy, and helps prevent depression.

Something as simple as a thirty-minute walk three times a week qualifies as exercise. If even that is too much, you can work exercise into your routine; for example, park the car far from office and store entrances, take the stairs rather than the elevator or escalator, walk to nearby stores and offices instead of driving, and incorporate physical activity into simple daily household chores. If you do these things on a regular basis, you will reap the benefits that regular physical activity bring and will most likely remain healthy during the caregiving process.

MAINTAIN A HEALTHY DIET

Generally, people who lead busy or hectic lives do not maintain healthy diets. They eat fast foods high in fat and sugar and eat on the run, and as a result they do not maintain good health. For the caregiver of an Alzheimer's patient, the problem is exacerbated by the fact that even when you would like to eat better, you find that your caregiving schedule leaves little time for preparing good, nutritious meals.

You must therefore make a concerted effort to maintain a healthy diet. Your meals should be balanced and rich in complex carbohydrates, fruits, vegetables, protein, and healthy fats. To cope with the hectic schedule and the inability to prepare a nutritious meal every day, look for recipes that do not take much time to prepare, make meals ahead of time and store them in the freezer, and keep healthy snacks in the cupboard.

GET SUFFICIENT SLEEP

A good night's sleep is essential for someone providing care for an Alzheimer's patient. With the hectic schedule of caregiving, the caregiver may try to pack as many chores—both for the patient and for the caregiver's own household—as possible into a day, in the process stretching out the night. The caregiver should not yield to such a temptation. In order to give the patient the best care possible, the caregiver should get a good night's sleep each and every night. In fact, the caregiver should follow the same routine every day, going to bed at the same time each night and waking up at the same time each morning. To that end, the caregiver should avoid ingesting substances like caffeine and alcohol that could prevent him or her from getting a good night's sleep.

DEVELOP OR IMPROVE YOUR CAREGIVING SKILLS

People who work or have worked in caregiving professions—nurses, social workers, counselors, ministers of religion—might

find the task of providing care for an Alzheimer's patient relatively easy. For others, though, the task of caregiving may be a
challenge.

The person called upon to provide round-the-clock care to a
relative who has developed Alzheimer's disease often comes to
the task unprepared and untrained, with very little knowledge
about the disease and very little time to prepare for what lies
ahead. Yet it is possible for every caregiver to provide a very
satisfactory level of care. All it takes is the development or im-
provement of the caregiver's caring skills. One of the best ways
to do this is to improve your communication skills with the Alzheimer's patient. Indeed, too often caregivers speak to Alzheimer's patients as if they are speaking to imbeciles who have no
feelings. No caregiver should adopt this approach. The Family
Caregiver Alliance provides the following tips to caregivers for
developing or improving their communication skills with Alzheimer's patients:

- **Set a positive mood for any interaction.** Speak in a pleasant and respectful manner. Use positive facial expressions,
  a positive tone of voice, and a gentle touch to help get
  your message across and to demonstrate your underlying
  affection for the patient.

- **Get the person's attention.** Limit distractions and noise by
  turning off the radio or TV, drawing the curtains, shutting
  the door, or moving to a quieter place. Before saying anything to the patient, make sure you have his attention. Use
  eye contact and gentle touches to keep his attention focused on you.

- *State the message as clearly as possible.* Use simple words and phrases, and speak to the patient slowly, distinctly, and in a reassuring tone. Do not raise your voice. If necessary, repeat the message a few times, making sure to use names of people and places instead of pronouns and abbreviations.

- *Keep questions simple and answerable.* Learn to ask one question at a time. Questions that can be answered with "yes" or "no" work best for the Alzheimer's patient. Do not ask her open-ended questions or those that have too many options. If possible, use visual cues and prompts to help clarify the question and guide her response.

- *Listen with your eyes, ears—and heart.* Be patient if your Alzheimer's-stricken relative is struggling to come up with the right words. Simultaneously, pay attention to nonverbal cues that may speak more than words.

- *Redirect and distract when things get rough.* If you sense that an emotional meltdown is coming, try changing the subject or environment or suggesting a new activity.

- *Respond to the patient with affection and reassurance.* People who have Alzheimer's often feel confused, anxious, and uncertain of themselves. Do not try to convince the patient that she is wrong. Rather, focus on how she is feeling, and respond with verbal and physical expressions of support, comfort, and reassurance. Hold the patient's hands, hug her, or give her some other form of feedback in the form of a compliment.

- *Remember the good old days.* While recalling what happened an hour ago might be impossible for the Alzheimer's patient, if he is still able to talk, the patient may well be able to recall what occurred many years ago. Recalling old memories is often a soothing and affirming activity.

- *Maintain a sense of humor.* You should never laugh at the person who has Alzheimer's. However, you should use humor whenever possible to communicate with him. Chances are the patient will laugh right along.[5]

Even with these improved communication skills, you must often depend on your intuition to decide what to do in any given situation. On the other hand, dealing with Alzheimer's disease is counter-intuitive. Often, the right thing to do is exactly opposite to what seems like the right thing to do. To that end, the Alzheimer's Association offers the following practical advice for caregivers:

- *Don't try to be reasonable, rational, and logical.* When a person is acting in ways that do not make sense, as human beings we tend to explain the situation carefully, assuming that the person will understand. However, the Alzheimer's patient cannot respond to this argument. The fact that it is logical is not important. Instead of trying to reason with the patient, use simple, straightforward statements about what is going to happen.

- *Don't try to ground a person with Alzheimer's in reality.* A person with memory loss often forgets important things, such as the fact that her mother is dead. Reminding her of this loss also reminds her about the pain associated with that loss. Likewise, you will often have an argument with an Alzheimer's patient when he says that he wants to go home and you reassure him that he is at home. It is a better idea to try to calm the person by redirecting her, asking the patient who asked about her mother to tell you about her or asking the patient who wanted to go home to tell you about his home.

- *No one can be a perfect caregiver.* Parents can't be perfect, and neither can caregivers. Indeed, caregivers—who have the right to the full range of human emotions experienced by everyone—may sometimes be impatient or frustrated. It is important, therefore, that during the caregiving journey you learn to forgive both yourself and the patient.

- *Lying can reduce your stress.* We are taught that we should be honest with all people at all times. We hold on to the maxim that honesty is always the best policy. However, when someone has Alzheimer's disease, honesty can lead to distress both for the patient and the caregiver. Ask yourself this: Does it really matter that the patient thinks she is helping out at the day care center instead of going there as an Alzheimer's patient? Is it okay, as a way of getting the patient to the doctor, for you to tell her that you are going out to lunch and then stop by the doctor's office on the way home to pick up something? Sometimes such "therapeutic lying" can serve a good purpose.

- *Realize that making agreements does not work.* It is true that an Alzheimer's patient will soon forget if a caregiver asks him not to do something ever again or to remember to do something. It sometimes helps if you leave notes as reminders for people in Stage I Alzheimer's. However, as the disease progresses, this tactic will not work. It is usually a better approach to take action rather than talking and discussing. For example, it is better to buy an electric tea-kettle with an automatic "off" switch than to warn the patient of the dangers of leaving the stove on.

- *Educate the doctors.* It is important that you tell the doctor what happens at home. Remember, the doctor cannot tell during an examination that the patient has been up walking around all night or has been forgetting to turn off the stove. Without this information, the doctor will not be able to treat the patient properly.

- *You cannot do it all, so it is fine to accept help.* When people offer to help, always answer "yes." In fact, you should keep a list of things people can do to help, whether it is bringing a meal, picking up a prescription, shoveling snow, or staying with the patient while the caregiver goes out for a while. Asking people to do specific things, in fact, will reinforce offers of help. In addition, remember that although it is harder to ask for help than to accept it when it is offered, you should not wait until you really need help before you ask for it.

- *Realize that it is easy to both over- and underestimate what the Alzheimer's patient can do.* Often, it is easier for you to do something for a loved one than to let her do it herself. However, if you do it for her, she will lose the ability to be independent in that skill or task. Conversely, if you insist that the patient does some things for herself and she becomes frustrated, you run the risk of agitating her and probably have not increased her ability to perform the task. The key, then, is to find the balance between helping and interfering. It is also important to know that this balance may change from day to day; the patient may be able to do something one day and then be unable to do it the next.

- *Tell the person—don't ask.* Asking, "What would you like for dinner?" may be a perfectly normal question. However, asking that question of an Alzheimer's patient will not produce results. Indeed, it will only increase your frustration if you ask the patient to come up with an answer when he might not have the words for what he wants or might not be hungry. You will also be frustrated if the patient answers but doesn't want the food when you serve it. It is better to simply tell the person what is about to happen. Saying "We are going to eat now" encourages the person to eat and does not put him in the position of having failed to respond.

- *Recognize that it is perfectly normal for you to question the Alzheimer's diagnosis when the patient has moments of clarity.* One of the hardest things to remember about Alzheimer's is that you are responding to a disease and not to the person who existed before the disease struck. Often, people who have developed Alzheimer's—and especially those in the early stages of the disease—have moments when they make perfect sense and respond appropriately. When they witness these moments, caregivers and onlookers sometimes feel that the person has been faking the memory loss or that you and other family members have been exaggerating the nature of the patient's "problem." When this happens, remember that while these lucid moments do occur, they are not indications that the person was either never ill or that he or she is now healed.[6]

THE CAREGIVER AND THE LEGAL SYSTEM

Two areas of the law should be of particular interest to the caregiver of an Alzheimer's patient: tort law and contract law. In Chapter 7, we discussed the legal consequences that arise when an Alzheimer's patient commits a tort. We discovered that while such an act may not always have consequences for the patient, his or her caregiver might well be liable for the harms perpetrated by the patient on third parties. Here, we'll discuss the consequences of contracts on caregivers.

THE CAREGIVER AND THE LAW OF CONTRACTS

When people hear the term *contract*, they often think of a lengthy document written in hard-to-understand language detailing the rights, duties, and obligations of various parties. Alas, this conception is so incorrect! In reality, a contract is simply a promise or set of promises made by one person to another that the law will enforce or at least recognize in some way.

The contract process has three parts:

1. The *offer*, wherein one person (called a *party*) makes a proposition ("I would like you to move to Santa Fe, New

Mexico, to care for my mother who has Alzheimer's disease")

2. An *acceptance*, whereby the other party agrees to the proposition ("I shall indeed move to Santa Fe, New Mexico, to care for your mother who has Alzheimer's disease")

3. The *consideration*, which is the inducement to get the second party to agree to the proposition ("In return for your moving to Santa Fe, New Mexico, to care for my mother who has Alzheimer's disease, I shall pay you $500 a week, buy you a train ticket, and provide you with board and lodge at my place of residence")

Contracts can be both written and spoken. The caregiver of an Alzheimer's patient may become involved in contract disputes arising from either (1) contracts the patient enters into, or (2) contracts the caregiver enters into for the patient's care.

PATIENT CONTRACTS

Sometimes, Alzheimer's patients enter into contracts without realizing what they have done and the legal ramifications of their action. Consider this scenario:

Junji is an Alzheimer's patient. One morning, the phone rings, and before his caregiver, Emiko, can get to it, Junji picks up the receiver. It is a telemarketer pitching a change in telephone companies. Junji, the subscriber of record, agrees to the switch. Two days later, an employee of the telephone company arrives to switch some cables in the telephone box at the back of the house. Emiko, upon learning that Junji had authorized the switch, asks him about it. Junji has no recollection of the telemarketer's call or of his agreement to change telephone service providers. Moreover, Junji asserts that he is quite satisfied with the service provided by the current provider.

What recourse do the patient and/or caregiver have? As we discussed in Chapter 3, when a person who, because of some mental illness or defect such as Alzheimer's disease, is unable to understand the nature and consequences of a contract or to act in a reasonable manner in relation to its terms and the other party should know the person's condition, the contract is *voidable*—not void, but voidable. Hence, Junji or Emiko could simply inform the telephone company that, based on the patient's condition, they have no desire or intention to fulfill the terms of the contract. The providers either could agree to void the contract or could take the matter to court.

If the matter proceeds to court, the situation could become tricky for Junji and Emiko. The law states that if the contract is made on fair terms and the healthy party is unaware of the patient's condition, and if the healthy party has already performed in whole or in part and it would be unjust to void the contract, a court would determine what is fair and grant relief as justice requires. This does not sound too good for Junji and Emiko. After all, it is possible that the court would enforce the contract so that the provider would not suffer loss.

To avoid such outcomes, caregivers must be vigilant. They must keep their charges away from the telephone and monitor all incoming and outgoing mail. One caregiver shared this story and the steps he took to eliminate it:

I noticed that the telephone bill was unusually high one month, and I carefully reviewed each call, checking the numbers called and the times they were made. I noticed several calls to a 999 number, made between midnight and 6 a.m. I began pacing the corridor outside the patient's room after midnight. One night, I thought I heard the patient groaning or moaning. I stepped into the room and found the patient with the telephone receiver in his hand. Quietly, I asked, "What's up? Whom are you speaking to?" The patient did not answer. "Can I listen, too?" I asked. The patient handed over the receiver, and I heard a husky voice on the other end uttering words I will not repeat.

That same night, I took the telephone from the patient's bedroom and began monitoring his use of the telephone, effectively preventing him from ever using the telephone again.

CAREGIVER CONTRACTS

Caregivers sometimes enter into contracts pertaining to their charges' care. Foremost among these are contracts entered into with healthcare providers like physicians, nurses, and attorneys. Caregivers must understand that they have a duty to fulfill their obligations to pay for the services received on their charges' behalf. If they cannot pay, they may seek public assistance or negotiate with the service provider. What they must never do is ignore the attempts of the service providers to collect what is owed them.

Caregivers may also enter into contracts—mostly oral contracts, this time—with nonprofessionals to assist in providing care for their loved ones stricken with Alzheimer's disease. To the extent that these nonprofessionals are paid for their services, these contracts give rise to two duties that you should be aware of:

1. ***The duty to ensure that these nonprofessionals have the legal right to work in the United States.*** Too often, caregivers, seeking the cheapest labor available, employ undocumented immigrants to help care for their loved ones. This violates a law that carries severe penalties. Therefore, instead of encouraging one's cousin's girlfriend from Antigua or Grenada to come to the United States on a visitor's visa and not return home at the end of her "vacation" so that she can care for an Alzheimer's-stricken relative, go through the legal channels and either find a way to legally help her move to the United States to work or hire someone else.

2. ***The duty to ensure that all taxes are paid on the employee's behalf.*** Too often, caregivers pay their nonprofessional helpers "under the table"—that is, with unrecorded cash payments. That, also, is a violation of the law. The caregiver should either deduct from the helper's wages and pay payroll taxes on the helper's behalf, or make it clear to the helper that he or she is an independent contractor who will need to pay his or her own employment taxes upon filing the required tax returns at the end of the tax year.

A NEED FOR DEDICATION

Being an informal caregiver of any sick person is difficult. Being an informal caregiver of an Alzheimer's patient is daunting. Indeed, the caregiving experience can have severe consequences for the caregiver. To add to the burden, providing care has legal consequences. Yet because of the desire to care for a loved one at home as well as the cost of institutionalized care, many family members do become caregivers of a relative who has developed Alzheimer's.

If you are ever *blessed* with the responsibility of caring for an Alzheimer's patient, dedication to the task is essential. Notwithstanding the difficulties of the caregiving experience, only your dedication will allow you to care for the patient and protect you from developing depression or some other condition that would render you useless to yourself and to the patient. I wish you well.

NOTES

1. See National Institute on Aging, *Alzheimer's Disease: Unraveling the Mystery* (Bethesda, Md.: Department of Health and Human Services, 2003).

2. See Alzheimer's Association website, www.alz.org (last visited November 26, 2007).

3. Richard Schulz and Scott R. Beach, "Caregiving as a Risk Factor for Mortality—The Caregiver Health Effects Study," *Journal of the American Medical Association*, Volume 282, 1999.

4. Todd E. Feinberg and Winnie Yu, *What to Do When the Doctor Says It's Early-Stage Alzheimer's: All the Medical, Lifestyle, and Alternative Medicine Information You Need to Stay Healthy and Prevent Progression* (Gloucester, Mass.: Fair Winds Press, 2005, ISBN: 978-1-59233-161-1). Reprinted with permission.

5. Family Caregiver Alliance website, www.caregiver.org (last visited May 11, 2008). Adapted with permission of Family Caregiver Alliance. For more information, visit www.caregiver.org or call (415) 434-3388.

6. Ibid.

CHAPTER 11

THE FUTURE: IS THERE
ANY HOPE?

THE FINAL STRAW

*L*ast Thursday was a rough day. I had just sat down at
my desk at the law school when the phone rang. "Good
morning, this is Professor James," I said.

"Good morning," a voice I did not recognize responded.
"Professor, this is Dr. Soriano calling from New York."

"Yes, doctor," I said.

"It's about your brother, Viktor," the doctor stated.

Viktor, one of my older brothers. Forty-six years old. Just
ahead of me on the list of James children. Why would a doctor
be calling me about Viktor? The doctor continued, "Viktor has
given me permission to speak to you about his condition."

"Condition?" I asked, wondering what on earth was wrong
with Viktor. The last time I'd seen him, he was acting kind of
slow, but then, Viktor had always been slow. I did not think
anything of it.

"Yes," Dr. Soriano continued, "Viktor is very sick. I can say
with 95 percent certainty that he has Alzheimer's disease."

The receiver fell from my hand. I sank deep into my chair.
First, Grandpa, then Aunty Arlette, Aunty Dail, Uncle Andy,
and now Viktor? This was the last straw. Viktor was so young!
Only forty-six years old! I recalled reading that people with a
family history of Alzheimer's were prone to suffer from early-
onset Alzheimer's. Who would be next? (I admit it crossed my
mind that I was next oldest!) Who would care for Viktor? He
lived alone, had no wife, no children. What would become of
Victor? If our mother or some other family member decided to
become Viktor's caregiver, what would he or she face? Finally,
I asked myself, was there any hope—for Viktor, for the rest of
the family, and for whoever would become his caregiver?

This was truly the last straw.

By now, you may be thinking, "This book is bleak. Alzheimer's
disease sounds terrible. What's worse, I might develop it before
I die." I wish I could say, "Don't worry about it. Chances are
you will never develop Alzheimer's."

But I cannot do that. The truth is you may well develop Alzheimer's disease before you die. Scientists project that unless
they find ways to prevent or treat the disease, by 2050, some
13.2 million Americans will have Alzheimer's disease. Over the
coming years, as the population ages, the number of older people
with the disease will grow dramatically. By 2050, the incidence
of Alzheimer's globally will quadruple to more than 106 million,
meaning that one in eighty-five persons worldwide will be living
with the disease. This increase will be most dramatic among peo-

ple age 85 or older; by 2050, 8 million people in that age group may have the disease. Forty-three percent of the people stricken with the disease will require a high level of care equivalent to that of a nursing home.[1] Surely, if society is to head off these very high rates of Alzheimer's disease in the future, something needs to be done now—today!

THE OUTLOOK FOR TREATING ALZHEIMER'S DISEASE

Scientists have been hard at work trying to find a cure for Alzheimer's disease. They have yet to find a definitive cure for the disease, but all hope is not lost.

MEDICATIONS FOR TREATING ALZHEIMER'S

Currently, doctors are using a number of drugs to slow down the symptoms of Alzheimer's disease: Aricept, Exelon, Razadyne (formerly Reminyl), Namenda, and Cognex.

ARICEPT

As this book goes to press, Aricept is the most widely used drug for treating Alzheimer's. The drug contains a substance called an inhibitor, which stops the breakdown of acetylcholine, a chemical in the brain used for memory and other mental functions. In a person who has developed Alzheimer's disease, there is a deficiency of acetylcholine in some areas of the brain, which accounts for some of the symptoms of the disease.

Aricept is the only drug approved by the Food and Drug Administration (FDA) for treating mild, moderate, and severe Alzheimer's. While Aricept does not cure the disease, it can improve mental function in some patients. Side effects, which are usually mild, include diarrhea, vomiting, nausea, fatigue, insomnia, and weight loss.

EXELON AND RAZADYNE

Exelon (which is given in the form of a patch) and Razadyne (formerly called Reminyl) are newer drugs that also work by inhibiting the breakdown of acetylcholine. The drugs are most effective when they are given to the patient during the earlier stages of the disease. Their side effects are similar to Aricept's. (Note that in one study, Razadyne was linked to heart attack and stroke.)[2]

NAMENDA

Namenda, which is used to treat moderate to severe Alzheimer's disease, works differently than other Alzheimer's drugs. It apparently regulates a chemical called glutamate, which acts as a kind of "gatekeeper" of some of the brain's other chemicals, such as calcium, which the brain requires for information storage. Glutamate allows these chemicals to enter the brain's nerve cells. Glutamate plays a role in learning and memory. Because the Alzheimer's-diseased brain pushes away too much glutamate, Namenda is prescribed to help regulate glutamate activity. That, in turn, can improve the brain's ability to process information and retrieve memories.

Namenda is the first drug approved by the FDA for treating more severe Alzheimer's. It may be especially beneficial when used with one of the other Alzheimer's drugs, such as Aricept, Exelon, Razadyne, or Cognex. Side effects include tiredness, dizziness, confusion, and headache.

COGNEX

Like Aricept, Cognex is an inhibitor that works by slowing the breakdown of acetylcholine. Nausea, vomiting, diarrhea, abdominal pain, skin rash, and indigestion are among the side effects. In addition, Cognex may also cause liver damage.

THE CURRENT STATE OF
PRESCRIPTION DRUG TREATMENT

Of the prescription drugs we have discussed, the FDA has approved Aricept to treat all stages of Alzheimer's disease: mild, moderate, and severe. Exelon, Razadyne, and Cognex are used for people in the mild or moderate stages of the disease, while Namenda is prescribed for patients with moderate to severe Alzheimer's. The American Academy of Neurology has also stated that Vitamin E supplements may delay the worsening of the disease.

New research findings are giving reason for hope. Several drugs are being studied in clinical trials to determine whether they can slow the progress of the disease and its symptoms or improve memory.

THE FUTURE: AN ALZHEIMER'S VACCINE

Scientists are also working hard to develop a vaccine that would blunt or even prevent Alzheimer's disease. In November 2007, scientists at the Oklahoma Medical Research Foundation reported that they had immunized mice with a protein believed to play a key role in slowing down the disease's progression. According to the scientists, the mice that received the vaccination had a significant reduction in the build-up of certain protein plaques that, when present in the brain for long periods, are believed to cause certain conditions seen in Alzheimer's disease, such as cell death, memory loss, and neurological dysfunction. The mice also did better cognitively than mice that did not receive the vaccine.

Although pleased with the results, Jordan Tang, Ph.D., the researcher who led the study, emphasizes that the vaccine approach should be viewed as a supplement to—rather than a substitute for—the inhibitors and other treatments currently being used and developed for the treatment of Alzheimer's. According to Dr. Tang, the next step will be to progress the work to the point that it can be tested on humans.[3]

POSSIBLE PREVENTIVE MEASURES:
LIFESTYLE CHANGES

Some scientists are now reporting that some simple lifestyle changes may delay or prevent the development of Alzheimer's disease. According to these scientists, a diet rich in fish, omega-3 oils, fruits, and vegetables may lower the risk of developing the disease.

Meanwhile, some medical practitioners are advising people to take steps to maintain their mental health. According to William Theis, Ph.D., vice president of medical and scientific affairs at the Alzheimer's Association, "The best thing people can do is to try to plan for their later years and try to remain as functional as possible." Dr. Theis advises people to "stay connected to the world, because . . . social isolation is a contributor to unhealthy aging."[4]

Steven Ferris, Ph.D., director of the New York University Alzheimer's Disease Center, makes the following three recommendations:

1. Stay mentally active. As Ferris says: "The more you challenge the brain, the more you'll be able to maintain it. When you're stimulating the brain, you're growing more interconnections and maybe even growing more neurons. The more brain cells and connections you have, the longer you'll be able to function well, even if you get Alzheimer's."

2. Stay physically active. Physical exercise improves brain function as well as benefiting the rest of the body.

3. Eat a healthy diet and stay in good physical health, which are both extremely important in maintaining good brain function.[5]

THE FUTURE: OUTLOOK FOR THE CAREGIVERS

In Chapter 10, we looked at ways caregivers can care for themselves even as they provide care and comfort for their loved ones who have developed Alzheimer's. In addition, caregivers face myriad other issues including dealing with the diagnosis and maintaining the safety of the person with Alzheimer's. This section explores these two issues and offers some ideas on preparing for and coping with them.[6] Other issues of concern to the caregiver regarding the Alzheimer's patient are also discussed.

DEALING WITH THE DIAGNOSIS

The first thing you as the caregiver have to do is deal with the diagnosis. This is not the time for denial. If the disease has already struck, there is no turning back. Hence, you have to simply face the facts and deal with the disease. To begin, you should:

- Ask the doctor any questions you may have about the disease, and find out what treatments might work best to lighten the patient's symptoms or help him—and you—cope with his behavior problems.

- Call a family meeting to discuss the diagnosis and its implications with as many other family members as possible. If feasible, arrange for a conference call so that those family members who are unable to attend the meeting in person may do so by phone. It is important, also, that the newly diagnosed patient be involved in the meeting in order to participate in the planning of his or her life.

- Contact organizations such as the Alzheimer's Association and the Alzheimer's Disease Education and Referral (ADEAR) Center for more information about the disease, treatment options, and caregiving resources. In addition, some community groups may offer classes to teach caregiving, problem-solving, and management skills. You should take advantage of these opportunities.

- Find and join a support group where you can share your

feelings and concerns. Members of these support groups are themselves caring for Alzheimer's patients and, based on their own experiences, often have helpful ideas or know of useful resources. In these days of advanced technology, online support groups are also a good option; they make it possible for you to receive support without even leaving home.

- Develop a routine that makes things go smoothly. If the Alzheimer's patient is less confused or more cooperative at a particular time of day, plan your routine with this time in mind. You should also know that the way the person functions may change from day to day, and you should try to be flexible, ready to amend your daily routine as needed.

- Although your loved one has just been diagnosed with Alzheimer's it is not too early to begin planning for the future. Get financial and legal documents in order, investigate long-term care options and costs, and determine what services are covered by health insurance and Medicare (if the patient is eligible).

- Begin researching adult day care or respite services. As your caregiving role becomes more demanding, these services will allow you to have a break knowing that the patient is being well cared for.

MAINTAINING THE PATIENT'S SAFETY

HOME SAFETY

In many ways, caring for an Alzheimer's patient is like caring for an infant or a toddler: The home must be made "Alzheimer's-patient safe." To achieve this goal, you should:

- Examine all locks in the home and install secure locks on all outside windows and doors. This will prevent the Alzheimer's patient from wandering (some Alzheimer's patients are prone to wander). You should also remove locks on bathroom and bedroom doors to prevent the patient from accidentally locking him- or herself in.

- Use childproof latches on any cabinets and other places where you keep cleaning supplies or other chemicals.

- Label all medications—whether for you, the Alzheimer's patient, or anyone else living in the home—and keep them locked. You should also put all knives, lighters and matches, and guns in a secure and out-of-reach place.

- Maintain a clutter-free house. To minimize the chances that the patient might fall and injure himself, you should remove scatter rugs and anything else that might be slippery. Also, you should ensure that lighting is good both inside and outside the house.

- Because the patient might forget to turn off the stove after cooking, install an automatic shut-off switch on it—and thus prevent burns or fire.

PROTECTION AGAINST AND PREPARATION FOR WANDERING

To be successful in caring for a loved one who has developed Alzheimer's, you must be prepared to keep that person safe at all times. Unfortunately, some people with Alzheimer's disease have the tendency to wander away from their home or their caregiver. Some steps to limit or eliminate wandering include the following:

- Make sure that the Alzheimer's patient carries some kind of identification or wears a medical bracelet (similar to those worn by heart patients, diabetics, and others). If the person gets lost or is unable to communicate adequately, the identification card or bracelet will alert others as to her identity, address, and medical condition.

- Keep a recent photograph or videotape of the patient so that if she gets lost, the police will know what she looks like and who they are looking for.

- Keep doors locked. In addition to any locks already installed on the doors, install a keyed deadbolt or an additional lock up high on the door where it is difficult—impossible, even—for the patient to reach it.

OTHER ISSUES OF CONCERN

DRIVING

As previously stated, the time will come when you and the rest of the family must take away the patient's driving privileges. This is a difficult decision to make and even harder to implement. It must be communicated carefully and sensitively. Even though the patient may be upset about her loss of independence, safety (and aversion of tort liability) must be your priority. You should:

- Look for clues—such as getting lost in familiar places, driving too slow or too fast, disregarding traffic signs, or getting angry or confused—that the person can no longer drive safely.

- Be sensitive to the patient's feelings about losing the ability to drive, but be firm in requesting that he no longer drive. You should also be consistent and should not allow the person to drive on "good days" but forbid it on "bad days." "No more driving" means just that—no more driving!

- Ask the doctor to help. While the patient may not accept your request not to drive, she may regard the doctor as an authority figure and may be willing to stop driving upon the doctor's request or mere "suggestion."

- If necessary, take the car keys. If just having keys is important to the patient, you can give him a different set of keys (but of course, a set that does not start or fit any of the cars in the garage or driveway).

- If all else fails, disable the car or move it to a location where the patient does not have access to it.

ACTIVITIES

Caring for an Alzheimer's patient can be boring. What does the patient—and you—do all day? Sure, by the time the patient enters Stage III of the disease, he or she will not be able to do anything other than lie in bed or sit in a chair. Until that time, though, you will expend much time and energy trying to come up with some activities the patient can engage in and is interested in doing. The following tips may help:

- Do not expect too much. Simple activities are often best. Crossword puzzles, board games, and sing-alongs can be beneficial for both you and your charge.

- Be prepared to help the patient start the activity. Also, praise the person as he completes each step of the activity.

- Watch for signs that the person is becoming agitated or frustrated with the activity. If this happens, help or distract the patient to do something else.

- Include activities the patient seems to enjoy in the daily routine and try to do them at the same time each day.

- Take advantage of adult day care services. These provide various activities for Alzheimer's patients and gives you an opportunity to gain temporary relief from your caregiving responsibilities. Adult day care services often provide transportation and meals for the patients. Accordingly, you can be assured that your loved one is being well taken care of.

INCONTINENCE

As the disease progresses, many Alzheimer's patients begin to experience incontinence—that is, they lose the ability to control their bladder and/or bowels. Incontinence can be upsetting for the patient and difficult for you. You should:

- Develop a routine for taking the patient to the bathroom and stick to it as closely as possible. You may, for example, take the person to the bathroom every three hours. Do not wait for the patient to ask to go or be taken to the bathroom.

- Watch for signs that the patient may have to go to the bathroom. The patient may become restless or may begin pulling at her clothes. If you see these signs, respond quickly and take the person to the bathroom.

- Be understanding when accidents occur, as they most likely will. Stay calm and reassure the patient if he is upset. Keep track of when these accidents happen and, if possible, plan ways to avoid them.

- Help prevent nighttime accidents by limiting certain types of fluids, such as those with caffeine, the patient ingests in the evening.

- Plan ahead. Before going out with the patient, find out where the restrooms are located, and have the patient wear simple, easy-to-remove clothing. Also, take along an extra set of clothing in case the patient has an accident.

- Stock up on incontinence products ("adult diapers") that the person may use as underclothing.

SLEEP PROBLEMS

As we have already seen, taking care of an Alzheimer's patient is hard work—*very* hard work! By the time bedtime rolls around, many caregivers can hardly wait to get into bed, and sleep cannot come too soon. However, for many people with Alzheimer's disease, nighttime is a difficult time. The patient finds it difficult to sleep, or he may be restless and agitated. If you are the caregiver of such a person, you must do some advance planning in order to get the patient to go to bed and stay there.

- As bedtime arrives, set a quiet, peaceful tone to encourage sleep. Keep the lights dim, eliminate loud noises, and play soothing music if the patient seems to enjoy it.

- Try to keep bedtime at a similar time each evening.

- Encourage the patient to exercise during the day, and limit daytime napping. However, do not eliminate daytime napping. Alzheimer's patients tend to nap during the day. If you eliminate these naps, the patient will be fatigued and may become restless and unable to sleep at night.

- Restrict the patient's access to caffeine late in the day.

- If you notice that the patient finds darkness frightening and disorienting, use nightlights in the bedroom, hall, and bathroom.

HALLUCINATIONS AND DELUSIONS

As Alzheimer's disease progresses, the patient may experience hallucinations and/or delusions. When someone hallucinates, he sees, hears, smells, tastes, or feels something that is not there. Delusions are false—often irrational—beliefs that the person holds and will not let go of.

To care for the patient properly and to maintain his or her own sanity and well-being, you must be able to deal with these hallucinations and delusions. The following suggestions may help:

- Recognize that hallucinations and delusions are sometimes signs of physical illness. You should keep track of what the Alzheimer's patient is experiencing and discuss it with her doctor.
- Avoid arguing with the patient about what she sees or hears. Instead, try to respond to the feelings the patient is expressing, and provide reassurance and comfort.
- Try to distract the person to another topic or activity. It might help to move the person to another room or to take him outside for a walk.
- Turn off the television when violent or disturbing programs are on. Note that the Alzheimer's patient may not be able to distinguish television programs from reality.
- Ensure that the patient is safe and does not have access to anything he could use to harm anyone.

VISITING THE DOCTOR

Although there is no cure for Alzheimer's disease, it is important that the Alzheimer's patient receive regular medical care. However, the trips to the doctor's office can be trying for both the patient and you. Fortunately, with advance planning, the trip could go relatively smoothly. With this in mind, you should:

- Try to schedule the doctor's appointment for the time of day when the patient is lucid and at his best. In addition, find out what time of day the office is least crowded, and make the appointment for that time.

- Let the office staff know in advance that the patient is suffering from Alzheimer's and may be confused. They might be able to do something to make the visit go smoothly; you should not hesitate to ask for such help.

- Do not tell the patient about the appointment until the day of the visit or even shortly before it is time to leave home for the doctor's office.

- Bring along something for the patient to eat and drink and something that he may enjoy doing while waiting.

- Have a friend or another family member accompany you and the patient on the visit. That person can be with the patient while you speak with the doctor.

CHOOSING A NURSING HOME

Many caregivers come to a point in time when they are no longer able to care for the Alzheimer's patient at home. Should that time come for you, you will have to choose a residential care facility—a nursing home or an assisted care facility—to which your loved one must relocate. Keep in mind that the patient is someone near and dear to you—a spouse, parent, sibling, child, or close friend, for example—and that moving the person to a residential facility is a big decision. The following tips should be helpful in the decision-making process:

- Gather information about residential care facilities, the services they provide, cost, and options for payment before you actually need to transfer the patient to such a facility. This gives you time to explore fully all the possibilities before making a decision.

- Seek information about facilities in the immediate area. Doctors, friends and relatives, hospital social workers, and religious organizations may be able to help you identify specific facilities.

- Make a list of questions to ask the facility's staff. You should think of things that are important to you, such as activity programs, transportation, or special units for people with Alzheimer's disease, and be prepared to ask about these.

- Contact the places that interest you and make an appointment to visit. On that visit, you should talk to the facility's administration, nursing staff, residents, and relatives of residents.

- Observe the way the facility runs and how the staff treats the residents. It is a good idea after your initial visit to drop by the facility unannounced to see if your initial impressions are the same.

- Find out what kinds of programs and services the facility offers for people with Alzheimer's disease and their families. You should ask about staff training in dementia care and check to see what policies the facility has about family participation in planning patient care.

- When you have narrowed your options down to two or three facilities, check on room availability at each, cost and method of payment, and participation in Medicare or Medicaid. You may want to place your name on a waiting list even if you are not ready to make an immediate decision about long-term care or may end up placing your loved one in a different facility.

- Once you have made a decision, you should be sure that you understand the terms of the contract and financial agreement. You should have a lawyer review the documents before you sign them.

- Recognize that moving is a big change for both you and your loved one. A social worker may be able to help you plan for and adjust to the move. In addition, it is important that you have support during this difficult transition.

WHAT DOES THE FUTURE HOLD FOR THE PROFESSIONALS?

The increased prevalence of Alzheimer's disease over the years will be very costly to society. These costs will be a result not only of medical treatment and institutionalization but also of lost income for both Alzheimer's patients and their at-home caregivers. Current annual estimates for caring for an Alzheimer's patient (not including costs of morbidity, premature death, and lost employment income) range from $38,000 to $47,000. The majority of these costs will go toward medical care and institutionalization of the patient.

THE IMPACT ON MEDICAL PROFESSIONALS

The large sums of money that will be spent on medical care and institutionalization of Alzheimer's patients over the next several years is an indication of the amount and type of health services Alzheimer's patients will need in the future. Although informal caregivers (that is, family members and friends) will care for many Alzheimer's patients, many more will be institutionalized in assisted living facilities and nursing homes. To meet this growing demand, society will have to build and staff more of these facilities. Meanwhile, say some researchers, the provision of health services will change somewhat over the years, with the development of new forms of outpatient services for Alzheimer's patients, such as disease-specific clinics and centers.[7] The medical profession has already increased its focus on gerontology and geriatrics to meet the demands of the ever increasing elderly population; going forward, the profession will focus more on providing services for people stricken with Alzheimer's disease.

As a result, society and the medical profession will experience a need for more doctors, psychiatrists, psychologists, and other medical personnel, as well as more nursing home operators and staff. Even now, society needs to invest in encouraging college-age students to enter these fields. This need is quite urgent, for over the coming years, not only will more consumers be in need of these services, but as current providers themselves develop Alzheimer's disease and other forms of dementia, a void will exist that will need to be filled.

THE IMPACT ON THE LEGAL PROFESSION

Over the past few years, the law has developed a specialty known as elder law. Bar associations have elder law sections, and law schools have developed elder law courses. The practice of elder law currently encompasses a mixture of other legal practices such as estate planning, property management, healthcare planning, and public benefits. The typical elder law practice goes beyond traditional legal issues and also provides advice, referral, or direct assistance in addressing the problems of the elderly and securing health and social services for them. Elder law practitioners often work closely with other professionals such as social workers and healthcare providers.

With the predicted prevalence of Alzheimer's disease in society, elder law attorneys will have to incorporate the legal issues related to Alzheimer's into their practices. These issues are not necessarily new—they are mainly the same issues elder law attorneys have already been facing—but they will now be more focused. In addition, the need for these services will increase dramatically over the coming years. Finally, as with the medical practitioners who will have to leave their professions because they have themselves developed Alzheimer's, legal practitioners will face the same plight with many practicing lawyers becoming afflicted with the disease.

A NEED FOR HIGHLY SPECIALIZED PRACTITIONERS

With the projected increases in the incidence of Alzheimer's disease, a need will exist for highly specialized medical and legal practitioners with expertise in providing services to Alzheimer's patients. Law schools, medical schools, and nursing schools need to develop specialty programs in equipping their graduates to serve clients and patients with Alzheimer's and other forms of dementia. These institutions must not wait for the crisis to hit before they act. They must begin the process now.

NOTES

1. Ron Brookmeyer, Elizabeth Johnson, Kathryn Ziegler-Graham, and H. Michael Arrighi, "Forecasting the Global Burden of Alzheimer's Disease," Johns Hopkins University, Department of Biostatistics Working Papers, January 2007.

2. See WebMD, "Alzheimer's Disease Treatment and Medicines," www.webmd.com/alzheimers/guide/treatment-overview (last visited November 12, 2007).

3. "New Alzheimer's Vaccine Study," Science and Medical News Update, www.ahafinfo.org/NewsUpdates/AHAF/ShowNewsUpdate .asp?NewsID = 3247 98&page = 38strProgram = ADR (last visited November 12, 2007).

4. Quoted in Linda Bren, "Alzheimer's: Searching for a Cure," *FDA Consumer*, www.fda.gov/fdac/features/2003/403_alz.html (last visited November 12, 2007).

5. Ibid.

6. These ideas are mostly taken from the National Institute on Aging, *Alzheimer's Disease: Caregiver Guide*, available at the National Institute on Aging website, www.nia.nih.gov/Alzheimers/Publica tions/caregiverguide.htm (last visited May 11, 2008).

7. See Philip D. Sloane, Sheryl Zimmerman, Chirayath Suchindran, Peter Reed, Lily Wang, Malaz Boustani, and S. Sudha, "The Public Health Impact of Alzheimer's Disease, 2000–2050: Potential Implication of Treatment Advances," *Annual Review of Public Health*, May 2002.

CHAPTER 12

WHEN THE DIAGNOSIS IS ALZHEIMER'S, YOU NEED A LAWYER! THE SEARCH

*M*y family was in crisis. Thus far, we had five family members exhibiting Alzheimer's-like symptoms: Grandpa, Aunty Arlette, Aunty Dail, Uncle Andy, and Viktor. With Uncle Andy's relocation to the United States several months ago, all were now living in the United States. They were all at different stages of the disease.

Throughout our ordeal, I had served as the family's unpaid attorney, giving advice freely and flying from city to city and state to state to do legal work for the patients, caregivers, and family members. I had sat in on many family conferences and been turned to for advice.

Now I was getting tired. I still had a book to write. My sabbatical would soon be over, and I would return to teaching law five days a week. I still had a family to care for. Vijhay was at college in Atlanta. Etienne was four and demanding more and more of my time. Maelys-Claire would be born any time *now. My wife, Marva, had been a tower of strength throughout my trials, but with Maelys-Claire due to be born in the next two weeks, Marva was understandably occupied with other things. I loved my extended family and loved practicing elder law. I decided to call Francis to explain my predicament and let him know what I intended to do.*

"Hello," I heard him say.

"Cuenka," I responded, calling him by a nickname we've used for him since our high school days. "Que pasa?"

"Cool, Bro," he responded. "What's up?"

I told him my story and concluded with, "All things considered, it is time for us to retain an attorney in the New York area to do the work."

Francis understood. "Have you any friends who could do this?" he asked.

"Listen," I said to Francis, "I have many friends who practice law in New York, and I love them all, but this time I think we should look for someone who practices elder law."

"Elder law?" Francis asked. "What on earth is that?"

Elder law. I began the explanation. . . .

When someone is diagnosed with Alzheimer's disease, he or she (if lucid) and his or her family members rarely consider retaining an attorney. Yet for many reasons, that is just what they should do. As we have already discussed, someone who has developed Alzheimer's disease needs, at the very least, an estate plan and a set of advance directives. The person may also need an advocate to ensure that he or she receives all the public benefits for which he or she is eligible—Medicare, Medicaid, Social Security, and whatever else may be available. The person therefore needs an attorney to draft the necessary documents and to interpret state and federal laws to ensure that the wishes of the patient and his or her family are carried out.

Many people mistakenly believe that they can simply go to the stationery store or go on the Internet and find all the forms they need to prepare legal documents, or that they can simply do the research themselves. However, it is important to remember that laws vary by state, and changes in our life situations (such as divorce, birth or adoption of a child, or relocation to a different state) can influence how documents are prepared and their potential impact. For these reasons, the Stage I Alzheimer's patient and his or her family members should retain a competent attorney to represent the patient's interests. Not only that, but as the patient goes through the different stages of the disease and his or her situation changes, it will be necessary that he or she (and/or family members) review the documents and have the attorney update them as necessary.

We have thus far been focusing on the Alzheimer's patient and his or her need for legal assistance. The patient's family members also need legal assistance. For example, we have already determined that when the patient is mentally incapacitated, it may become necessary for a family member to commence guardianship proceedings in order to care for the patient effectively. This, of course, requires the family member to retain the services of an attorney. Such services would also be needed by the healthy spouse of an Alzheimer's patient who would need advice on how to avoid becoming impoverished while taking care of the patient.

We see, then, that both the Alzheimer's patient and his or her family members need to retain the services of one or more attorneys. Of course, the attorney(s) must be qualified to handle

the special legal needs of the Alzheimer's patient. Ronald Fatoul-
lah, an attorney and a member of the National Academy of Elder
Law Attorneys, expresses this need as follows:

> Once a person has been diagnosed with [Alzheimer's dis-
> ease], we recommend that the person and his or her family
> seek the advice of an elder law attorney–a lawyer qualified
> to handle the special needs of older people–to devise
> plans. For instance, an attorney can help people under-
> stand what Medicare will and will not cover, how to cover
> expenses like long-term care, and the differences between
> skilled and custodial care. An elder law attorney can also
> provide advice to help the well spouse avoid becoming im-
> poverished while trying to care for a loved one.[1]

FINDING A LAWYER

Several resources exist to assist the Alzheimer's patient and his
or her family members in finding a qualified lawyer to represent
their interests. Most state and county bar associations now have
elder law sections consisting of attorneys capable of assisting the
elderly with their legal problems. Some members of these sections are certified as elder law practitioners. The bar associations
are happy to make referrals.

People who for some reason do not trust "local" lawyers or
"local" lawyer associations to help them find a lawyer can turn
to the national bar associations:

American Bar Association
Commission on Law and Aging
740 15th Street, NW

Washington, DC 20005
Phone: 202-662-1000
www.abanet.org/aging

Hispanic National Bar Association
1111 Pennsylvania Avenue, NW
Washington, DC 20004
Phone: 202-223-4777
www.hnba.com

National Bar Association
1225 11th Street, NW
Washington, DC 20001
Phone: 202-842-3900
www.nationalbar.org

Those who want to look beyond the bar associations for a referral have a number of resources available:

AARP
Legal Counsel for the Elderly
601 E Street, NW
Washington, DC 20049
Phone: 888-OUR-AARP (888-687-2277)
www.aarp.org/lce

Alzheimer's Association
225 North Michigan Avenue
Chicago, IL 60601
Phone: 800-272-3900
www.alz.org

Eldercare Locator
U.S. Administration on Aging
Phone: 800-677-1116
www.eldercare.gov

Family Caregiver Alliance
108 Montgomery Street
San Francisco, CA 94104
Phone: 800-445-8106
www.caregiver.org

National Academy of Elder Law Attorneys
1604 North Country Club Road
Tucson, AZ 85716
Phone: 520-881-4005
www.naela.com

It would do well for the patient and/or his or her family members to receive three referrals from whatever resource they choose to use. They should then visit all three prospects; get sufficient information on each attorney's background, experience, and ability to undertake the representation; and then make a decision as to which attorney they will retain.

WHAT TO EXPECT AND WHAT TO ASK

Having found an attorney, the patient and/or his or her family members must ask the right questions and insist on receiving truthful answers. Even before asking questions, though, the patient and family members must be aware of what they should expect from an elder law attorney. The following guideline on the relationship between an attorney and his or her elderly client, promulgated by the American Law Institute–American Bar Association Committee on Continuing Professional Education, is instructive:

> An attorney who specializes in the problems of the elderly is aware of their special needs and issues and, at a minimum, can counsel the client to seek specified, nonlegal assistance from identified sources. The client can reasonably expect the lawyer to assist in arranging services, and the lawyer should expect the client to return for further assistance as circumstances change. . . .
>
> Perhaps the greatest single impediment to a sole practitioner assuming broad responsibility for elderly clients with complex service needs is the necessity of a 24-hour-a-day, on-call system for the firm. Emergencies, particularly medical emergencies, are not restricted to a nine-to-five schedule and can sometimes require a staff member to respond in person. . . .
>
> Even the most conscientious attorney cannot ensure that community services will be delivered flawlessly or will be effective in meeting the client's needs. The limits of the attorney's responsibility should be included in a written agreement executed by the client at the onset.[2]
>
> In essence, then, the Alzheimer's patient and family should expect the attorney they retain to be able to:

- Provide the legal services required.
- Counsel them as necessary.
- Refer them to nonlegal professionals to assist them in nonlegal matters.
- Be available twenty-four hours a day.

At the same time, though, the patient and family members should understand that apart from the issues that come up within the framework of the attorney's representation, they would be presenting the attorney with an ethical dilemma. Let me explain. Pursuant to the ethical code of the legal profession, a lawyer must fulfill for each client the duties of diligent representation, zealous advocacy, and communication that would enable the client to make informed choices. The lawyer must fulfill these duties whether the client is a healthy twenty-five-year-old or a sixty-eight-year-old who has developed Alzheimer's. Moreover, the lawyer's duties are to the client and the client only, and communications between the lawyer and his or her client are privileged and confidential. Absent the client's consent, no one may be privy to discussions between the lawyer and the client.

Alas, when an Alzheimer's patient (or most likely, his or her family members) contacts a lawyer for legal assistance, the lawyer will first have to sort out just who is the client: To whom does he or she owe these duties? Frequently, the Alzheimer's patient's family members are involved in advising, assisting, and even directing financial and practical arrangements for the patient's care and his or her property management. In fact, family members are typically the ones who make the appointment with the attorney, and one or more of them often accompany the patient to the lawyer's office. This companion—son, daughter, niece, nephew, grandchild, or parent—often provides much of the information the lawyer receives about the patient, the patient's property, the proposed estate plan, and the patient's alleged desire to have in place some advance directives. The patient—the subject of the plan and the property owner—may say very little, apparently acquiescing to the arrangements being proposed by his or her family members. Sometimes, the lawyer might doubt that the patient really agrees with what is being proposed. At other times, the situation is further complicated when, some time after the patient and accompanying family member or members have left the lawyer's office, other family members contact the lawyer to question or oppose some aspect of the proposed plan or the involvement of the family member or members who accompanied the patient to the lawyer's office.

On still other occasions, the proposed plan or the requested plan of action, though concerning the patient's property or person, is apparently of more benefit to the family member than to the patient. Consider this situation, which is similar to Aunty Dail's:

Alexandria is in private legal practice in Syracuse, New York. Once a month, she volunteers at the local Legal Aid Society's *pro bono* clinic. Last week, Alexandria received an interesting case. Pamela said she needed a durable power of attorney drawn up for her mother, Alethia, who had developed Alzheimer's disease several years ago. Alethia was now unable to talk, unable to write, and in fact, unable to do much of anything. Meanwhile, the Social Security Administration kept sending Alethia's benefit checks to her address. Unfortunately, Alethia was not able to endorse the checks. Hence, the checks had been piling up in the nightstand drawer as Pamela struggled to pay the bills. Pamela believes that if she is appointed Alethia's agent under a durable power of attorney, she will be able to endorse the Social Security checks and thus have sufficient funds to pay the bills without having to struggle as she currently does.

This scenario is truly heart-wrenching. Alethia, whose Alzheimer's disease has left her mentally incapacitated and unable to write, is not able to execute a durable power of attorney. Not only that, but even if she were able to execute a durable power of attorney, without more information, Alexandria cannot know whether Pamela really wants the power in order to benefit her mother of if she is seeking to benefit herself.

Lawyers representing Alzheimer's patients and their families frequently face issues and questions like these. At an initial conference with a lawyer you are seeking to retain to provide such representation, you should be prepared to be asked such questions and to provide answers—truthful ones, at that. You should also be prepared for the lawyer to choose to represent the patient—and only the patient—in which case the lawyer would explain the limitations this decision would impose on interactions with them. Conversely, the attorney may choose to represent the family, in which case the lawyer would explain the ethical rules concerning conflicts of interest and, in the event such conflicts exist, to have one or more family members sign waivers. In the alternative, in light of these conflicts of interest, the attorney could simply decline the representation.

For their part, both before retaining the attorney and throughout the course of the representation, the patient and family members should ask the attorney questions. After all, the lawyer is working for them. Initially, the questions should be phrased to determine the attorney's capability to present the required services:

- *The lawyer's training in elder law and in representing clients with Alzheimer's disease and their family members.* Note that the emphasis is not so much on the lawyer's experience in these matters. Elder law is still a relatively new specialty within the law. Many of today's lawyers never took a course in elder law while in law school. Currently, at law schools where elder law is offered as a course, enrollment is limited. Thus, many lawyers who wish to practice elder law have actually been trained in estate planning and other aspects of the law. Several have developed their elder law skills by taking Continuing Legal Education courses after they graduated from law school. In any event, by asking questions about the lawyer's training, the Alzheimer's patient and family members can determine whether the lawyer is capable of providing the required services.

- *The lawyer's ability to network with nonlawyers in providing services for the patient.*

- *The lawyer's availability for providing counseling and assistance outside office hours.*

- *The lawyer's experience, if any, with Alzheimer's disease or another form of dementia.* People who have experienced Alzheimer's firsthand—say, in a family member—are more understanding of the disease in others. They have seen the effects of the disease and, if the person is a lawyer, has most likely had to prepare legal documents and file court papers on behalf of the relative who has or had the disease. They are therefore more empathetic toward the patient and his or her family members. Although this is not an absolute requirement in the choosing of an attorney, it would be advantageous for the patient and family to retain an attorney who "has been there" and witnessed the ravages of Alzheimer's disease up close.

Last, but not least, you also must ask about the lawyer's fees.

THE COST OF LEGAL ASSISTANCE

Legal services are expensive. While the dollar amount charged by a lawyer varies based on location, when the cost of living and cost of other services in each particular location are considered, legal services rank among some of the most expensive services. Hence, when someone retains the services of an attorney, he or she should be prepared to pay a relatively high—but reasonable—fee. While lawyers' fees are not regulated by any federal or state agencies, the market serves as a dampener on some lawyers asking fees that are too much in excess of what their colleagues are asking. The result is that in any given locality, lawyers' fees for elder law services will be relatively even within the profession.

That said, as part of the process whereby someone retains the services of an attorney, the attorney would ask the client to sign a retainer agreement. This agreement sets forth the terms of the representation, ways in which the attorney-client relationship may be terminated, and the attorney's fees and how they will be billed and paid. The agreement will typically require the client to deposit a retainer fee with the lawyer. This is usually equal to ten hours' worth of fees. As the attorney provides services for the client, he or she will reduce the retainer in payment of the bill. The retainer agreement specifies an amount at which the client will be required to replenish the account. Whenever the attorney-client relationship is terminated—whether at the death of the client or for some other reason—the attorney will return any unused portion of the retainer to the client or his or her estate or representative.

WHEN FUNDS ARE UNAVAILABLE

Alzheimer's disease does not discriminate. It strikes people like former President Ronald Reagan and John O'Connor, husband of former Supreme Court Justice Sandra Day O'Connor, as well as it strikes some of the nuns taking part in the study discussed in Chapter 1. In all likelihood, patients and their family members from low-income groups cannot afford the services of private lawyers. What, then, can they do?

First, they can engage in a little self-help. As soon as possible after the person is diagnosed with Alzheimer's, he or she should prepare a handwritten last will and testament. While a patient who is able to afford a private lawyer will most likely have the holograph converted into a formal will, for the low-income patient, this might be his or her only chance to prepare a will.

Second, there are several sources of legal assistance available for low-income patients and their families. State, county, and citywide legal aid societies offer free services to low-income persons. Several law schools run civil clinics, estate-planning clinics, and wills clinics to give free services to low-income persons while their students gain experience. In addition, some local nonprofit agencies, foundations, and social service organizations provide umbrella services that provide referrals to organizations that offer reduced-fee or free legal services to low-income persons.

Finally, many attorneys offer their services free to low-income persons (this is known as *pro bono* service). Indeed, national, state, county, and local bar associations have responded to the needs of low-income persons in providing free legal services to them. Most state bars maintain referral panels of attorneys who volunteer to provide free and discounted legal assistance to low-income and elderly clients. In Florida, for example, panels are available for low-income and elderly individuals who receive an initial consultation for little or no fee. If the client then needs more complex legal assistance, he or she negotiates a reduced fee with the attorney. Meanwhile, many state bar associations have elder law committees that typically provide public information through pamphlets and talks to civic groups.

There are, of course, drawbacks to *pro bono* services. Two drawbacks, in particular, deserve attention here. First, there are never enough lawyers volunteering for *pro bono* service. Accordingly, those who do volunteer end up with heavy *pro bono* caseloads at the same time as they are either in private practice with a full load of paying clients or are law professors with their class loads and research projects. When choices have to be made between the obligations to paying clients or the law school and the client receiving *pro bono* services, the latter is not first in line.

Second is the question of the quality of service provided. Volunteer and reduced-fee attorneys are often still building their practices. Even when experienced attorneys volunteer to assist the elderly and those stricken with Alzheimer's disease, they may be very inexperienced in serving the particular needs of these patients. In the absence of experienced advisors to assist these volunteer attorneys, the result may be delay and less than optimum solutions for the client.

All things considered, though, legal services are available to each Alzheimer's patient and to that patient's family members. If someone does develop Alzheimer's disease, it is advisable that he or she (if still in control of his or her mental faculties) or his or her family members consult with and retain an attorney as soon as possible.

LEGAL ASSISTANCE AND THE CAREGIVER

We have thus far looked at the need for the Alzheimer's patient and his or her family members to retain the services of an attorney on behalf of the patient. But what about the informal caregiver—the spouse, son, daughter, sibling, or other family member who must for the next several years make a full-time commitment to caring for the patient? Does he or she need to retain an attorney also?

The answer is an unequivocal "yes," although the attorney's role will be different from the role of the one representing the patient. In Chapters 7 and 10, we discussed the legal liability of caregivers of Alzheimer's patients for torts committed by these patients as well as some issues in the area of contract law. For these reasons, it is advisable that you retain the services of an attorney to guide you in your relations with the patient and third parties. The attorney-client relationship here need not be a full-time one. What you really need is someone you can turn to for advice on tort or contract law in the jurisdiction where you live, and someone you can call or meet with for advice when you need guidance on whether a certain course of action—such as letting the patient drive his or her car to church services—would be wise. The retention of this attorney should not prove to be costly and would give you some peace of mind as you go about the task of caregiving.

SOME CLOSING THOUGHTS

Alzheimer's disease is the world's next big health issue. Scientists are yet to demonstrate that anyone can prevent the development of Alzheimer's disease. Moreover, because Alzheimer's disease robs the patient of his or her cognitive abilities, long before the patient's death, he or she will be unable to make decisions, direct business affairs, or recognize loved ones. Thus, for a few years before the Alzheimer's patient dies, the person will be completely dependent on others.

It is for these reasons that the Alzheimer's patient needs legal assistance. It is for these reasons that the family members of the Alzheimer's patient need legal assistance. It is for these reasons that the Alzheimer's patient—if lucid and in possession of his or her mental faculties—and his or her family members and close friends, as well as members of the general public who are not yet exhibiting any symptoms of the disease, need to understand the legal implications of Alzheimer's disease.

NOTES

1. "Legal and Financial Planning for the AD Patient: How the Health Care Team Can Help," *Connections*, Volume 15, 2007.
2. Alison P. Barnes, Lawrence A. Frolik, and Robert Whitman, *Counseling Older Clients* (ALI/ABA, 1997).

EPILOGUE

One week before Thanksgiving 2007. I have finally finished writing the book. Over the past thirteen months, I have spent most of my time researching and writing. I have traveled many miles, met many people who either have Alzheimer's disease or are family members or close friends of persons with the disease. I have been told many true stories about people who have the disease—sometimes funny stories, sometimes not, but always sad. I have attended the funeral of one of my uncles who died from pneumonia after suffering from Alzheimer's for several years, and I have seen other family members either develop the disease full-blown or begin exhibiting Alzheimer's-like symptoms. The disease has struck, not very close to home, but right at home.

It has been an exhausting thirteen months. Now it's over. The story has been told. One week from tonight, we'll celebrate Thanksgiving. I'll sit at the table with my family (minus our eighteen-year-old, who is at college and will not be coming home for the holiday) and we'll have Thanksgiving dinner. We'll thank God for His mighty and many blessings, pray for our loved ones who have Alzheimer's or Alzheimer's-like symptoms, and pray that should we develop the disease, we will be ready because we followed the advice in *The Alzheimer's Advisor* seriously and thus made all the preparations we'd need to minimize the stress on our loved ones and caregivers. We might shed tears as we reflect.

For now, though, my discourse is over.

FOR FURTHER READING

BOOKS

Boyer, Kim, and Mary Shapiro. *Alzheimer's and Dementia: A Practical and Legal Guide for Nevada Caregivers*. Reno: University of Nevada Press, 2006.

Castleman, Michael, Dolores Gallagher-Thompson, and Matthew Naythons. *There's Still a Person in There: The Complete Guide to Treating and Coping with Alzheimer's*. New York: Putnam Publishing Group, 2000.

Feinberg, Todd E., and Winnie Yu. *What to Do When the Doctor Says It's Early Stage Alzheimer's: All the Medical, Lifestyle, and Alternative Medicine Information You Need to Stay Healthy and Prevent Progression*. Gloucester, Mass.: Fair Winds Press, 2005.

Frolik, Lawrence A., and Alison McChrystal Barnes. *Elder Law: Cases and Materials* (4th ed.). Newark, N.J.: LexisNexis, 2007.

Frolik, Lawrence A., and Richard L. Kaplan. *Elder Law in a Nutshell* (4th ed.). St. Paul, Minn.: Thomson/West, 2006.

Hughes, Julian C., and Clive Baldwin. *Ethical Issues in Dementia Care: Making Difficult Decisions*. London, England, and Philadelphia, Penn.: Jessica Kingsley Publishers, 2006.

Kapp, Marshall B. *Key Words in Ethics, Law, and Aging: A Guide to Contemporary Usage*. New York: Springer, 1995.

Kapp, Marshall B. *Lessons in Law and Aging: A Tool for Educators and Students*. New York: Springer, 2001.

Kapp, Marshall B. *The Law and Older Persons—Is Geriatric Jurisprudence Therapeutic?* Durham, N.C.: Carolina Academic Press, 2003.

Lee, Jeanne L. *Just Love Me: My Life Turned Upside Down by Alzheimer's.* Purdue, Ind.: Purdue University Press, 2003.

Mace, Nancy L., and Peter V. Rabins. *The 36-Hour Day: A Family Guide to Caring for Persons with Alzheimer Disease, Related Dementing Illnesses, and Memory Loss in Later Life.* Baltimore, Md.: Johns Hopkins University Press, 1999.

Premack, Paul. *The Senior Texan Legal Guide.* San Antonio, Tex.: Longview Publishing, 2001.

Pruchno, Rachel A., and Michael A. Smyer, eds. *Challenges of an Aging Society: Ethical Dilemmas, Political Issues.* Baltimore, Md.: Johns Hopkins University Press, 2007.

ARTICLES

Appelbaum, Paul S., and Thomas Grisso. "Assessing Patients' Capacities to Consent to Treatment." *New England Journal of Medicine,* Vol. 319 (1988).

Cooney, Leo M., Jr., and John M. Keyes. "The Capacity to Decide to Remain Living in the Community." *Ethics, Law, and Aging Review,* Vol. 10 (Marshall B. Kapp, ed., 2004).

Kapp, Marshall B. "Legal Standards for the Medical Diagnosis and Treatment of Dementia." *Journal of Legal Medicine,* Vol. 23 (2002).

Roth, Loren H., Alan Meisel, and Charles W. Lidz. "Tests of Competency to Consent to Treatment." *American Journal of Psychiatry,* Vol. 134 (1977).

INDEX

ABOUT THE AUTHOR

Professor Vaughn E. James is a full-time member of the faculty at Texas Tech University School of Law in Lubbock, Texas, where he teaches or has taught various courses including Elder Law, Estate and Gift Taxation, Estate Planning, Federal Income Taxation, and Wills and Trusts. During the summer months, he often teaches Gratuitous Transfers and/or Elder Law at the University of Tennessee College of Law in Knoxville, Tennessee. For several years, he joined fellow Texas Tech Law Professor Larry Spain, Texas Tech University School of Law Clinical Programs staffers Elma Moreno and Samirah Abdallah, and the staff of Legal Aid of Northwest Texas in running a Wills Clinic, where they guided law students in preparing wills and other estate planning instruments for low-income residents of Lubbock and its environs. Many of the clinic's clients were elderly and actually received assistance in the field of elder law. Professor James is a popular speaker at Estate Planning and Elder Law seminars, symposia, and Continuing Legal Education courses. He was recently appointed director of the Texas Tech School of Law Low Income-Taxpayer Clinic.

Professor James is also a minister of religion and a graduate of the Seventh-day Adventist Theological Seminary at Andrews

University, Berrien Springs, Michigan. In his role as a minister, he has often had to counsel parishioners on issues involving Alzheimer's disease and other forms of dementia.

His greatest experience with Alzheimer's has come not from his legal or ministerial roles but from personal experience. Over the past ten years, eight people very close to him have developed Alzheimer's or exhibited Alzheimer's-like symptoms. The youngest of these is an older sibling who was not even fifty years old. These personal experiences have left him acutely aware of not only the legal aspects of the disease but also its physical and mental toll on its victims and the physical and emotional toll on their loved ones.